# BARRIERS
# A Novel

Steven Wasserman

# DEDICATION

TO MY WIFE, CINDY, AND MY KIDS

# CONTENTS

# ACKNOWLEDGMENTS

Thanks to all the family and friends who reviewed various drafts, over the years, and offered up suggestions that made a marked improvement in the story and presentation. Special thanks to my wife, Cindy, and oldest son, Marc, who endured multiple readings and provided valuable insight and recommendations that made the book better and more readable. A special callout to my old friend, Michael Nissenbaum, who also read the novel several times and added his thoughts and constructive criticism that was much appreciated.

# CHAPTER ONE

For weeks, my mother had been nagging me to look through the half dozen boxes of my belongings that were stored in the house she and my father had moved to in 1963. Years before, I had carried those same boxes up the narrow pull-down staircase, the one that wobbled and creaked horribly, and then placed them in the dusty, cobweb filled attic of her soon to be vacated house. It was more than likely that those boxes contained nothing worth holding on to and I considered telling her to simply toss whatever was there. But it was clearly unfair to leave it to her to deal with my junk. Expecting a woman, at sixty years old with an arthritic hip, to navigate those narrow stairs with cartons that were certain to weigh fifteen, maybe twenty pounds each, was an accident waiting to happen.

As with many things throughout my life, I had postponed the chore for as long as possible. But time was up, she was due to leave next week to move to her new house in a Florida retirement community so I reluctantly gave up my free Saturday morning to head over and tackle what was there. Which was not much of anything as I had assumed. Some Revelle model cars and monster models of the Wolfman and Frankenstein that I had assembled and meticulously painted as a kid. My old baseball glove, a stack of 45 rpm records and paperback copies of Dr. No and Goldfinger. All of which I earmarked for the garbage. The only things that possibly had some value and might be worth hanging onto were my collection of baseball cards and an autographed photo of the 1958 Baltimore Colts.

After rummaging through those boxes, the only thing left to sort out was a box that contained the contents of my old desk. A periodic table—trash. A metric conversion chart—*trash*. A Kodak Instamatic camera with a dozen rolls of undeveloped film and a JFK for President button—*possible keepers*. A lot of pens and pencils and binders. And finally one photograph.

I held the photo in my hand and looked it over. Propped in the lap of the kid in the center of the first row was a sign that read *Mrs. Garrett's Third Grade Class*. And there I was standing in the last row. Crew cut. Slightly lazy left eye. And front teeth that stuck out from pressing my tongue against them whenever I swallowed. My parents would spend the next five years and thousands of dollars trying to correct the problem.

Looking at the photo reminded me that for all the things that could traumatize a student back then, it was only picture day that did it for me. It was never tests or homework. Not even the girls who would try to sneak a kiss during recess. No, for me it was only picture day. I had hated it from the very first time in kindergarten and nothing had happened to change my mind by third grade.

The day always started off the same way with my mother pulling out a nice looking shirt and pants, ones without stains or frayed cuffs, and commanding me not to get dirty running around the playground with the other boys before school, an instruction I had failed to follow in first grade when I fell off the jungle gym into a mud puddle and had dried dirt visible on my knees as I sat in a front row chair in that year's class photo.

As was always the case, getting dressed and then trying to stay clean was the easiest and calmest part of the day. The rest was sheer chaos. Once the bell sounded, each class was herded into the auditorium starting with the kindergarten and moving up the grade school ladder. Almost immediately, the noise level rose as the students shuffled in their seats becoming increasingly more impatient. Which always led to one boy poking a girl in the ribs and the girl responding with a shriek. Or two kids arguing over a thumb wrestling match. Or another boy pulling the hair of the girl in the row in front of him. Or simply kid after kid turning up the volume of their voices so he or she could be heard by someone at the other end of the row. And rising above all of this was the constant chirping of the teachers, *Kids. Quiet Down!*

When my class lined up for the picture, the photographer directed me to the back row. *Tall guys in the back*, pointing to me and four others. Upon taking my place, the mischief imp took hold of me and goaded me into placing my hand above Amy Berlin's head with fingers spread to resemble devils horns. It got a lot of laughs from my classmates. Unfortunately, Mrs. Garrett didn't see the humor in it and ordered me to the front row. *Michael why don't you join us up front*, she announced in no uncertain terms. I obeyed her command although I couldn't figure out how she saw me in the first place. She never once looked in my direction yet somehow she knew what I had done.

She sure was one tough, old lady. Later, it surprised me to learn that she was only thirty-nine, which certainly was not an old age except perhaps to a third grader. But she definitely looked it and more. It could have been the long floral print dresses that draped around her ankles. Or the silvery blonde hair she tied up in a bun on top of her head. Or the thin wire glasses that seemed like a relic from the Civil War era. Even if old might have been in question, there was no doubt about her toughness. She had a head that seemed able to swivel three hundred sixty degrees on her neck. So, she saw everything. And what she didn't see, like me putting the devil horns on Amy Berlin, she sensed. She was demanding, no-nonsense, rigid and structured. She had her rules and no one, and I mean no parents, kids, or administrators, dared to challenge them.

Looking at this photo triggered another memory. It made me recall that it was Mrs. Garrett who forced me to declare what I wanted to do with my life. Or it might be better said that she doomed me to what I would do with my life.

It was a rainy day, early in the spring, when she decided to ask each of us what we hoped to be when we grew up. Now, it probably seems premature to be asking a bunch of third graders what they aspired to be. But, Mrs. Garrett was always one who believed kids should have a direction in life and the sooner the better. She pushed back her chair and rose from her desk and announced, "Today I want to learn what each of you plan to do when you become an adult. What kind of career are you looking for?"

She started on the opposite side of the classroom meaning I would be last to answer, giving me plenty of time to figure out what to say. In the meantime, the responses were what you might expect from kids growing up in the 1950's. Most of the girls were hesitant, saying they would probably just get married and become a housewife, raising their own kids (much like their own mothers). One did say she hoped to become a nurse, another said she wanted to be a teacher and a third girl wanted to be a movie star. Ellen Wagner, as one might expect, proclaimed she would be the first woman President of the United States. Geez, I didn't know girls were even allowed to become President. But, if they were, I would sure want Ellen Wagner to be my president. She was smart and good looking.

The boys were far more definite in their career plans. Two wanted to become doctors and three said they would become lawyers, following in the fathers' footsteps. There was a scientist, an astronaut and a veterinarian. Two boys hoped to be professional baseball players. And that left me. To be honest, I had never given one second of thought to what I would be when I grew up. I guess I could have taken the easy way and picked one of the careers already mentioned by my classmates. But I had this feeling that, twenty years later, Mrs. Garrett would pop up and check out whether I had followed through on what I said that day in her classroom. And find that I hadn't become what I said I would be. *Michael, why don't you come join us up front*, she would reprimand me. Put me on display. Losers in the front row. Put devil horns on Amy Berlin, move to the front row. Don't follow through on your career choice, come on up to the front row. So I thought it over. I needed a good answer. And then it hit me. So, when it was my turn, I announced, with a small degree of optimism and a larger dose of enthusiasm, that I wanted to become a writer.

"And what type of writer do you hope to become, Michael?" Mrs. Garrett asked. I answered that I wasn't sure.

"Is there a type of writing that appeals to you? Do you write poems or short stories?"

Why was she asking these questions? She didn't ask the others what type of doctor they wanted to be. Why was I the one getting the scrutiny?

"I like to write stories about people."

Writing was actually a new hobby for me. Earlier in the year, I started writing because it was difficult for me to remember the names and exploits of the key historical figures during our study of the American Revolution. I was having trouble keeping track of who did what. Was it Thomas Paine who wrote the Federalist Papers and Nathan Hale who said, *Give me liberty or death*? Was it James Madison who wrote the Declaration of Independence with Thomas Jefferson? And who won that duel between Andrew Hamilton and Aaron Burr?

I needed to do something to prepare for Mrs. Garrett's upcoming test. Then I found the solution. It was at the end of the chapter in our history book, the place where they ask questions about what you had just read. It was the place I always went to first figuring if I saw the questions, it would reveal what the author thought was most important to remember and save me from wasting time on the less important stuff. There was also a section, underneath the questions, where the author made suggestions to be used as study aids. In one of the chapters, he recommended writing a story about one of the famous characters. I gave it a try composing a story about John Hancock based on the information in the textbook and then using my imagination to add details about his family, hobbies and career. And it worked. After writing the story, it was a snap to remember everything about him. So I kept writing. Benjamin Franklin, George Washington, Paul Revere—I wrote stories about each of them. In the end, I aced the exam.

"Sounds like we may have a future biographer," Mrs. Garrett announced. "One day, when we have some time, I hope you will share one of your stories with the class."

"Sure thing, Mrs. Garrett. I'll be glad to". But there was no way I was going to let my classmates hear my stories. The stories may have worked their magic as a study technique but I harbored no illusion that they were any good. In fact, I was certain that, being an average student at the time, half my class probably wrote better than me.

But writing the stories was fun and I threw myself into it full bore. I wrote after school and on weekends, when I was in the car or sitting in my grandmother's house. When I couldn't sleep at night. Or when there was nothing worth watching on television. On many Saturday afternoons, while my friends were playing Monopoly or touch football, I was in my room writing. Before long, I had exhausted the list of everyone in my history book. There were stories on presidents like Abraham Lincoln, Ulysses S. Grant and Teddy Roosevelt. Stories about Alexander Graham Bell, Thomas Edison and George Washington Carver. Stories about Pony Express riders, sheriffs in the Wild West and gold-seeking miners in California. By the end of third grade, I had over one hundred stories.

So, I changed my focus and began writing about people from my everyday life. While waiting my turn at the barbershop, I wrote about Mr. Willie, the guy with a pock marked face and sparse oily strands of hair that swept across an otherwise bald noggin. He was the guy who always cut my hair. On the fifteen minute trip on the number seven bus to the Crest Movie Theatre, I wrote a story about the craggly faced driver who stared straight ahead as I placed my fare in the receptacle and looked peeved as if my climbing aboard the bus had encroached upon some sacred turf. Before long I had stories about the mailman, the butcher at the kosher market and the coach of my Little League baseball team. Some people doodled. Other people gabbed. I wrote.

By the time I entered high school, my collection soared past three hundred stories. Either I needed to move to a new city and find new people to write about or I had to find new subject matter.

Then, in tenth grade English class, we read a group of novels that captivated me. First up was *The Scarlett Letter*, and then *Huckleberry Finn*. We read O. Henry short stories and Thurber essays. Using these authors as a guide, I began to write stories where, for the first time, there was a plot. Up to then, my stories were strictly about characters—how they looked, how they walked, what they ate, what they wore. To someone else, my early stories were probably boring and repetitious. Change that. My early stories were boring and repetitious. After all there are only so many ways to describe facial features. But now, the stories were, well, stories. Things happened. And the characters became better. Now they reacted, they thought, they felt. No longer were they just a catalog of mannerisms and appearance, they were alive.

It was also in tenth grade that each student met with a counselor, for the first time, to discuss career paths. I was ready. After all, thanks to Mrs. Garrett, I had known for years what I wanted to do. So, when Mr. Bailey asked, I replied, "I want to be a writer. I want to write novels."

"And when did you decide to become a writer?" Given the tone of his voice, it was obvious that Mr. Bailey was not impressed, or even comfortable, with my choice.

"In third grade."

"Third grade huh? Don't you think it rather peculiar that an eight year old boy has decided how you are going to spend the rest of your life?"

"Well, it's what I always wanted to do. I've been writing stories for years. I can't imagine not continuing to do it." What I should have added was that I had to become a writer because Mrs. Garrett might show up down the road to make sure I had followed through on my proclamation that day in her class.

"Listen, Michael. Writing is an admirable pursuit. But it's a career that is unlikely to happen, much less provide a living for you. It's really difficult to get published. Even if you can get published, you can't depend on earning enough income from it. You need to find something else. Let writing be your hobby. Find something else to do for a career. Keep an open mind and I'm certain something will come along that will interest you."

Mr. Bailey would not have had much of an argument from my father, the man who had spent the majority of my life convincing me that I was nothing more than average. My mother rarely contradicted him. And so, for a lot of years, I rewarded both of them with exactly what they believed to be my nature. Mediocrity. Mediocrity in school. Middling in my appearance and looks. In my effort. In my attitude and in my aspirations. That is until I made my declaration that day in Mrs. Garrett's class.

On the one occasion my father showed any interest in my plans, the conversation turned into an unmitigated disaster. When I told him I wanted to go to college, he snapped, "So, what is all this education going to do for you Michael?" Considering that my father had dropped out of high school to work in the family store, then went off to fight in World War II, and, upon returning home, resumed working at the store, his reply was hardly a surprise. Education didn't mean much to him beyond being able to read a newspaper and being able to think for yourself.

"I want to be a novelist."

"Isn't that just great? You picked a career where probably one guy in a million makes it and the rest of them wind up on the scrap heap, looking to guys like me to pay their way. Doesn't sound like much of a life to me."

"But it's not your life. It's what I want to do with my life. I'm not asking for your approval. Or your support. I can do it on my own."

"I doubt that. Let's face facts, Michael. You're an average student. Average students don't become writers. They don't become Presidents or lawyers or doctors. Average students work in grocery stores, like me. Or they become accountants."

Even though I didn't hold much stock in my father's appraisal, the seeds of doubt had been sown. My father and now Mr. Bailey. Two people, who were earning a living and providing for their families, thought following the career path of a writer was unwise. And I had to admit it. My youthful attempts at writing gave no indication that I had any special ability or aptitude. I liked writing. It was fun. Yet, despite all those stories, I hardly had an unwavering confidence that I could build the rest of my life on it.

Still I would lie awake in my bed at night thinking about writing. There were nights when I could envision everything falling into place and realizing my goal. Then there were nights when the doubts overwhelmed me and I would imagine myself, years from now, living in some dingy, walk-up, one-room  apartment with peeling paint, scuffed floors and dilapidated plumbing. And there I would be, hovering over a dimly lit desk, pecking away at a Royal typewriter with an "s" key that kept sticking while the aroma of bubbling oil wafted through the open window from the restaurant three floors below. And my father and Mr. Bailey standing in the doorway shaking their heads in a way that said, *I told you so.* Not very inviting but I couldn't imagine doing anything else. So, I had to give it a try. I didn't need to become famous or rich or even deemed successful by my peers. I just wanted to write.

And that's how easy things can get started. Gaining a life of its own. Snowballing. Years from now when I might wonder how I ended up where I am, I will think back to a third grade teacher who asked me what I wanted to be. And the next thing you know, in the pressure of the moment, this somewhat optimistic eight year kid gives an answer that sends me down a path that I follow, in some manner, for better or worse, for the rest of my life.

# CHAPTER TWO

The first legitimate step toward my goal began by accident. Or by luck.

The State of Maryland ran its state fair during the last ten days of summer vacation leading up to Labor Day. It was held at the Timonium Fair Grounds, not far from where I lived. As a kid, my parents would take me to the fair one evening each year. For educational purposes, my dad insisted. Plodding through the sawdust, dodging the piles of manure, we would check out the cows and pigs and visit the agricultural displays. If my father was in a good mood, I was allowed to visit the midway and go on three rides before we headed home. But we never stayed very long, my father always insisting that we beat the rush out of the parking lot. By the time I was ten, I had seen enough farm animals to last a lifetime. By the age of twelve, I told my parents that I no longer wanted to go and, so, the family trips to the state fair came to an abrupt end.

It had been six years since my last visit, when in the summer prior to entering twelfth grade, I decided to go with friends. My parents had no objections. They never cared about my comings and goings as long as I found my own way there and home. That was the rule of the house. I could come and go as I pleased but, under no circumstance, would my parents take me or pick me up. Fortunately, my best friend, Lenny, had his own car, a gift from his parents for his sixteenth birthday. So, I was set to go.

We arrived about seven o'clock and did a once-around the midway and ride area to check things out. There were hundreds of kids roaming around and quite a few were friends from school. After stopping to grab two corn dogs (part of the allure of state fairs being the chance to consume large quantities of the unhealthiest food on earth, food that also was never allowed in my mom's kosher kitchen), we headed over to the main pavilion where various community groups, radio stations, government agencies and businesses set up booths. They always had give-aways and Lenny thought he could score one or two for his car—a bumper sticker, an ice scraper or a hanging deodorizer.

Halfway down one of the aisles, we came to the Baltimore Gazette booth. And who should be standing there but Wes Unseld, the center for the Baltimore Bullets professional basketball team, and Bill Perl, the sports editor for the Gazette. I recognized Perl from the photo that was always pasted to the top of his sports column. I recognized Unseld because, well, it was impossible not to given his size and stout afro hair style. There were several dozen people queued up to get Unseld's autograph. Lenny got in line. Perl stood to Unseld's side, dwarfed by the wide bodied center, and not one person was waiting for his autograph or even bothering to talk to him. So, I walked up to him and shuffled my feet, thinking about what to say.

"You got something you want to ask me?" he snarled. He sounded like he had a reservoir of smoke in his throat, coating every word that swirled from his lips. His clothes wrinkled, almost to the point of looking disheveled, his eyes red and sunken, he looked like he had been at an all-night poker game.

"Yes sir. My name's Michael Sanders and I want to ask you how you got started writing sports."

"So ask me."

"I just did."

"No. You said you wanted to ask me. But you didn't ask."

"Ok. So how did you get started writing about sports?"

"I got the good old U.S. Army to thank for that, pal. Shipped my ass off to Korea in 1951. But the bastards gave me the chance to write for the base newspaper. Human interest type stuff. Blurbs about the basketball games between the troops. Kept my ass off the front line though. When I got back to Baltimore in fifty-three, I tried to get a job at the Gazette but all they offered me was a copy boy position. I took it. Had nothing better in the hopper. Eventually they gave me a chance to write a bit about high school sports. Then, in 1954, the Orioles moved to town from St. Louis and they needed to increase the staff. I was in the right place at the right time. You looking to become a sports writer?"

"Well, I really want to write novels. But everyone says that it will be a struggle to earn a living that way. I play basketball and lacrosse for Pikesville high school. Thought that sports writing might be a way to combine my interests. What do you think?"

"Ah. The new Ernest Hemingway."

"What?"

"Ernest Hemingway. They still teach him in high school, don't they?"

"Yeah. Of course. *Old Man and the Sea.* I read it."

"Well Hemingway was a journalist. In Kansas City. And a foreign correspondent too. Before he started writing novels.

"Ok. That's cool. So, I want to ask how I should get started."

"First you got to drop that *I want to ask* shit. Just ask it. Get to the point. Brevity. It'll serve you well if you're going to be a journalist. Since I doubt you want to get your ass over to Vietnam and write for the army base newspaper there, I suggest you go to journalism school. You sure as shit can't get into the business the way I did. Not anymore. You need to go write for your school newspaper. Yeah, you gotta get credentials today. A resume. A portfolio. A degree. Not just some shit articles from an army newspaper."

"Hey thanks for the insight." I started to walk away since Lenny had his autograph and was now waiting for me.

"Just make sure that's what you really want to do."

"How's that?"

"It ain't as glamorous as it may seem, kid. It ain't an easy life. You've got games at night and on weekends. So, you're working when everyone else is kicking back and relaxing. And you can count on having a shitty social life as well. If you have one at all. Three days in one city then three days in the next city. Living out of a suitcase. Then back home for a week or two. Not the best way to attract women. Or keep them, you can ask my first wife about that. And the athletes. What a bunch of prima donnas. They aren't the best at taking criticism either. So, don't expect to be hanging out with them. No, you'll be hanging out with a bunch of over-the-hill guys, in the same sorry ass spot as you. Tipping the bottle. Chowing down on greasy food at midnight. Everyone thinks it's a great job because you're around a game that people are passionate about. But it's just the same kind of shit ass job that everyone else has."

"It wouldn't be that way for me." I thanked him again for talking with me and walked away.

One week later, school opened and, on the first day, I went to see Mrs. Chilton, the adviser for the student newspaper.

"Hi Mrs. Chilton. I'm Michael Sanders and I'd like to join the newspaper staff."

"I'm sorry Michael, but you have to complete Journalism One to be on the paper." Mrs. Chilton taught the journalism classes so she knew what was required to work on the paper. This was a definite problem since my schedule was set for the coming semester.

"Isn't there something I can do?"

"The only thing you can do is to go see your guidance counselor and get into the journalism class for second semester. Then you'll be eligible to join the paper in the fall semester next year."

"There is no fall semester for me next year. I'm a senior."

"I'm sorry Michael. There is nothing I can do."

This was not good news. There were probably thousands of kids, across the country, writing for their school newspaper, gaining experience, compiling a portfolio. Thousands of kids vying for a few hundred spots in good journalism schools. What would I have to show when I applied to college? Nothing and that meant it would be tough to convince a college to let me enroll in their journalism program.

That night, I struggled to fall asleep as I pondered my situation. I wondered if that eight year old boy had any ideas up his sleeve.

# CHAPTER THREE

A few weeks later, I was sitting around the house and picked up a copy of the Baltimore Gazette and turned to Bill Perl's column. He called it "Perls of Wisdom" and the Gazette published it three times a week. Today's column was his analysis of the recently completed Orioles season:

*So we finally get to put a lid on the Orioles season. And now, the front office and the disappointed fan base can spend the next four months figuring out what went wrong. After all, on paper, the season sure looked promising. Coming off a world championship, highlighted by a four game sweep of the favored Dodgers, expectations were, as expected high. But as my Uncle Fred used to say, "The only thing that looks good on paper and gets you the same result every time is a twenty dollar bill with good old Andy Jackson's face on it.*

*So seventy wins and eighty-five losses. From virtually the same team that went to the World Series. From champions to also-rans. Tied for sixth with the Washington Senators. That's right. The Washington Senators. It's a sad day when you tie the sorriest franchise in the major leagues. But that's what the Orioles have to show for their efforts in 1967. Oh there will be plenty of excuses. The front office will point to all the sore arms that led to twenty-one different pitchers taking the mound. But what explains such a drop in production? The four starters in 1966 contributed only seventeen wins one year after winning forty-eight, not a formula that spells success. And how fitting that the season was marred by so much rainy weather—eighteen home games were cancelled or interrupted. Highlights. How about losing a no-hitter? The O's accomplished that when they lost to the Detroit Tigers 2-1. Just one of fifteen losses to Detroit. Then there was the 318 minute, nineteen inning victory over Washington. It was the longest game in Orioles history. Again, fitting for a season that went on too long.*

*I think what fans found most disappointing was the reversal in competitiveness for the franchise. Third place finishes in 1964 and 1965, followed by a championship in 1966 and four game sweep of the Dodgers in the World Series, created the expectation that the O's would be battling for championships for years to come. To revert to being a second division ball club, well, it was about as welcome a development for me as going back to my first wife.*

*So who takes the blame? Among the suspects, how about Hank Bauer? He should be sitting on the hot seat for the way he handled the team. Early on, he let them become too relaxed, too confident in their ability. As the losses piled up, he watched helplessly as the team tried too hard. Guys were trying to hit grand slams with the bases empty. Among the players, there is no shortage of candidates that should be shown the door. Boog Powell couldn't even hit his weight. The starting pitching was horrible. Someone in the front office needs to take a long, hard look at the staff. The situation cries out for change.*

*As would be expected, the impact of the poor performance was felt at the gate.*

*Home attendance dropped by over 300,000. Unless this team is ready to watch a further exodus of fan support, they need to make drastic changes. They need to jettison the underperforming players, and I say start with Boog Powell. Find some new talent. Only then will Baltimore fans find a team ready to compete consistently in the American League.*

Perl's comments made me angry. Not only did I worship the Orioles but Boog Powell was my favorite player. Like most good fans, I was disappointed with the O's play. But, that was hardly a reason to abandon the team. They still had the makings of a quality group. So I composed a letter to the editor to let Perl know what I thought about his column.

*To the Editor:*
*I was disheartened to read Mr. Perl's comments about the Orioles. As a young fan, I am not ready to jump ship. We all want the O's to win a championship every year. But, we know it's not likely. The days of one team's domination are over. In the last three years alone, we've had three different teams represent the American League in the World Series—the Twins in 1965, the Orioles in 1966 and the Red Sox in 1967. I am confident that, with our veteran presence, we will be back in the mix next year. And as for Boog Powell, I am sure that Mr. Perl does not hit home runs with every column he writes. I think Mr. Perl has had his share of bad days, maybe even bad seasons. This column is surely one of them.*

To my surprise, the letter was printed in the next day's edition. Over the next several weeks, I found myself disagreeing with many of Mr. Perl's columns. Each time, I wrote a letter expressing my opinion. The Gazette printed three additional letters.

Then, one night, the phone rang and my mother answered. She called for me to come to the kitchen.

"Michael, it's a Mr. Perl calling for you." When I approached, she covered the mouthpiece with her hand and whispered, "Are you in some kind of trouble?"

"No," I laughed, "he's the sports editor of the Gazette but I have no idea why he's calling." I grabbed the phone and said, "Hi, this is Michael." Stretching out the cord to its full ten foot length, I stepped out of the kitchen, out of easy eavesdropping range for my mother.

"I remember you. From the state fair."

"Mr. Perl, how did you find me?"

"Hey give me some credit. After all, I am a journalist with a lot of experience. When I saw your letter to the editor, I remembered the name and our conversation from the state fair. From there, it was easy. I called the school and got your contact information. Anyway it appears that you don't like my writing much, do you kid?" Mr. Perl rasped.

"Your writing is fine Mr. Perl. It's your opinions that bother me."

"You think some seventeen year old kid knows more than I do?"

"I'm not saying that I know more than you. I just know what I think."

"Well, kid, your letters impressed me. The writing was pretty good for someone your age. And the arguments were solid. I have a proposition for you."

By this point, I had wrapped the cord around my torso four times. I spun out of its grasp. "What kind of proposition?" I asked, feeling the anticipation building.

"Find yourself a story and I'll print it. That is, if it's any good. This is not a job offer and I'm not giving you an assignment. I don't care what you write about or where you find your story as long as it's about sports. You got thirty days. Make it happen. When you have it, come by the office." And with that he hung up.

"Holy shit," I screamed. I was ready to do a jig across the living room floor.

"Michael. What's with the foul language?"

"Sorry about that, Mom," I said as I walked back into the kitchen, my face too small to contain the smile that spread from ear to ear. "But you are not going to believe this. Mr. Perl, the sports editor of the Gazette, just told me that if I write a story, he'll publish it. I mean he'll publish it if it's any good."

"What kind of story?"

"Anything he said. No limits. "

"So, what are you going to write about?"

"I have no I

# CHAPTER FOUR

Several weeks passed and I was no closer to coming up with a story. Basketball season had begun and the team was getting ready for the first regular season game. Between school and practice, I had little time to think about writing a story for the Gazette. I was anxious to do as Mr. Perl said, to make it happen, but my focus was spread in too many directions.

Our first regular season game was scheduled for Friday night against the Lions, the perennial champions in the county. It was a home game and I was excited. Our team looked good—much improved over the previous year. We had played two exhibition games, winning both against schools generally considered among the elite in the area. But the game against the Lions would be a bigger challenge and a true test of how good a team we were.

We kept the game close for the first quarter and held the lead for several minutes. But, in the second quarter, the Lions surged ahead to lead by eight points at halftime. After that it was all downhill and they poured it on in the second half. Final score—the Lions beat us by seventeen points.

After the game, Jimmy Klein, a fellow senior and our best player, sat dejected in front of his locker. "I really thought we had a chance to beat them this year. Shit. Can you believe we lost by seventeen points."

I was disappointed but what was there to say. Although basketball was a game I loved to play, it had never been a highly emotional experience for me like it was for others. Like it was for my teammates. I never worried about wins and losses. When the game was over, it was over.

"Face it Jimmy. They're just a really good team. It's not hard to see why they're county champions every year. Look at that point guard and center that they have."

Anyone who had watched the game would have agreed that those two players were far better than anyone on our team.

"Just explain to me how they never get weaker. Every year, they're the same. It's like playing the Boston Celtics."

"Jimmy, they're good. Hey we're good, we're better than last year. Just not good enough yet to overtake them. Take consolation in the fact that we played hard and didn't make it easy for them."

"Sorry, Michael, but it just doesn't make sense to me. Every team has guys graduate and new guys come in. Their fortunes ebb and flow. Some years are better than others, some worse. But with the Lions, it is always the same. They don't even slack off enough to finish second. "

There were no answers for Jimmy, none that would satisfy his curiosity or provide a realistic explanation for the Lions perennial success. So I let it drop. I was drained and I intended to head straight home. After taking a shower and changing my clothes, I headed out the door into the brisk November air. It would take twenty minutes to walk home.

"Michael. Michael. Over here."

It was my older cousin, Elliot, leaning against his car. Elliot, who was in his junior year at William and Mary, had been the best basketball player in the area and held every school record for scoring and rebounding.

"Want a ride?"

"Man that would be great. I'm beat. I wasn't looking forward to walking home." We shook hands and his left hand grabbed my shoulder and gave a squeeze. "What are you doing here?" I asked.

"Came in for the weekend. My girlfriend, Jenny, is throwing a party for her parents' anniversary tomorrow night. Figured I'd catch your game while I was here."

Over the years, Elliot was one of those guys who always seemed bigger than they really were.

Growing up, five houses down the street from my house, he had always looked out for me, letting me join in his pickup games and always choosing me for his team, when no one else wanted me.

He was such a presence-- in school, on the court, with the girls—that I think I always saw him as larger than he really was.

"The team looked good out there tonight. Tough game but you guys did okay. Much better than I did back in the day."

"Thanks but most of the guys are pretty upset. They thought this was finally going to be the year we knocked off the Lions."

"That ain't gonna happen. Not in our lifetime. "

"Jimmy Klein said he can't understand how they're so damn good every year."

"They have their way. "

"Whatta you mean?"

"You really don't know how they do it?" I shook my head. "I guess you could say that they bend the rules a bit. They recruit players from

Baltimore City and bring them into the school just to play basketball. Been doing it for years. Us county guys can't hang with those city kids on a basketball court."

I was stunned.

"How do you know about this?"

"I played intramural basketball my freshman year at William and Mary. There was a guy there who played for the Lions. He was a year ahead of me and I remembered playing against him my junior year in high school. We'd shoot around together after the games and we got to talking. He clued me in."

"But, but, how can they get away with it?"

"They have a pipeline. Seems everyone, who knows about it, looks the other way."

"Yeah. Great. That's not very fair and maybe it's illegal. Aren't you supposed to have a team made up of people that live in your own district?"

"Sure, but hey that's just life. You know not everything is always on the up and up. Don't let it bother you. Forget I told you. Or remember that I told you and go out and kick their butts next time. It will be that much sweeter when you win."

We hopped in the car and headed to Gino's where Elliot bought me a burger and fries. He talked about college and, on the way back to my house, he asked about my plans.

My plans? My head was roiling and all I could think about was that I had to do something about what he had told me. My immediate plans would be to investigate the Lions basketball team to see what I could uncover. It could be my story for the Gazette and I couldn't think about anything else beyond that.

As Elliot pulled up to the curb, my mind was still churning.

"Elliot, suppose I don't want to forget what you told me. Suppose I want to check into what's going on there."

"For what end Michael. I told you no one cares. You have a better chance to beat them on the court than getting anyone interested in what they're doing. So you know how long the odds are."

"I care because it's not fair. And I might have a chance to do something about it. I have a connection with the Gazette so there's an opportunity for me to write a story about it. To expose it."

"You're opening a can of worms. You have no idea what will happen. Maybe you won't find what you hope to find. Maybe you find it but the Gazette doesn't run it. Or maybe they run it and you get a result that you don't expect or won't like. Are you sure you want to do this?

"I do. I just need you to get your friend to talk to me, to help me get started."

Elliot agreed to ask his friend to talk to me when he returned to school on Sunday night. Meanwhile, I considered what else I could do to get information about what was going on.

On Sunday night, Elliot called. He had talked with his friend, Dennis, and Dennis said he didn't want to get involved. But, after some gentle persuasion from Elliot, Dennis softened. He agreed to talk with me provided that I was able to find another source or additional details to back him up.

That sounded pretty hard to do. But what choice did I have? As I laid in bed on Sunday night, I tossed around what I knew. There was a pipeline bringing players from the city to the county. That meant there was someone in the city feeding players to the county school and someone in the county processing the necessary paperwork to get them enrolled. I knew there was no way to uncover who was involved on the city side which meant I had to find out who was involved on the county side. The logical place to start was with investigating the coach. He had to be the mastermind and, if not, he had to know what was going on. It was doubtful he would talk to me, but at least it was a starting point.

# CHAPTER FIVE

On Monday morning, before heading off to school, I checked the sports page of the Gazette to see the schedule of high school games for the week. We had a bye on Tuesday but the Lions were scheduled to play a home game that day. I planned to be at that game.

Since I needed a way to get to the game, I asked Lenny to come with me. I told him my plan and swore him to secrecy. Basketball practice would be over around 4:30 pm. It would take about thirty minutes to drive to the Lions' gym so we could be there in time for the five o'clock start.

We each paid the one dollar entrance fee and settled into the section behind the visitor's bench. The gym was impressive, covered with championship banners on every wall. There were banners announcing county championships, regional championships, and state championships. On the way into the gym, we walked past three glass cases filled with championship trophies from preseason and holiday tournaments, basketballs signed by each team, action photos and other memorabilia. There was no getting away from it—it felt like going to the National Basketball Hall of Fame.

Oh and the game itself, well like most games that the Lions played, it was not very competitive. By half time, the Lions led by twenty-five points. The fourth quarter turned into pure garbage time. Despite using their bench players for the entire quarter, they expanded the lead and won by forty-two points.

Before they left the court, most of the players greeted their parents and friends. But there were two players who headed straight for the locker room. Both were black guys, both starters and both key players—the point guard and center that had dominated the game when they played us the week before. I knew their names. One was Jones and the other's name was Hicks. It appeared that no one was there to watch them. None of the students milling around went over and talked to them. They seemed out of place, now that the game was over.

"Lenny, let's scoot. I want to hang out by your car and watch these guys come out."

We reached the parking lot and climbed into Lenny's car and within minutes, most of the crowd left. Then, over the next twenty minutes, every player walked out of the school except the two black guys. It was odd since they had hit the locker room before any of their teammates.

We sat slumped in the car seats, our eyes barely skirting over the dashboard in our best private eye stakeout mode, and we waited. And waited. And waited some more. The parking lot was virtually empty, when finally, Jones and Hicks stepped out of the locker room door. Right behind them was the coach of the Lions—Jim McCaskill. They crossed the sidewalk to the teachers' lot where all three got into McCaskill's car, a sky blue Mercury Cougar, with a large dent on the driver's door and rusted spots above the rear bumper. Hardly the car of a champion. As they pulled out onto the street, Lenny moved into a trail position, keeping a safe distance behind.

McCaskill headed west on the Baltimore Beltway and then down the Jones Falls Expressway to the North Avenue exit. Winding through the city streets, he eventually turned onto Fulton Avenue, a street I was well familiar with. My father's grocery store was on Mount Street about two blocks west of Fulton. First he stopped at 1732 Fulton. The rear door opened and Hicks stepped from the car. He hopped onto the sidewalk, flinged the door closed and climbed the five marble steps of the brick row house in two bounds. He pulled his key out of his pocket, slid it into the keyhole and entered. Once the door closed, McCaskill drove off and headed a few more blocks down Fulton to Fayette, made a right and stopped again. Jones stepped from the car and entered the house at 4409 Fayette Street. McCaskill pulled away, made a u-turn and headed back in the direction of the expressway.

We sat in the car about a block away from Jones' house. The streets were empty, there was no other activity, no cars, no people. I jotted down the two addresses in my notebook. My mind was racing, certain that I had uncovered the first piece of the puzzle.

"Mikey, what's going on? What are two county kids doing in the city on a Tuesday night?"

Lenny was never the swiftest of thinkers.

"That's the point Lenny. These kids don't live in the county. Looks like they live here and that McCaskill drives them back and forth. The rumor was that he was bringing in kids to play basketball to prop up the quality of his team. What he's been doing is against the rules and this is the first piece of evidence. But we can't tell anyone yet. This stays between us until I have the rest of what I need for my Gazette story."

Lenny stammered, "You're fucking crazy man. You're gonna write a story about two black kids playing in the county? Do you think anyone gives a shit? And, if someone does, you are about to create a real mess? You're gonna get your ass kicked."

In a way, Lenny was right. It's not like McCaskill had robbed a bank or embezzled money. Not much harm had been done other than to some kids who may have been impacted by the scheme and lost their chance to play for the team. Still, it tainted what the Lions had accomplished on the basketball court. Rules were rules and if everyone else abided by them, shouldn't the Lions? Most people might consider it a minor infraction and hardly worth the time to investigate. For me, though, it was about to become an obsession.

"Who knows what else is going on? I'm not looking to be the arbiter of what's fair, but this is not a kosher situation. In any event, I'm not doing anything more about it today. So, let's head home before my parents kick my ass."

There were plenty of loose ends left to clean up but, at least, it was a start and maybe even enough to get Elliot's friend to talk to me. I couldn't wait to call him that night.

It was almost nine o'clock by the time I got home. My father was asleep on the sofa. My mother was in the kitchen washing dishes.

"Where have you been, Michael?"

"I was at Lenny's working on a project for social studies. I'm pretty sure I told you I was heading there after basketball practice."

I knew the excuse would hold. My mother never paid much attention to what I told her. She may have doubted my explanation but she was too uncertain to challenge it.

"Have you had dinner?"

"Yeah, Lenny's mom made us grilled cheese sandwiches. Is it all right if I make a phone call? It's long distance."

My mother agreed, although she cautioned me to keep it short so that my father would not complain about the charge. I dialed Dennis' number and after two rings, he picked up. "Hello?"

"Hi Dennis. This is Michael, Elliot's cousin."

"What's up man?"

"You said I could reach out to you if I found out anything about the basketball team. Well, I followed McCaskill today when he left the school. He had two of his players with him and he dropped them off in the city. Right near my father's grocery store."

"That sounds about right."

"So, what's up with that? Anything that will shed light on the situation would be appreciated."

"All I can tell you is that, when I was a senior on the team, there was one other senior. Name was Ted Scott. He was a guard. Played off the bench the two previous years, maybe seven to eight minutes a game, but senior year was going to be his year. Co-captain with me. Then, on the first day of practice, McCaskill walks in with this black kid. About six-two and lightning fast. Popping shots from all over the court. I had never seen him before that day. McCaskill introduces him and says he just transferred in. Donte. Donte Barnes. Best player on the court. Best player I had ever seen. Anyways, Donte beats out Scott for the starting point guard position and Scott goes ballistic. His parents come in the next day and are all over McCaskill. McCaskill decides to move Donte to shooting guard and let Scott play the point. So, everything dies down. But it was always strange to me. Never saw Donte in any of my classes. Kept to himself. Didn't hang out with the team after games. Scored his twenty per game and headed home. After the season, word leaked out that McCaskill hooked up with some coach in the city and got the kid into my school. Carried him back and forth to the city every day that year. And the following year too, until he graduated. Scott told us McCaskill had been doing it, on and off, for years. And no one ever minded. At least not until Scott got upset about losing his starting position."

"So Jones and Hicks must be the newest recruits in McCaskill's game?"

"I guess so. So, listen, use my information if you want. Never liked what McCaskill did. What he stood for. There were rumors about him pressuring teachers to fix grades and money he was paid under the table to steer kids to certain AAU teams. And illegal practices--that I can tell you plenty about. But you're gonna need more than just my word."

Dennis was right. I would need more than his story, something more concrete. His story was a start but could hardly stand on its own. The Gazette would demand corroboration. As I saw it, there were two ways to accomplish that. One was to dig up something through the school—something that showed what was going on with McCaskill doctoring records and bringing in students. For that, I needed someone on the inside who was willing to cooperate. That was unlikely since anyone with any knowledge of the situation would be looking to protect the school not expose it.

But there was another way and that was to reach out to Hicks or Jones and get the inside information from them. Not that they were any more likely to reveal what they knew and how they were involved, but it was worth a shot, and it was the only viable option out there. Since they lived in the Mount Street area, near my father's grocery store, I was pretty sure I had a way to contact them, a way to reach out to them—and that way was through Darnell Watkins.

# CHAPTER SIX

Darnell Watkins lived about a mile from Mount Street but his father owned the barbershop directly across from my father's store. The barbershop was like City Hall with Darnell's father serving as the mayor. He knew everyone—sooner or later, everyone in the neighborhood passed through his door. Some came for haircuts but many more came for help. Active in city ward politics, the civil rights movement and his church, he was the one person who could offer advice and counsel for virtually any problem. He knew the right people and he was always glad to do what he could to solve a problem. His father knew everyone's business and, most of the time, so did Darnell.

Darnell and I first met in 1961. I was eleven and in sixth grade at the time—so was Darnell. My father had decided that it would be a good idea if I earned my allowance by working at the store. When the school year began, I started working every Saturday. Darnell's father, having discussed the plan with my father, decided it was a good idea to have Darnell do the same at the barbershop.

My responsibilities included restocking the shelves, cleaning the bathroom and sweeping the floor. When the older women would purchase their groceries, my father would call me to the front register and have me carry the bags back to their houses. This soon became my favorite job because it got me out of the store and out from under my father's watchful eye.

The first time my father asked me to help, it was for Mrs. Washington, a frail, eighty year old lady who used a cane to walk. I couldn't imagine how she had been able to carry her groceries when one hand was always needed to hold the cane. Somehow she had managed but it made me happy to be able help her out. When we reached her house, I placed the bags on her kitchen table and as I turned to go, she said, "Now hold on for just a minute, sonny."

She fumbled through her purse and pulled a nickel out and gave it to me.

"Mrs. Washington, this isn't necessary."

"Nonsense. You deserve a reward for your excellent service. It ain't easy lugging those bags for blocks."

"But you did it and you're a lot older than me. If I take your nickel,

you have to promise me that you'll do your shopping on the days that I
work so I can help you get the groceries back to your home. And no
more tips."

"You got a deal. Now before you go, can I interest you in a piece of
chocolate cake?"

"My father will be expecting me back. I better go."

"Pshaw. Now you just sit yourself down and don't worry none about
your father. If he gives you any flack, you just come and get me and I'll
tell him what's what."

Each one of the customers treated me the same, giving me a tip and
a plate of food. The tips were not much, a nickel or a dime, but then my
allowance was only one dollar. As for the food, it was as if these women
had entered into a secret pact to put some meat on my skinny bones.
So, I was never able to leave and return to the store until I agreed to eat
something. It didn't take much to twist my arm.

Mrs. Brown had the best fried chicken and Mrs. Jackson ruled with
the best sweet potato pie. Each and every one of them was a great
cook. On a busy day, I could double my earnings and probably put on
five pounds. When I would return to the store, my father always asked
why it had taken so long. I told him that the customer always demanded
that I eat something before leaving. When he complained that I was
neglecting my other duties, I just told him that I was only trying to keep
the customers happy. Isn't that what they call good customer service?

Darnell did similar jobs at the barbershop. On my way back from the
customers' homes, I would often see him sweeping the hair off the floor
or toting the towels to the basin, where he would wash them by hand
and hang them in the alley to dry. Even though we had not met, he
would wave as I passed by. Finally, one Saturday, he came into the store
to buy a candy bar and soda at lunchtime.

When he reached the register, my father asked, "You're Willie's boy
aren't you?"

"Yes sir."

"And what's your name?"

"Darnell, sir."

"So how do you like working for your dad?"

"It's fine sir."

"I'm glad to hear it. Now you just put your money back in your
pocket. The soda and candy bar are on me. "

"Thank you sir. But are you sure?"

"Of course I'm sure. Now, just wait one more second. I want to introduce you to my son. MICHAEL. MICHAEL. Can you come up to the register?"

I raced out of the back room and skipped to the register, figuring there was another customer who needed me to carry groceries. "Michael. This is Darnell. His dad owns the barbershop and Darnell works there on Saturdays, just like you. Why don't you grab your sandwich and go have lunch with Darnell."

I returned to the back room and picked up my lunch box which held the egg salad sandwich that my mother had made that morning along with an apple and three home baked chocolate chip cookies. I grabbed a small carton of chocolate milk, out of the refrigerator, and headed back to the front of the store.

"I'm ready Darnell. Where to?"

"Follow me."

We crossed the street and entered the barbershop below the illuminated cylindrical sign with its revolving spirals of red, white and blue. Mr. Watkins was busy cutting a man's hair. The customer sat in one of the brown leather barber chairs while, across from him, two other men sat on blue naugahyde chairs, partially shredded from years of use, arguing about a recent ordinance enacted by the City Council. The place itself was simple. A black and white tiled floors, a coat rack by the door and a wall decorated with framed pictures of players from the Baltimore Colts football team. The wall behind the barber chairs held a long shelf filled with clippers, scissors and hair products. Darnell quickly introduced me to his father and told him that I worked at the grocery story (which, of course, his father already knew) and that we were having lunch together. Then we went out the back door toward the alley to a small concrete yard.

There were cinder block walls, about three feet high, that framed the yard on the right and left and a chain-linked fence connecting the two sides at the rear by the alley. The yard was maybe twenty feet wide by thirty feet long, sloping towards a drain right in the middle and with two clothes lines running the entire width of the area. They were filled with the wet towels that Darnell had washed and hung out to dry. A backboard that looked like someone had taken bites along the edges was affixed to the wall of the barbershop right above the doorway.

Darnell gathered the towels off the line closest to the building and draped them over the towels on the second line. He unhooked the line, which then retracted into a weathered spool that was attached to a wood pole extending out of the concrete wall. He hopped up onto the wall, opened his soda and took a bite out of his candy bar. I followed him onto the wall, opened my lunch box and began eating my sandwich.

"So, what grade you in?" Darnell asked. "Sixth" I replied.

"Where at?" "Fallstaff. How 'bout you?"

"Pimlico Elementary. I'm in the sixth grade too."

Looking at the two of us, it would be hard to believe that we were both the same age. My lanky body had grown to just over five feet and Darnell was a good five to six inches shorter than me, with a chunkier body. He had puffy cheeks, barely visible eyebrows above sleepy, watery eyes and he wore his hair close cropped. But his manner was clearly more assertive than me. I had always been one of those kids who melted into the crowd, never at the top of my class in anything. But not at the bottom either.

"I'm going to Pimlico Junior High School next year. Is it near your school?"

"Yeah, a few blocks away. I'm going there next year too. Maybe we'll be in the same classes."

As I took a bite of my sandwich, I thought about sharing classes with Darnell, who I had known for all of five minutes but who seemed genuinely excited about that prospect. For me, the idea of moving on to junior high was already causing stress. I worried about fitting in. In elementary school, each class stayed together from first through sixth grade. Since I was on the shy side, that arrangement gave me a certain security knowing that my classmates would be the same from year to year and I wouldn't have to worry about making new friends. But, junior high would separate us based on academic performance. My grades had steadily improved over the years so I was confident that I would be selected for the enriched program with most of my friends. But you could never know enough people and I figured a friendly face, like Darnell's, would be welcomed.

A moment later, Darnell shook me from my thoughts. "So you want to shoot some baskets while you eat?"

"Yeah."

Darnell scampered off the wall, opened a wooden bin and pulled out a basketball. "A game of horse", he suggested. "I'll start. Home court advantage."

His first shot was a right-handed layup that clunked off the backboard, hit the front rim and spun back through the net. I swallowed the last bite of my sandwich, climbed down the wall and grabbed the ball as it rolled toward the fence. My layup went cleanly through the net.

"You like school?" he asked, moving about twelve feet away from the right side of the basket and taking a set shot, which hit the back of the rim and bounced away. Darnell tossed me the ball and I positioned myself about five feet directly in front of the bucket, aimed, shot and watched the ball pass through the rim. The key to winning a game of horse was to get control and then keep it, so I always started with easy shots. Of course, you had to make them but if you could get ahead, it put the pressure on the other player. Then go for the harder shots. That was always my strategy.

"Yeah school's alright."

Darnell stepped to the same spot where I stood a moment before. His shot barely reached the front of the rim and bounced back.

"That's "H", I announced.

"Yeah man, I know how to keep score. Go on. Take your next shot."

I decided to try a left hand layup and called "left hand only". My shot went through the basket again. Darnell took a few dribbles, shifted the ball into his left hand and fumbled it before he reached the basket.

"HO," I said. Then we each traded a few missed shots

"So Michael, you got a favorite subject at school?"

I moved to the baseline to the right of the basket, eyed the hoop and again the ball went through.

"I like to read and write stories about people. It's my hobby. At school, I guess because of that I like English best. "

Darnell missed again and was now down three letters.

"How about you?" I asked as I took a shot from right on top of the drain in the middle of the concrete yard. It went in again and Darnell missed again.

"Well I like current events so probably social studies. My parents and older brother are always talking about what's going when we're at the dinner table. Mostly civil rights issues. So I have a lot to say about things when we talk about it in class."

Darnell flipped me the ball and I walked underneath the basket, took two giant steps forward and stood with my back to the basket. I planned to try a shot that I had practiced hundreds of times in my driveway. I gripped the ball in both hands at waist level and started my arms towards my head with my back still toward the basket which kept me from seeing the flight of the ball. As my arms passed over my head, I released the ball and it soared through the hoop again. I called it the nail in the coffin shot. Darnell shook his head, retrieved the ball and gave it a try. He missed. Game over.

"Well, you're pretty good for a white boy," he teased.

"And Jewish."

"What's being Jewish got to do with basketball?"

"Did you know who scored the first basket ever in the NBA?" I didn't wait for Darnell to answer. "It was Ossie Schectman. A Jew. Basketball was a big deal back then in the Jewish community in New York City. You probably didn't know that. That's what they played. That was their game. You got guys like Wilt the Stilt and the Big O now. But we had guys like Dolph Schayes and Red Holzman."

"You're right I didn't know that. Always cool to learn something new," Darnell admitted.

"Hey Darnell, it was fun playing with you but I better go. I gotta get back to work. My father will be looking for me."

"Yeah, me too. Maybe I'll see you next Saturday."

The following Saturday and every Saturday after that, Darnell and I ate lunch together and shot a game of horse. My easy win, the first time we played, turned out to be a fluke. In fact, it turned out to be a setup. Before we started, Darnell suggested we play for a quarter. I had no sooner agreed when Darnell grabbed the ball, stepped about twenty feet from the basket and crisply sent the ball through the hoop. A clean shot from twenty feet? The previous week he couldn't make it standing in front of the basket. I smelled trouble and it threw me off my game. I missed my try. Darnell reclaimed the ball and said, "That's 'h'. I told you I knew how to keep score." 'O', 'r', 's' and 'e' followed in short order. I pulled out five nickels, which represented my morning tips, and handed them over to Darnell.

"There's always next week," he said.

We became Saturday afternoon buddies and basketball cronies. After the first two weeks, the games of horse proved to be competitive. We mixed in some games of one-on-one but it made me too sweaty and I hated going back to work with my shirt clinging to my back. Darnell was a good guy and I had a lot of fun hanging out with him. When summer came, we both started working six days a week. We ate lunch together every day. And every day we shot baskets.

In September, we both entered Pimlico Junior High, a school which was sixty percent Jewish, twenty percent black and twenty percent rough and tumble white kids, who we called drapes, guys who wore tight pants and black tee shirts with rolled up sleeves, had greased back hair and tacked metal taps on the heels of their ankle height boots .

Each group tended to keep to themselves except when the drapes decided to shake someone down, a situation I encountered early on when, one day after gym class, I wasn't swift enough to avoid an encounter in a stairway. I could hear them coming, the steady click of the shoe taps signaling their approach. But there was nowhere to go to escape them. Fortunately, friends had told me to carry my money in my shoes so when the two drapes (they always seemed to travel in pairs) demanded my money, I showed them empty pockets. They pushed me against the wall and then walked away. I was a coward, I hadn't stood up to the threat, but I had survived. Better to be thought a coward and live to tell about it.

There also were other challenges that I was not ready to face up to at school. For instance, around my friends, I was too hesitant and meek to own up to my friendship with Darnell and include him in our group. We shared every class together and, in each of those classes, Darnell was the lone black kid. Everyone else was white and Jewish. I knew most of them from elementary school. For each of us, it was the first time we ever had a black kid in our class. Rather than introduce him to my friends, I avoided him because I felt uncomfortable explaining our friendship. It was not a problem in the classroom since our seating was assigned. It was everywhere else. When we walked the hallways to each class, I walked alongside my white, Jewish friends and never invited Darnell to join us. When we sat in the cafeteria for lunch, I chose to sit with these same friends leaving Darnell to fend for himself. I would look over and he would be sitting alone— ignored by the white kids as well as the black kids, who didn't share any classes with him. I felt bad for Darnell but I didn't do a thing.

It didn't take long to learn the hurt I had caused. When I went to work on Saturday, after the first week of school, Darnell failed to show at lunchtime so I headed over to the barbershop.

"He's in the alley", Darnell's father said.

I walked through the store and out into the alley. Darnell was shooting baskets. He turned to face me.

"Whaddya want man?"

"You want to shoot hoops? A game of horse. Like we always do."

"You sure it's cool with your friends to shoot hoops with me? I don't want you to have to cross any lines."

I didn't know what to say. Darnell was right and I had failed him as a friend. But I was too afraid to remedy the situation. Lacking confidence in myself, I worried how my friends would react if I introduced Darnell into the group. Would they accept him? If not, would they ostracize me? I worried what they might say to him but, to tell the truth, I was more afraid of what they might say about me.

And it wasn't like I thought my friends were prejudiced. It was just that interacting with a black kid was not something any of them had experienced. We had all gone to a totally white elementary school. We had all lived in a totally white neighborhood. The main connection we had with anyone black was with the housekeepers that tended to our homes. Not exactly the background that gave me confidence that Darnell would be accepted. We had all told jokes about black people and often made fun of them. We had derided kids in our own group by using mean racial terms. Who knew what might slip out of someone's mouth if Darnell joined our group. Given all that, I didn't have enough confidence that I could pave the way for Darnell's acceptance. In my own inconsiderate and self-centered way, I only worried about myself.

Ashamed and not knowing what to say, I lowered my head, walked past Darnell and out the rear gate. Once I cleared his property, I ran up the alley, turned left and circled back to Mount Street and down to the grocery store. When I walked through the door, my father looked surprised and asked why I was back so soon. "Darnell had some extra chores to finish," I said and headed off to the back room to eat my lunch.

When Monday morning came, and school resumed, I did nothing to ameliorate the situation. I avoided even looking in Darnell's direction. I wasn't sure what would happen between us. Part of me wanted to make amends and reclaim my friendship with Darnell. But, the other part of me was stricken, by my cowardice, to inaction. I knew if there was to be an easing of the situation, I would have to be the one to make the move.

A few weeks later, fate, or rather Mr. Sparks, our social studies teacher, intervened and gave me an opportunity to make things right with Darnell. It was early October and I had not spoken to Darnell for about one month.

Mr. Sparks walked by each row of desks and handed a stack of mimeographed sheets to the person sitting at the front desk of each row. The sheets were passed back and each of us took one.

"What you have in front of you is a list of projects. You are to pick a project, find a partner and together research the subject and prepare a presentation to the class. You will have the rest of this semester and most of next semester to work on the project. Starting in May, each team will present a fifteen minute report to the class. Now I want you to take the time now to read the list." After a few minutes had passed, Mr. Sparks asked if there were any questions. Once he had answered all the questions, he said, "Ok I want you each to find a partner. Quietly."

Everyone jumped from their chairs and most made their way toward the kids generally considered the smartest in the class to plead their case. Though Darnell was one of the smartest kids, no one headed toward him so, as I watched everyone else avoiding him, I made the move.

"Whatta you say Darnell? You want to work with me on a project? I know I've been a real asshole to you. I'm sorry and I'd like to work with you on this project."

Darnell looked skeptically at me, sizing up the offer. But he didn't answer.

"Look I feel really bad about what I did to you. I know it wasn't right and I promise it won't happen again."

After what seemed like an eternity, he smiled, "Yeah. As long as I get to choose the project. If you're ok doing something on civil rights, I'm ok doing it with you."

We started work on the project the next weekend. When I finished at the grocery store on Saturday, I met Darnell at the barbershop and we headed back to his house. We had decided that we would spend each Saturday night and Sunday morning working together on the project. That first night, we decided we would write about segregation in Baltimore and what was being done in the community to address the situation. It was not a hard choice to make. It was all Darnell's father and brother talked about at dinner.

"I understand you boys are doing a project on civil rights," Darnell's father posed.

"Yes sir."

"Well, I think that's a good idea. There's a lot to be learned and a lot that has to change. You know your brother can tell you stories about his experience in the movement. Maybe you can use it in your project."

Darnell's brother, George, had attended Morgan State College starting in 1955. That year, students, at the college began staging sit-ins at restaurants around the city. Baltimore was not unlike most cities. Whereas the school system had been integrated, there remained a de facto segregation in housing as many communities were closed off to people of color. Restaurants and movies continued to deny them access. Even government operated facilities, like the public golf course in Baltimore, refused to allow blacks to use the facility. The effort made by the Morgan students, along with students from other colleges in the area, reached a crescendo with the sit-in at the Reads Drug Store on Howard and Lexington Street. Although George was in a group that demonstrated at one of the other Reads locations, he had a front row seat to the unfolding events.

"I was in a group that went to the Reads in Northwood while Mr. Everinghim (the president of the Baltimore chapter of CORE) and Dean Kiah, from Morgan, led a group that demonstrated at the main store downtown. Meanwhile, we went to the Northwood store for a week straight and other groups were sent to the other locations. We held a sit-in at that lunch counter day after day. The counter was in the rear of the store so we walked past all the shoppers and sat down on the stools. The first day, one of the waitresses was so stunned she didn't know what to do. She stared at us like we were aliens from outer space. Then she says something like what do you boys want and we said we want to order some food. *I can't be servin' no colored folk, it ain't allowed,* she says and then goes and calls for the store manager. The white people sitting at the counter are glaring at us, they didn't know if they should go on eating, walk out, or say something to us. They started up murmuring to each other, loud enough for us to hear though, saying things about how disgraceful it was and didn't we know it wasn't allowed and how the world was changing for the worse with these uppity Negroes trying to come into white establishments. We just went on sitting there and within a few minutes, the store manager approached us and asked us to leave, telling us that they did not serve Negroes.

"That be ok," said my friend, Charlie, in his best lackey voice imitation. "We all jes be lookin' for a nice ham sandwich, sir. We ain't too keen on eatin' Negroes. No sir. We ain't got no hankering to eat no Negroes."

Of course, he called the police because we refused to leave. The police came and escorted us out of the store. All of us were arrested. We posted bail and the next day we were back. And so were the police. Every day we sat at that counter and every day we were escorted out of the store."

"What happened after that week," I asked.

"Someone in management at Reads called Dean Grant at Morgan and complained that our demonstration was costing them business. Asked Dean Grant what he could do about it and Dean Grant told him that he wouldn't intervene and that Reads should own up and declare its true colors. Said that they should put a sign in the front window that said colored people could spend their money in the store but were not allowed to eat at the lunch counter. The Reads official said he couldn't and wouldn't do that. Then Dean Grant suggested that they run an ad in the Afro-American newspaper saying the same thing that colored people could shop in the store but couldn't eat at the counter. The Reads executive said he couldn't do that either. You see, he didn't want to serve food to us colored folk and offend his white customers but he didn't want to lose the business we gave them. Finally, Dean Grant proposed that their best option would be for Reads tell all their customers that everyone was welcome at their lunch counters and until he did, he could expect the demonstrations to continue. Two hours later, the Reads official called back and announced that the store would fully integrate and begin to serve all customers."

"It must have been really exciting to be a part of that. To change history."

"It was exhilarating. It was a victory. But there were so many more battles waiting to be waged and victories waiting to be won."

"You know, Michael, there was a demonstration at a restaurant in your own area. Just last year," Darnell's father added.

"I didn't know that."

"Yeah, things like that kind of get covered up. It was at Mandell-Ballow restaurant and it showed how blinded people can be about color. A group of Israeli sailors entered the restaurant and were refused service because they were dark skinned. The manager thought they were just colored folk from Baltimore. But it turned out that they were of Yemeni descent. Once the manager found out that they were really Israelis, they were served. Still strikes me funny that an Israeli colored person is ok but we are not. I guess a bunch of folks felt the same way and that's why they picketed the restaurant."

"I never heard anything about it."

"That's not surprising. People don't talk about it. The newspapers rarely mention it. You know, Michael, it is hard to stand up for principles and people. I think you already found that out." I assumed Darnell had told him about our falling out.

"I hope you'll learn a lot more from your project. There are people in the Jewish community stepping up to support our efforts. People like your father and someday maybe you. Darnell is your friend so you know a colored person firsthand. You know the type of person he is. He's

35

smart but he can't get into the same schools you can get into. He can't go to places you go to all the time. He is not accepted into groups who should welcome him with open arms. All because he is judged by his skin color. You turned your back on him once. I would hope you've learned a lesson and will treat him just like all your other friends from now on."

Darnell was probably more uncomfortable than I was listening to his father's lecture. So, he came to my rescue and asked his father if we could be excused from the table. We went up to Darnell's bedroom and spent the next half hour making an outline of what we wanted to research. We split up the topics and then decided that was enough for the first night.

From that point on, when I finished work on Saturday afternoon at my father's store, I would cross over to the barbershop, wait for Darnell and then head back to his house. I would spend every Saturday night with his family, eating his mom's wonderful dishes and watching television. Then, on Sunday mornings, we would spend a few hours going through the week's newspapers and cutting out articles on civil rights. We wrote letters to the local activists and asked them to recount their experiences. We accumulated mounds of paperwork that we sifted through over the months. By early March, we began to write our presentation. We made poster boards with pictures from sit-ins and demonstrations and a tape recording with George, where he recounted his experience at the Reads' sit-ins. We even had a letter that Dr. Martin Luther King had written in response to questions we had sent him. We made our report to the class in early May. Mr. Sparks was pleased with our work and rewarded us both with "A's." Both Darnell and I were thrilled. Over the months, we had become closer friends. I shared my writings with him. He was the first person I felt comfortable letting read my stories. And he shared a little secret with me.

# CHAPTER SEVEN

Except for Thanksgiving weekend and Christmas vacation, I had spent every Saturday night at Darnell's house since early October. After the first few weeks, I was treated as a member of the family and expected to share in the chores. Darnell's sister, Celia, was responsible for setting the table for Saturday night dinner. Darnell and I were responsible for clean-up. Unlike cleaning the bathroom, at the grocery store for me or at the barbershop for Darnell, washing and drying dishes was a snap. It was actually the first time I ever had done it since an electric dishwasher did it at my house.

Although Sunday dinner, served after Mr. and Mrs. Watkins returned from church, was their big family meal for the week, Saturday night was a close second. I usually had departed by midday on Sunday to meet my father at the store and return home. So, I rarely joined the Watkins' Sunday meal. But, the Saturday night meal was one to savor, both for the food and the discussions. Darnell's brother, George, would join most of the Saturday meals since he attended CORE meetings on Sundays, after church, and could not make it to the house in time. Celia, who was seventeen, would be there before going out with her friends. And on many nights, the Watkins would be joined by some of their neighbors. The meals were hearty—Southern style meatloaf, beef stews, pork chops, hams and chicken pot pies alternated weekly on the menu. Homemade biscuits were a staple along with a lima bean, corn and raisin casserole. Each meal was capped off by one of Mrs. Watkins famous desserts—pecan pie, chocolate cake and lemon chiffon pie, being the most common. Sitting at the table was better than sitting in history class. Mr. Watkins would opine about the state of affairs for the black community and George would update us about CORE's action plans. We would hear what was happening in Birmingham, Montgomery and on the Eastern Shore of Maryland. There were stories about leaders like Dr. King and Stokely Carmichael. We would hear about voter registration efforts and freedom rides.

After finishing the clean-up from dinner, Darnell and I would usually head up to his bedroom. We would do a little bit of work on the project, leaving most of it to Sunday morning. Then we would usually play board games until bedtime. This was our routine until one night in February.

Celia, who usually left the house right after dinner, was home on this night. It was snowing heavily and Mr. Watkins had ordered her to stay in. Darnell and I were playing a game of chess when I heard the bathroom door close. Darnell's bedroom adjoined the bathroom so you could hear the sputtering of the water when the shower was turned on.

Almost instantly, Darnell perked up and said, "I want to show you something. Just between us."

He opened his closet door and motioned me to move closer as he crawled in. I slid up beside him against the rear of closet. There was no insulation, the back of the closet sharing a common wall with the bathroom. A sparkle of light seeped through a crack. Over the years, the steam from the shower had expanded and shrunk the vertical wood planks. Darnell looked through the crack and then pulled away. "Take a look."

I placed my right eye against the crack. The bathtub was visible directly in front of me. In the next instant, Celia was standing in my line of sight. She stepped in front of the bathtub, sat on the edge and stuck her left hand behind the curtain to test the water temperature. Satisfied, she stood up and pulled off her robe. Standing in front of me was the first woman I had ever seen without clothes on. The fact that she was beautiful was icing on the cake. I had been attracted to her from the first time we met and sexual thoughts, like seeing her naked (not uncommon for a twelve year old boy), had crept through my mind many times over the previous weeks.

I caught a side-view glimpse of her breast, and, as she stepped into the tub, a full view of her rear. I took a long breath as Celia disappeared behind the curtain. I turned back from the wall and propped my back against the side of the closet. Darnell grinned, "I thought you might like that. Take another look. Take your time." Darnell obviously realized my attraction for his sister.

As I kneeled in front of the crack, I could hear the water dripping off Celia's body. I imagined her hands shampooing her hair and massaging her scalp. I pictured her soaping up a washcloth and then gliding it across her chest and up and down her legs. Five minutes passed and I stayed glued to my spot. Then the water shut off and Celia pulled the curtain open.

There she stood, face forward, right in front of me. She grabbed a towel and padded the water off her chest and then moved the towel over her head and began drying her back. I peered at her breasts. They were smallish but with nipples that looked like jujubees. She had slender arms and slender legs. I was enthralled. Finally she stepped out of the bathtub and put on her robe. The show was over. For this Saturday at least. Over the next few months, I found myself daydreaming, more than usual, about Celia. Fantasizing. And during that time, I had the opportunity to watch Celia three more times. Each time was as thrilling as the previous one. I couldn't get enough of her. I had found Celia attractive and alluring, the first time we met, and these viewings sealed the deal. Each time, Darnell sat patiently beside me. I assumed he did his viewing during the week.

On the last Saturday, in April, Celia left early, skipping dinner. Since it was still light out, Darnell and I decided to shoot some baskets after we finished the clean-up. When we returned, Mrs. Watkins called to Darnell as we were heading up the stairway. "Darnell don't forget you have to attend church tomorrow. We're leaving around eight. Michael, you can stay until it's time to meet your father. Celia will be home and I'll ask her to fix breakfast for you."

The next morning, Darnell awoke around seven. As Darnell dressed, I stayed in bed, deciding that it was best not to get in the way as three people needed to share the one upstairs bathroom. After grabbing a quick breakfast, Darnell poked his head through the doorway and said, "I'll see you at school on Monday." Moments later, I heard the front door open and close. The house was silent. I stayed in bed for about thirty minutes, figuring there was no rush since I was not meeting my father until later in the morning.

I walked to the bathroom in my pajamas, carrying my clothes. There was no sound coming from Celia's room. I wondered if she was there. Maybe she had not come home Saturday night.

I turned on the water, stripped off my pajamas and stepped into the shower. As the water poured down, over my head, I heard a creaking sound. Then the shower curtain rippled and pushed against my body as air swept against it. I stared as a hand grabbed the curtain and pulled it open. Celia peered in. I was startled. I didn't move and I didn't speak.

"Did you think I didn't know about the crack in the wall? I know you've been watching me."

For the second time in my life, a Watkins had left me speechless. Guilt pulsed through my veins. I knew I had acted badly again but had no idea what to say.

"Cat got your tongue?" Celia asked.

I prayed for some kind of divine intervention. Maybe the water would melt me and I could swim away down the drain like the wicked witch in the Wizard of Oz.

"I guess your eyes work better than your mouth does. Let's see what else works." With that she pulled off her robe and stepped in.

If I was at a loss for words before, I was completely frozen now. Celia stepped toward me. One more inch and our bodies would touch. She grabbed my hands and placed them on her breasts. I didn't move. So, she again placed her hands on the back of my hands and began to move them slowly. "Got the idea?"

As I started rubbing and squeezing her breasts, with great gusto now, she lowered her hands and took hold of my penis. Taking that as a signal, I started moving my hands down her belly towards her legs. "Keep your hands where they were." I obeyed and went back to caressing her breasts. She continued to lightly swirl her fingers around my penis. Then, just as suddenly as things got started, she stepped away. Her eyes pierced my eyes and the faintest smile etched onto the corners of her mouth.

She pulled the curtain open, stepped from the tub and grabbed a towel. Leaving the shower curtain open, she quickly sopped up the water on her shoulders, chest and legs. As I stayed put in the same spot, water still pouring out of the showerhead, she put her robe on. She turned towards the door and, as she twisted the doorknob, she curled her head back towards me.

"You really need to find your way out of the dark, Michael. I hope you do figure it out some day?" and she flicked the light switch off and walked out of the bathroom.

I didn't have a clue what she meant about finding my way out of the dark. I doubted that turning the lights back on was what she meant. What I did know was that I was excited and confused beyond belief. I was also certain that this was not what Mrs. Watkins intended for Celia to make for my breakfast. And I knew I couldn't tell Darnell anything about what happened.

After dressing, I decided it was best to leave the house and avoid any more contact with Celia. Although my father would not arrive for another two hours, it would be uncomfortable to hang around. So, I walked to the grocery store and dropped off my overnight bag on the rear loading dock. To kill off time, I decided to go shoot baskets behind the barbershop.

The next day, at school, I ran into Darnell on the way from the bus stop. I didn't mention anything about Celia, and, if Darnell knew anything about what happened, he didn't bring it up either. In fact, when I went to his house the next Saturday, everything went on in normal fashion. When I saw Celia, she greeted me cheerfully as she always did. There was nothing in her behavior that indicated anything had happened between us. I acted the same. Except for one change. When Celia went to the bathroom and Darnell asked if I wanted to go to the closet, I declined and suggested we just keep playing our game of chess.

I never again made a visit to the closet to look at Celia. It had been wrong of me to do it in the first place. Then as soon as we made our presentation in May, I stopped spending Saturday nights with Darnell. He was disappointed but I told him my parents wanted me to spend more time at home. I couldn't tell him the real reason. The simple truth was that I felt I would burst every time I saw Celia.

When school ended in June, Darnell decided to enroll in an experimental summer program for high achieving students. He went to classes daily and only worked at the barbershop on Saturdays. Meanwhile, I decided to take a creative writing class that met every Monday, Wednesday and Friday morning. My father reluctantly agreed to let me skip work those days. With different schedules, I saw a lot less of Darnell.

On the last Saturday in June, Darnell and I spent our regular lunchtime together. When it was time for me to get back to work, Darnell said, "Michael, how about coming home with me after school on Wednesday. The next day is the fourth of July so I don't have classes. When you finish your class, meet me outside the main entrance and we'll go back to my house. My brother says you should spend the night and the next day. He won't explain it but he says he wants us to see something that day."

"Let me check that it's okay with my father. I'll let you know before I head home tonight."

I was sure my father would not have an issue with me spending the holiday with Darnell. But, before accepting Darnell's invitation, I needed to make sure I could handle seeing Celia. I decided I could. In fact, I felt Wednesday could not come soon enough.

After summer school on Wednesday, I met Darnell and we caught the bus to Mount Street. When we reached Darnell's house, Celia wasn't there and later, when we sat down for dinner, she still wasn't home. Mrs. Watkins told us that she was spending the night with friends but would meet up with us the next morning.

"Tomorrow is going to be a special day," George chimed in. "It will be a fourth of July like none that you experienced before, Darnell. Or you either Michael."

My interest was piqued. "What's going to happen tomorrow?"

"Have you been to Gwynn Oak Park, Michael?"

"Yeah. Lots of times." Gwynn Oak Park was an amusement park on the west side of Baltimore.

"Well we've never been to Gwynn Oak Park. Do you know why? It's because Negroes aren't allowed into that amusement park. Tomorrow we are going to try to do something about that."

"What's going to happen? What will we be doing?"

"You will be doing nothing more than watching. From a distance. I will be part of the demonstration. From what I am told, there will be a lot of white people joining our protest as well. I think it will be a good opportunity for you to witness the things you wrote about in your social studies project. It'll be good for both of you."

It was likely that my parents would not be thrilled to hear that I would be in the vicinity of a desegregation rally. Even though my parents supported the actions of the civil rights movement, being there was a different story. "I think I better ask my parents if it's okay."

"Michael, if you ask your parents, they will forbid you to go," Mr. Watkins said. "I know your father. He is a good man. He supports our efforts. Financially. And morally. But he, himself, is not ready to do more than that. That makes him no different than most other people—white and colored. There are thousands who are barred by the policies of that park but only a handful who will stand up and raise a voice. George will be in the march and I decided to take you and Darnell and we will watch from a safe distance. You will be fine. Nothing will happen to you. I will see to that. And you will get to witness history being made."

The next day, George left early. Around eleven in the morning, Mr. Watkins drove the rest of us to Metropolitan Methodist Church, a church that had been started in 1825 by a former slave. It was a quick drive and by the time we arrived, there were already hundreds of people milling around. Black and white. Not only people from Baltimore but also groups from New York City, Philadelphia and D.C. who came on buses to participate. We entered the church and joined the demonstrators in the basement for a workshop on protest methods. Then everyone moved up to the sanctuary and joined in singing several hymns before a stream of religious leaders spoke to the crowd. Around two p.m., the demonstrators began boarding buses to take them to the rally. Mr. Watkins steered us back to the car. As we climbed into his

Chevy, Celia came running toward us and joined us for the ride over to the park.

The park was located off Liberty Heights Avenue at the corner of Gywnn Oak and Gwyndale and occupied about sixty-four acres surrounded by a residential area. We arrived before the buses and parked a few blocks from the entrance. Many of the neighborhood homeowners were already sitting on their porches in anticipation of the showdown, as if they were attending a heavyweight championship bout. George had said that the organizers of the march had notified the police department of their intention to demonstrate at the Park. The police, in turn, had mobilized about fifty officers, along with paddy wagons, to control the situation. They advised the organizers to expect to be arrested if they went forward with their plans.

Mr. Watkins suggested we remain in the car until the buses arrived in order to avoid drawing any attention. He scouted the area and picked a spot where he felt we would be safe-a sort of neutral corner, away from the homeowners but still in view of the entrance to the park. When the buses pulled up, a few minutes later, we climbed out of the car. Darnell and I sat on the hood and Celia and Mr.Watkins stood along the side of the car.

The first group off the bus was a group of white clergymen. Seeing collars on two of the men, I knew they were Catholic priests and two others appeared to be Protestant ministers. To my surprise, I saw the rabbi from my synagogue, Rabbi Lieberman, among them. They stood side by side, linked their arms together and began walking towards the entrance eventually entering the park through the main gate. What an interesting sight. A group of religious leaders on the one side, united in their cause for equality, and an angry, boisterous, almost rowdy group of short-sleeve clad men and boys pressed against the chain link fence, hurling obscenities from inside the park. If God had descended to earth at that very moment, would there be any doubt what side he would have joined?

Shortly after the clergymen entered the park, a man approached them and started reading from a sheet of paper, advising them to leave the premises. The clergymen ignored the warning and held their ground. Moments later, one of the police officers approached the group and motioned again for the group of clergymen to leave the park entrance but they refused to budge. Then, the first officer motioned with his arm and several other policemen stepped towards the clergymen and began escorting them to the waiting paddy wagons. The clergymen moved along peacefully and without incident. Flashbulbs exploded as the photographers from the local and national newspapers snapped photos.

By then, the rest of the buses had arrived and masses of demonstrators began pushing toward the park entrance. A crowd of patrons continued to build on the other side of the entrance and they began to shout. "Fucking Niggers!" "Fucking white niggers." As many of the demonstrators approached the entrance, they were met by the police, placed under arrest and ushered to the wagons. Some, however, sat down on the ground and refused to move. The shouts and taunts increased from inside the park as the all-white crowd of patrons began shaking the fence they stood behind. "Take 'em back to the zoo." "Send them back to Africa." The protestors countered the shouts by singing "We Shall Overcome" and locking arms. A rock was tossed from behind the fence, flying towards the group of demonstrators sitting on the ground. It struck one of the men and blood started flowing from the back of his head. At the same time, a group of teenagers began running along the fence line with a Confederate flag and shouting more taunts and slurs. The police moved in and began lifting each demonstrator and carrying them toward the paddy wagons. In the end, two hundred eighty-three people were arrested and charged with trespassing or disorderly conduct. George was one of them. Not one of the white people inside the park was arrested.

Once the demonstration was over, we climbed back into the car. Mr. Watkins was worried and said we needed to find George as quickly as possible. First we drove to the police station in Woodlawn but George was not among the group that had been sent there. The officers told us to go to the Wilkins station. We entered that station where dozens of the protestors sat on benches waiting to be processed. George had already been placed in a cell. After talking to the desk sergeant, Mr. Watkins posted the one hundred three dollar bond and George was released.

Mr. Watkins also handed over another thousand dollars to free ten others of the group. Turning to me, he said, "Some of this money is from your father, Michael," a fact that caught me by surprise—I knew my parents supported the civil rights cause and knew they contributed financially but since they never discussed it in front of me and, because Mr. Watkins had suggested that I not ask their permission to attend the demonstration, I didn't think they were aware of what was happening this day. But Mr. Watkins had talked about the demonstration with my father and solicited the contribution.

Many of those arrested were able to use the donated money to post bond and were released within an hour or two of their arrest. Others chose to spend the night in jail to further demonstrate against the segregation policies of the park and other businesses in the city. In the ensuing days, additional marches and protests would be held at the park. All the efforts would eventually be rewarded—the owners announced that the park would be opened to all races in late August. In the span of a few weeks, the demonstrators had succeeded in reversing the park's policy and opening its gates to black people for the first time.

We rode home from the police station listening to George describe the entire event in a way that added to the excitement of the day, for although we had all witnessed most of what had happened from the initial gathering at the church to the events at the park and later at the police station, George was able to tell the story as if it was a dream come to life. He related what went on behind the scenes detailing what the participants talked about at the planning meetings, at the church, on the bus ride to the park and in the paddy wagons and jail cells. When we arrived back at the Watkins house, Mrs. Watkins was ready with dinner so we all gathered around the table.

"Darnell I think you should lead us in grace tonight," Mr. Watkins suggested.

Darnell bowed his head. Joining hands, we all did the same. "Dear Lord. Thank you for the food that is set before us on this important day. May all other brothers and sisters who are denied the freedoms that so many others enjoy, soon share in those freedoms. May the day come when we can all sit together, black and white, in common bond and brotherhood. Amen."

As Mrs. Watkins began dishing out the main course, Mr. Watkins turned to me. "So, Michael, what did you think about what you saw today?"

"I don't know Mr. Watkins. It was overwhelming to watch all those people march toward the gate and be arrested. It was so brave. And inspiring. I was glad to see my rabbi among them. I really liked Reverend Bascom's speech too."

Reverend Bascom's spoke in the Church that day about how, over the many years of participating in the civil rights movement, he had done what he could to push the cause, but never at the risk of going to jail. Then, the very morning of the Gwynn Oak Park demonstration he awoke, looked in the mirror and took stock of his commitment and his fears and decided to put his entire being on the line  realizing that "all he really had to lose were his own chains."

"Bullshit." It was Celia. "Celia!" Mrs. Watkins admonished.

"I'm sorry Mama but what he says is bullshit."

"Perhaps you can find a better way to express it, Celia," Mr. Watkins said.

She turned to me. "You talk about being proud but you are a hypocrite. You pretend to care but really you don't. You don't extend beyond yourself. You play it safe. You are in the dark."

"I don't know what you mean." I felt certain I was about to find out what the dark was that Celia had brought up that day in the shower and again tonight.

"Let me ask you, Michael, why is it that you never have Darnell at your house? Why are you always at our house? It's because it's okay for you to be in his world but it's not okay for him to be in your world. Because in your world, you pay lip service to equality. In your world, you pay black people to make your bed and do your laundry. Black people can be your secret friend or your employee. They just can't be your equal."

"Celia, I don't think Michael feels that way about Darnell. And you can't hold him responsible for whom his parents hire as a housekeeper," Mrs. Watkins said.

"You mean maid, Mama. When black people work for white people, they aren't even housekeepers. They're maids, better to denote their subjugation. Isn't that right Michael? "

I just sat there. Did I dare say that the reason I chose to come to the Watkins house rather than have Darnell come to my house was that there was no Celia at my house.  If I didn't come to the Watkins house, there would be no chance to see her. Didn't she realize that? I remained silent. Because my excuse was pretty weak. Because, after all, she was right. The idea of having Darnell at my house never crossed my mind. It was no different than how I had treated him at school. There were lines that I was afraid to cross. I hadn't stopped to think how my actions were exactly what she said, hypocritical and hurtful and I knew I was still not ready to step out of my comfort zone and risk what might happen if I brought Darnell to my house.

Celia didn't back off. "It was easy for him to be friends with Darnell as long as it was on his terms. Who cared? So, they shot baskets together on Saturdays in an alley where no one saw them. And then in school, he ignored Darnell. For weeks. So, he tried to make up with

Darnell by working together on a school project. One of them white kids had to pick Darnell. So it might as well have been Michael. It was a false bravery."

"Celia, Darnell and Michael are thirteen years old. I doubt they think things through like you do."

"He's my friend, Celia. I don't care what you say or what you think," Darnell shouted. I still didn't say a thing.

"Why isn't he saying it, Darnell? Why doesn't he say anything? Because he can't defend it."

She was right. I had no defense. I had no answer about not inviting Darnell to my house. Well I did have an answer. I just couldn't say it. And I did consider Darnell my friend, my closest friend. After all, he was the only person I ever allowed read my stories, the only person I felt comfortable with to do that. But, I had never stopped for a moment to think about what it meant not bringing Darnell to my house. I think going to his house just became so normal, so expected. And a lot more interesting than going to my house.

'Then let me ask you this, Michael. Would you go out with a black girl?"

"I don't think I'm ready to go out with any girl." I was afraid of what was coming next.

"Well, I think you've learned a bit about the charms of us black girls. Isn't that right?" Darnell's mouth dropped. "So, would you go out with one of us?"

"That's enough Celia," Mr. Watkins interrupted. "You made your point."

"No I haven't." She turned towards me again. "It's about barriers, Michael. You erect them in your own mind and it keeps you from truly accepting us. You put us in compartments and as long as we stay in those compartments, you can accept us. George and his colleagues can do all the marching and sitting-in that they want. They may get the parks to let us in and the restaurants to serve us. But they will never be able to tear down the barriers in those peoples' minds. And, believe me, it's not something you can legislate either. Those people have to do it themselves, they themselves have to break down their prejudice and see us as equals. And you have to do it. If you don't break down the barriers you put up, then you can never be the man you want to be. Or could be."

"Celia, I said that's enough."

Celia pushed back her chair and stood up. "I think I've had enough supper for tonight."

"Well boys. I think I'll take care of the clean-up tonight. It's been a long day. Why don't you boys go upstairs and play."

We spent the next few hours playing chess. It was awkward. I could tell Celia had scored points and got Darnell thinking. But, he didn't bring up any of the things Celia had said. So I kept up appearances too. We talked about the things we usually talked about. But, it was hollow. My mind was turning over what Celia had accused me of. I was certain she had scored a TKO and I wanted to retreat and think things over.

The next day Darnell and I caught the public bus to school. I was looking forward to my writing class more than usual. The events of the last few days would give me plenty to write about. Writing was always my best companion. A perfect release. The ideal way for me to express myself since verbalizing was not something that worked best for me. And I needed that more now than ever.

After class was dismissed, I asked my teacher if I could wait in the classroom. I wanted to meet up with Darnell before he went home and show him what I had written. It was about the rally at the park and I thought Darnell would appreciate the message. But, Darnell would not finish classes for another hour. So, I sat at my desk and daydreamed and soon lost track of time. A little over an hour had passed and suddenly I was afraid Darnell had already left. My classroom was on the first floor and Darnell's classroom was on the second floor. I bolted from the classroom and ran to the stairway. As I opened the door, I could hear voices.

"So, are you one of those niggers that tried to get into Gwynn Oak yesterday?"

Another voice spoke up. Yeah. Maybe he's one of those chicken shit niggers."

"Maybe you want to lick the shit from my asshole, nigger. Whadda ya say?"

I crept up a few steps and I could see Darnell cornered by four kids. Summer school was a place for enrichment programs but it was also a place for the kids who had to take remedial classes. Darnell was facing four of those delinquent kids. I even recognized two of them. They were the two who had confronted me at the beginning of the school year looking to steal my money.

"I asked if you want to lick the shit from my asshole." Darnell was pinned against the wall. I wanted to run and get help but I knew there wasn't enough time. I crept up a few more steps. My feet felt like they were buried in cement. My heart was throbbing against my ribcage and my lips and mouth were bone dry.

"You hard of hearing, nigger? I asked if you want to lick the shit from my asshole."

"Only after you finish sucking my dick," Darnell replied. The kid, directly in front of Darnell, lashed out and landed a fist across Darnell's nose. Darnell winced. Blood began pouring out of both nostrils. The next blow landed in his solar plexus and Darnell crumbled to the floor.

I hurriedly climbed the steps and stopped just below where Darnell and his tormentors stood and blurted out "Leave him alone." Which came out in stutter-like fashion so it sounded like "Lllllleave him (gulp) alone." A declaration, but one without a lot of force behind it. And one that drew only laughs from Darnell's attackers.

"What are you some kind of nigger lover? Or maybe you're one of those white niggers who showed up to help them niggers yesterday at the park."

Before I knew it, two of them grabbed my arms and threw me against the wall. A fist landed against my left eye and the pain shot through my head. The punches started raining down on me. I tried to raise my arms but I couldn't throw a punch and I couldn't block their punches. I fell to my knees and they began pounding my back with haymakers. I rolled onto my left side and had enough strength left to lift my arms up around my head. The punches kept coming. I was conscious but motionless. Eventually, they tired of hitting me and turned their attention back to Darnell, who was still crumpled in a heap. Each of them kicked him, again and again, in the ribs and head and with each blow, Darnell yelped in pain. To this day, I don't know what made them stop. Probably boredom.

"Fucking niggers and nigger lovers. Next time, I'll remember to bring a noose." And then they were gone.

Both of us just laid there. For minutes. For hours. I don't know how long it was. Finally, one of the administrators making his rounds to clear the building found us. He ran down the steps and began shouting for help and instantly two other teachers appeared. "Go call for an ambulance and grab some towels and ice."

The ambulance arrived about ten minutes later and both Darnell and I were transported to Sinai Hospital. Darnell had four broken ribs, a broken nose and a concussion. My left eye was black and swollen shut and my back was covered with bruises and contusions. I was released to my parents a few hours later, the only visible sign of the attack being the large black and purple mark that covered my cheek up to my forehead and extended from my nose to my ear. Darnell needed to be monitored so he had to spend the next few days in the hospital.

We were each visited separately by the police, who wanted descriptions of our assailants. The principal also asked us to identify our attackers but we didn't know their names and knew it would be uncomfortable to be paraded from classroom to classroom to pick them out. So we asked if we could let it go. Reluctantly, they agreed but made us promise to come forward if we felt threatened.

My mother, on the other hand, did not let go of it. On the day of the attack, as soon as we returned home, she jumped on my father.

"We need to get Michael out of that school. We need to move to the county, where he'll be safe."

Within days, she put our house on the market and started looking for a new house. Two weeks later, we were preparing to move and I was soon enrolled at Sudbrook Junior High in Baltimore County. It was ironic. Here we were, probably the first white family to be fleeing Baltimore because of intimidation from white people. Hardly what most people considered to be the traditional definition of white flight. But was it an anomaly? Maybe those people were the real threat to decency and civility and the world had just not recognized it yet.

I was unhappy to be separated from Darnell and my other friends. More so, over time, I grew disappointed in the knowledge that my parents and I had failed to stand up to the hatred. Instead, we ran away when we should have stayed and fought the battle. We ran because we could, because we could afford to, an option that wasn't there for the Watkins family and many others.

# CHAPTER EIGHT

During the 1963-64 school year, my first in Baltimore County, I continued to work at the grocery store on Saturdays. Darnell and I continued to meet for lunch and basketball each week but my mother insisted that I come home with my father each night. The following summer was the same. Darnell and I saw each other every day but our time together was limited. The worst of it was that it had been a year since I had last seen Celia. Still I had no trouble recalling every detail about her-- from her black onyx eyes swimming in a sea of white to her lips which curled up in the corners and said *I may be smart and beautiful and outspoken but I am friendly and approachable.*

My last year at Sudbrook and the ensuing summer followed the same course. But, when I entered high school, the routine changed. I was playing three sports and I needed the weekends to catch up with the schoolwork. Working at the grocery store no longer fit into the schedule. On the days after Thanksgiving and during Christmas break, I would still pick up some hours at the store because I needed the money. So, I was able to stay in touch with Darnell, but the relationship was more distant. Darnell was focused on his studies. He was determined to go to Harvard in pre-law and his summer was filled with extra courses. He picked up an internship at one of the big law firms downtown. As a result, when I was at the store during the summer, Darnell was working at the law firm or attending summer school classes. And during the school year, when Darnell was working at the barbershop, I was spending Saturdays doing homework.

When I decided to enlist Darnell's help with my investigation, it had been two years since we had seen each other. My father had brought home news about Darnell and I wrote messages back. But, I was unsure how Darnell would react to seeing me again. I was sure that I had proven Celia's claim that I had not truly made Darnell a part of my life. And I guess she was right. Nevertheless, I decided to go forward with my plan.

On the first Saturday, following my pursuit of Coach McCaskill and his players, I popped out of bed early. I dressed and went down to the kitchen where my father was drinking a cup of coffee and reading the newspaper.

"Morning Dad. I thought if it's okay with you that I would work at the store today. I could use the money."

"You sure it won't interfere with your studies."

"No, I'm in good shape. I think I can finish everything tomorrow."

As soon as my father finished his coffee, we drove to the store. I did my normal jobs that morning, including two trips carrying customer's bags to their homes. When it was lunchtime, I headed over to the barbershop.

"Well look who's here. Haven't seen you in these parts for some time," Mr. Watkins said as I entered the shop. "How you been doing?"

"Great Mr. Watkins. Good to see you. "

"Still miss you round the house. It's kinda empty these days. George doesn't get by so often and Celia's away at school. Even Darnell's jumping out right after work to do things. Maybe you can get Darnell to invite you over soon. "

"I'd like that Mr. Watkins."

"Well go on now. I think Darnell's out in the yard."

I walked out the back door and saw Darnell shooting baskets, like all those Saturdays over the years. "Hey Darnell. How you doing?"

'Hey Michael. It's been a while." We shook hands. "You think you can handle a game of horse now that you're a big time varsity player?"

"I don't think that I'm big time but I'm pretty sure I can handle whatever you got."

We caught up on things as we traded shots. Darnell had applied to Harvard and nowhere else. He said it was all or nothing. But, he seemed pretty confident. His SAT scores were high and his grades were at the top of the class. He had the internship at the law firm to show on his resume. And in the last two years, he had become involved in the community, working at a soup kitchen organized through his church. George had recruited him into CORE and Darnell had participated in sit-ins on Maryland's eastern shore a few times. I told him that I was still doing a lot of writing and that I hoped to study journalism if I could get accepted at a college. I filled him in on the basketball team and how our season was going.

"So, what brings you down here? Your father said you have to study on Saturdays."

"I usually do. I'm always behind by the end of the week so I use the weekend to catch up. But I needed to see you. I need to ask for your help on something."

I told him about the first meeting with Bill Perl and then writing letters to the editor about his columns and how that led to the chance to write a story for the Gazette. "I didn't know what to write about. Then I learned about a situation with the basketball team at another school. I thought it would make a good story, one that raised some ethical concerns. But I need to reach out to two players and that's where I can use your help."

"What two guys?"

"I don't know their first names. But one guy is Hicks and he plays point guard on the team. The other guy is a tall dude named Jones and he plays center for them. Hicks lives over on Fulton and Jones lives on Fayette Street. Do you know them?"

"Yeah, I know those guys. They still come by the barbershop, from time to time, to get their hair cut. Always hanging out together. They went to Pimlico when you went there. Of course, they weren't as big as they are now. And since you weren't in any of their classes, there's no way you would have known them. So how do you know them now?"

"Well, I played against them and then I followed them home one night."

"Followed them home? Why would you do that? Are you crazy? "

I explained about losing to their team and how Hicks and Jones dominated the game. How I learned that they didn't live in the area and had been recruited to play basketball in the county and that it was a pattern that had been in place for years with kids coming from the city to play basketball at this school.

"So, I went to one of their games when we had an off day. I needed to make sure. After the game, the coach drove them back to their homes on Fulton and Fayette. Now, I need their help for the story. I need them to tell me what's going on."

"I don't know about this, Michael. I don't know about you messing around in those guys lives. Not so sure that much good can come from it."

"Listen Darnell. I understand where you're coming from. But this is my chance. Probably the only chance I've got to make it into a journalism school. I don't qualify to write for my school newspaper. So, I have no background, nothing to show. If I can get a story published, in the Gazette, I'm sure it will help me get into college."

"Let me think about it. Check back before you go home tonight."

At the end of the day, while my father was closing up, I told him that I needed a minute to check with Darnell. I hurried over to the barbershop. Darnell saw me coming and came out the front door to meet me.

"So did you think about it?" I held my breath waiting for his answer.

"Yeah, I thought about it. And I think it's a bad idea. Ain't no two colored boys gonna talk to a white boy that they don't know. Especially if they are part of something that's not right. But I still owe you. You did come to my defense when I was getting beat up by those four boys. Not that it was much of a defense. But I figure you took some blows that were meant for me. So, I'm gonna see what I can do. No guarantees."

"Hey I appreciate whatever you can do."

"Let me check it out and, if you're here next week, I'll let you know."

The following Saturday, I went to work at the store again. At lunchtime, I hooked up with Darnell, anxious to hear if he could help me out.

"All right man. Here's the plan. You got Christmas break coming up in a week. You gonna work at the store that week?" I nodded. "Then why don't you plan on staying at my house Tuesday night. Wednesday morning, we'll go to the rec center. Both of those guys play ball there every morning. I'll take you down there. We probably can get in the game. What else happens is up to you."

After work, on Tuesday, I met Darnell at his house just as the family was sitting down for dinner. "Nice to have you join us," Mrs. Watkins welcomed. "Feels like old times."

"Glad to be here, Mrs. Watkins. I've missed seeing you. And your food." She laughed. We all sat down. Mrs. Watkins, Mr. Watkins, Darnell and me. And Celia. Mrs. Watkins began piling the food on each of our plates.

Celia turned to me. "So, Michael, you still got that crush on me?" I hadn't seen her for years. And, right off the bat, she knocked me off balance. Again. I knew my attraction for her had not lessened since I had last seen her. In fact, she had blossomed. Her beauty was breathtaking.

"Celia, you're embarrassing Michael. As you can see, Michael, Celia hasn't become any subtler in her comments."

"Hey, I'm just messing with him. I know he's still got a thing for me. I can see it in his eyes. So what you been up to?"

I told the Watkins family about school, the basketball team and my plans for next year. Celia filled me in about college. She was on a full scholarship to Princeton. "When I graduate in the spring, I'm taking a year off to work down South on voter registration. Then I want to go to med school. Hopefully Hopkins. So, Michael, I'm just surprised to see you here, after all this time. What's really going on?"

"I asked Darnell for some help on a project."

"What kind of project?"

I wasn't sure how much to say about the story. It could be headed toward a dead end. Even if I was able to get information from Hicks and Jones, the Gazette might not take my story.

"I met the sports editor of the Gazette a few months back and he's giving me a chance to write a story for the paper. It's about basketball and I wanted to talk to some guys who live in the city. Darnell is hooking me up with some players at the rec center tomorrow. "

"What's your angle? What's this story about, exactly?" Celia asked. I think she sensed there was more to it than what I was saying.

"When we played the County champions this year, they had two guys playing on the team who actually live in the city. Just a few blocks over from here. I started checking into it and found that the school was bringing in players, from the city, for years. It's against the rules so I thought I would investigate and write about it. I'm not even sure the Gazette will take it. But I'm hoping they will publish it and that it will help me get into college, into a journalism school."

Celia absorbed what I was saying. "So, let me get this right. You are going to expose two colored kids for playing basketball in the county. That's their big crime?"

"No, you're missing the point. I'm exposing the school. I'm not after the players. I just want to show that all the acclaim the school has received is wrong. They cheated."

"You don't get it. That school is the white establishment. Nothing ever happens to the white establishment. You know that right? If you expose them, the only thing that will happen is that those two kids won't play for that school anymore. Whatever they are getting out of it, they'll lose it. Nothing will happen to the school except maybe losing a few games. Those kids will be right back in this neighborhood with less of a chance to get out. Those kids will be the only ones paying a price for all this mischief. Leave 'em be."

"I don't see it that way."

"Of course you don't. I'm not saying what the school is doing is right. But those kids are going to be hurt a lot more than the school. Right now they get to go to a school with better facilities and a better learning environment. If the price is that the school wins a basketball championship, then so be it. If you take it away, then those kids may be right back here following in the footsteps of all the others who have no way out."

"Maybe not. Besides, I would think, Celia, you of all people would see it the other way. You're always complaining about white people using black people. About not letting you into our world. That's exactly what that school is doing. They're treating them like a commodity, pretending to let them in just to win more basketball games. When the season is over, when those kids are of no further use to the school, the school won't give a damn what happens to them." I was yelling.

"Here's the thing, Michael. Those kids should be able to go to that school without any conditions or restrictions. They shouldn't have to rely on basketball to get them in. Educating them and every black kid in the city, should be just as important as educating every privileged kid in the county. Giving them equal access and a chance to learn should be the same no matter where they live. So, yeah I don't like it one bit that the school is using those kids. But I say, two can play that game. Let those two guys use the school to benefit themselves before the school uses them and spits them out." Celia was as animated and loud in her response as I had been.

'Okay. Okay. You know me, I'm all for a lively discussion. But, maybe it's best if we change the subject. We don't have the chance to spend time together anymore. So, let's be positive and enjoy each other's company," Mr. Watkins interrupted. We all settled down and moved onto calmer topics.

Early the next morning, Darnell and I headed down to the rec center, which was on the corner of Fulton and Lexington. When we arrived, both Hicks and Jones were there shooting around. Otherwise the gym, which smelled of stale sweat, was empty except for the supervisor. We pulled off our coats and sweats.

"You guys up for a little two-on-two?" Darnell asked.

"Sure, as soon as you're ready to go."

When we walked onto the court, Hicks checked me out. "Hey, I know you man. You play for that Jewish high school. What you doing down here?"

"My father has a grocery store on Mount Street and I work there on holidays and weekends. It's right across the street from Darnell's father's barbershop. We usually shoot hoops behind the shop but we thought we'd come down here today because it's too damn cold outside."

Hicks tossed me the ball and I stretched it over my head before taking a warmup shot. "So, what are you guys doing down here? " I asked, my voice full of innocence.

"We live here man. Down the street." The first slip up, an admission. I tried to act bewildered.

"You live down here? Don't you live in the county? I mean you go to school out in the county. Hell you just kicked our asses a few weeks ago. What gives?"

"It's an arrangement, man."

"What kind of arrangement?"

"Hey did you come to talk or to play basketball."

"To play basketball," I lied.

"Then let's play," Hicks suggested. "You guys can have the ball first. Game to ten. You score, you keep the ball."

If getting them to talk was a longshot, our odds of competing on the court were worse. I could match up against Hicks, although he was quicker and more athletic than me. But that would leave Darnell guarding Jones, who had at least eight inches and fifty pounds on him. Darnell was still a few inches shorter than me though he had slimmed down, lost all of his baby fat, and now had a trim, muscled physique thanks to the weight-lifting he did daily at home.

"Looks like we have our work cut out for us," Darnell said.

"We need to get them out of their game, get them to think it's a cakewalk so they'll let their guard down and then we can sneak up on them. That's our only shot. You take Hicks and just try to stay in front of him. If he goes to the basket, you won't be able to stop him. So dare him to take outside shots. He'll hit some but he'll miss some too. Maybe we'll get a lucky bounce on the rebound. I'll try to coax Jones outside because I won't be able to hold him off on the inside.

Darnell started with the ball at the top of the key and tossed it to Jones. "Check." Hicks tossed it back and Darnell started dribbling in place. Hicks stood back, daring Darnell to shoot. Darnell, who never needed much coaxing, arched a shot toward the basket and through, just like that shot he made the second time the two of us played horse. It went in. "Beginner's luck," Darnell offered.

Keeping possession, Darnell passed the ball to me on the right wing. I waited for Jones to step toward me. He stayed back so I took the shot and scored. On the next play, I again got the ball on the wing but this time, Jones moved up to guard me. I dribbled toward the basket, jumped and then twisted so that I could pass the ball back to Darnell, who lifted another shot to the basket and we went up three to nothing.

Our strategy was working but the results soon changed. I got free for another shot from about seventeen feet but bounced the ball off the front of the rim and Jones grabbed the rebound and, in a flash, they tied the score with three identical plays. Each time, Hicks tossed it into Jones who simply turned on me, spun to the hoop and dropped in a layup.

As we played, several other neighborhood guys entered the gym and stood on the sideline watching the game. One of them teased, "Hey Jones. Ain't you got any other type of shots in your repertoire?" When the next pass came into Jones, instead of spinning to the basket, he stepped back and launched a fade-away jump shot that missed everything and rolled out of bounds. "I guess that boy ain't got no other shots in his repertoire." The crowd hooted and continued to heckle them.

I felt I could take Jones on the dribble. He had the height but I had the speed. I motioned Darnell to the opposite side to make sure Hicks wouldn't slough off and help out his teammate. In an easy motion, I went past Jones and dropped in a layup. On the following play, I deked to the basket and Jones slid back giving me an open shot, which I hit to put us up five to three. But we lost possession, on the next play, when my pass to Darnell was batted away by Hicks. "Bout time you boys started playing some defense," someone in the crowd yelled.

Our opponents immediately went back to what was working for them. Two passes into Jones, two shots and the score was tied again. "What's up Jones, you gotta carry the whole load? Ain't your boy gonna try doing any scoring?" Hicks took the ball, smiled at his heckler, and flattened Darnell on his drive to the basket. Six to five. We were down.

Hicks dribbled the ball from his right hand, behind his back, pushing Darnell against his right hip and then faded to his left and put up a jumper. The ball bounced off the rim into Jones' hands. But when Jones lowered the ball down to his waist, I was able to swat it away. I beat him to the ball and found Darnell open on the baseline for an open shot. Six apiece. The crowd whooped it up and stomped their feet.

Hicks became intense, probably pissed off about how it was going in front of his buddies. He moved up tight against Darnell and swiped the ball and took it straight to the hoop for a dunk and then bumped his chest against my left shoulder as he headed back to the foul line. The crowd hollered. Next, Hicks took the ball and hit a jumper from fifteen feet and their lead went to eight to six. Things were becoming very reminiscent of how he played against us a few weeks ago.

Hicks was feeling it. He drove to the basket and bounced a beautiful pass to Jones, who was not expecting it and let it slip through his hands.

I knew this was our last shot. We would have to hit four in a row if we had any hope of winning the game. I took a pass from Darnell and stood a few feet from Jones. I faked a shot to draw him toward me and made my move. I went by Jones and leaped for my layup. Out of nowhere, Hicks came from behind and swatted the ball off the backboard into Jones' hands, for another easy layup. Hicks followed with a clean shot from the top of the key. Game over. Ten to six.

"Nice game."

"You guys did okay," Jones replied as we shook hands. I shook hands with Hicks, Darnell did the same and then I walked over to the water fountain with Hicks and Jones.

"I wish you guys had picked to come to my high school to play. I would have loved to win a county championship before I graduated. Are there are other guys down here looking to play in the county? Maybe I can get them hooked up with my school for next year."

"I don't know, man. You gotta have a connection like Coach McCaskill has with Mr. Berry." There it was. Another slip.

"Who's Mr. Berry?"

Jones glanced at Hicks and hesitated for a second. "He coaches a team out of the gym here. When we get to high school, he sees to it that we get to a school where we can play. Me and Hicks were on the "B" team. We were good but Mr. Berry knew we'd get less playing time at the city schools. We go out to the county and show what we got so we can get to college and maybe a scholarship."

"So you think I could have my coach contact Mr. Berry? We could use the players and I'm sure he could offer the same deal you're getting."

"I don't know man. McCaskill and Berry go back a long way. They played together in college. Everybody knows McCaskill's looking to coach on the college level and he promised to hire Mr. Berry to his staff, if he gets a job. Plus, you know McCaskill's brother owns a construction company. If things don't work out for us, we get a job working for his brother. Besides they help out my family whenever things are tight."

Hicks frowned at Jones, "I think you done enough talking for one day."

"Hey I'm just looking to help out my high school. If you guys don't think it's a good idea, no problem. But, I'm sure my coach would be interested. Let Mr. Berry know if you want. You know where to find me. If not, just drop it."

By this time, Darnell had joined us. "Hey, Michael, you better get to work. I think you're late already." We grabbed our sweats and headed out of the gym.

"You get what you wanted?" Darnell asked.

"I think I got a lot of what I needed. Now I just have to connect the dots."

The next day, I researched at the library searching through newspaper archives and found out where McCaskill and Berry had played in college. There were articles, from the Gazette, about Berry's amateur team as well. I was able to cross reference players from Berry's team who also played for McCaskill's team by checking through old box scores. That night, I wrote the story and the following day went to see Mr. Perl at the Gazette.

After waiting in the lobby for twenty minutes, the receptionist called my name and told me to take the elevator to the third floor. As I stepped off the elevator, a staff member pointed me towards Mr. Perl's office. He motioned me to sit down while he finished a phone call. His desk was littered with piles of articles waiting to be read and edited, a stack of newspapers, a brass desk lamp with a green shade, a baseball shaped pen and pencil holder and an ashtray filled with what was probably a week's worth of cigarette butts. On the wall were a few pictures of Mr. Perl standing with various local sports stars, a picture of him sitting in the press box at an Orioles game and a family photo.

"First thing you gotta learn about the newspaper business, kid, is that there are deadlines. I gave you thirty days and here you are now just showing up with your story."

"I'm sorry Mr. Perl. It took more time than I expected."

"Well hand it over. Let me read it." He leafed through the pages while I fidgeted in the chair.

"This is not at all what I expected from you. I figured you'd write some puff piece about one of the teams or one of the players at your school. This generally isn't the type of story I print on the sports pages. People want to read about games. About their heroes. It's all about escapism. They don't want to know that corrupt things are going on. I know this investigative reporting is big shit now. But, I'm not sure we're ready for this type of article on the sports page. Especially about high school basketball."

"Mr. Perl. You, better than anyone, know scandals have been a part of sports for a long time. What about Shoeless Joe and the Black Sox scandal. Or the point shaving at CCNY in the 50's. I'm not saying that what I wrote about is anywhere near on the same scale. But people love sports because they think it is about fairness and a level playing field. A competition to see who has the best team. They have a right to know when things aren't on the up and up and you have an obligation to publish it. If you think it is worthy."

"Well the second thing you have to learn about reporting is that sometimes you have to defend what you wrote. I'm glad that you feel so strong about your article. Who are these guys, Hicks and Jones and the others? Do they know they are being used as sources?"

"Not exactly. It was kind of off the record."

"Hmm. Off the record. That ain't good. Do they realize what's likely to happen to them if I print this story?"

"I don't think so. They realize their playing in the county is a violation. But they didn't know I was writing a story about it. I'm not looking to undermine them so I'm hoping they'll come out of it ok."

"Don't be naïve Michael. They'll get kicked out of the school and be back in the city. Who knows what will happen to McCaskill? But, I have to cover my ass. There is more that has to be done on this story before it can be published. Things that you won't be able to do. Like talk to McCaskill and Berry. So, I am going to assign one of my reporters to tie up the loose ends. I will give you a byline and I will include an editor's comment noting how this all came about."

Shortly after school resumed in January, the article appeared on the front sports page of the Tuesday morning edition. Neither McCaskill nor Berry responded in the article. The head of Baltimore County athletics promised a swift and thorough investigation. That investigation took three months, finishing long after the basketball season had concluded, a season that ended with another championship for the Lions. In the end, McCaskill and the school were reprimanded but suffered no further penalties. They forfeited no games and no championships. One month later, McCaskill resigned after getting hired as head coach at a low level Division 1 school in Pennsylvania. Mr. Berry was hired as his assistant. And Jones and Hicks? Well they were kicked out of the county and both decided to drop out of school rather than finish their high school education in the city. I got my byline, a great piece to add to my college applications and another reality check. Everything had worked out for me and even for the school. And the only ones who lost anything? Only Jones and Hicks. I felt bad about that but what could I do? In the end, it was exactly as Celia had predicted. I had traded the future path for Hicks and Jones for my own success.

# CHAPTER NINE

It was snowing on May 6. Not a surprising occurrence considering that it had snowed virtually every day since mid-October. But that was typical Syracuse weather. Like they said, the city had two seasons-- winter and the fourth of July. I never expected that my freshman year in college would end on a snowy day and just about begin on a snowy day. And I never expected that it would take an extra year for me to get my college career started in the first place.

Three months after the Gazette published my article, I had received my acceptance letter to the Newhouse School of Communications at Syracuse University. I was excited. I was ready to pack my bags that day. But things changed quickly. That night at dinner, my mother announced to my father, "Michael has some news to share with you."

"What kind of news, Michael?"

"Well I got accepted to Syracuse University. To the journalism school."

"Uh, well that's uh great. Good for you."

"You don't seem too excited, Dad."

"Look Michael. I thought I made my position clear about college. I don't think it's something you need to waste my money on. You have a job, a career, waiting for you at the grocery store."

"But, it's not something I want to do. I told you what I want to do."

"Well it was good enough for your grandfather. And it's been good enough for me. I think we all live a pretty nice life off that grocery store. If you don't think it's for you, then I can't force you. But I won't help you with college either. You said college was something you were prepared to do on your own. I guess now you have the chance to prove it."

I had to give my father credit for one thing. He was a man of his word and possessed an unerring memory. There would be no convincing him to change his mind either.

"And one more thing, Michael. I hope you will come to work full time at the store. But, whichever way you go, you will responsible for paying rent to stay here. Twenty-five dollar a week. Starting in July."

I excused myself and retreated to my room to contemplate my options. Regardless of the way things would work out, I knew I had to get out of my parents' house as soon as possible. It would be miserable facing my father each night. I could wait out the school year to plot my next moves but, at the same time, I knew the sooner I started lining things up, the better.

First up would be what to do about college. There was financial assistance available, maybe even scholarships if I could qualify. But I did not want to go into debt to pay for school. I preferred to earn the money up front to take the pressure off. Given the time, I believed I could earn enough to pay my way. So I contacted the University the next day and asked for an admissions deferment to give me the time to earn my tuition and room and board and then enter school in the fall semester of 1969. The University said I would have to reapply, but given the circumstances, I could expect to be readmitted.

In order to earn enough to pay for a college education, working at the grocery store would not suffice as my sole source of income. Begrudgingly, my father had started paying me the minimum wage of $1.60 per hour which allowed me to save some money. But, at that rate, it would take a lot of hours to accumulate the kind of money necessary to meet the costs of attending Syracuse. Finding another job to supplement my income would be essential.

After mulling over the situation, I decided to call Mr. Perl and see what advice he could offer. He certainly had taken an interest in me and my writing, and, to a certain degree, served as my mentor. Advice from a respected elderly source would be welcome. When I called a few days later, I told him about being accepted to Syracuse but that I would have to put off attending for a year in order to earn enough to pay my way.

"I need to find a job that will pay me enough so that I can pay for my education. Any suggestions?"

"Let me think about it," he proposed, "and call me back next week."

When I called Mr. Perl the following week, there was good news.

"How would you like to come to work for the paper? It would mostly be a lot of errands. But, I'll let you go with me to the Orioles games and you can help me with stats and learn a bit when I work as the official scorekeeper. There might even be a chance to write, depending on what happens. I'll pay you $120 per week and you can start as soon as school is over in June."

Without any hesitation, I accepted. I planned to keep working at the grocery store while also working at the paper. Combined the two jobs would generate the money needed. On top of that, with all of my friends gone, working two jobs would keep me busy and fill up all of the empty time.

My father quickly withdrew his offer to work at the store when I told him I would be working for the Gazette, starting in June. We were driving to the store, one Saturday, when I told him about Mr. Perl's offer. "But I want to keep working at the store too. So, I can save a lot of money. I will just to need to adjust my schedule to fit around the work at the Gazette."

"Michael. You don't pick the hours. I pick the hours. If you can't work a nine to five day, then I am afraid I don't have a position for you." I didn't answer. I figured I would just try to get through the day.

At lunchtime, I met up with Darnell and brought him up to date on what was going on. Darnell had been accepted by Harvard, on a full ride. He listened sympathetically to my predicament and then made a suggestion.

"Here's an idea. Why don't you take over my job? I'm sure my father could use the help. And I'm sure he'd accommodate your schedule so you could work at the newspaper. And if he needs convincing, I'll get Celia. I'm sure she'd be all for it. You know. A white kid working for a black man. She'd see some kind of justice in that."

"And I've got another idea. If things are that uncomfortable for you at home, why not live at my house? In my room. I moved into George's old room because it's bigger so mine is empty and it's not like you don't know the territory. And you'd have my Mom to keep you fed. With Celia and George gone and now me, I think my parents would welcome the company. They'll be happy to have some noise in the house."

It sounded good to me. As it turned out, Darnell's mother was only too glad to open her home to me. Darnell's father needed a little more convincing, not wanting to intrude on my family dynamics. But when he asked, my father presented no objections. "I think Celia would bite off my head if I didn't agree to this." A few days, after school was over, I packed my clothes in two suitcases and boxed up my few personal belongings and I moved into Darnell's room.

Since, Darnell had taken the internship at the law firm again, Mr. Watkins certainly needed the help. I started working at the barbershop immediately. On days when I had to report to the Gazette in the morning, I would be at the barbershop by six. It would take two hours but, in that time, I could get the blades cleaned and sharpened and the towels folded and placed on the shelves. I cleaned the mirrors and swept the floor. Put antiseptic solution in the comb and scissors containers. Wiped down the chairs. Emptied the trash. By the time Mr. Watkins arrived, around eight, the place was ready for business and I headed off to the Gazette. I would return at six in the evening to wash the towels and hang them on the clothes line in the alley. On other days, when I was scheduled to meet Mr. Perl at Memorial Stadium, to work an Orioles game, I would work at the barbershop until three and then catch the #22 crosstown bus to the ballpark. Usually, I would not finish up at the stadium until eleven or later. By the time I returned to the Watkins house, it would be past midnight. Still, I was at the shop at six the next day. I worked all day at the barbershop on Saturday. On Sunday, I was back at the stadium for a two o'clock game, when the Orioles were in town. As autumn rolled in, I started working at Colts games on Sundays as well. It was a demanding schedule. But, it eased up for a few months during the winter, with both the Orioles and Colts done for the year. Then, before I knew it, it was spring and baseball season had begun. The schedule became crazy again. I was tired. But, I had earned enough money to cover my college expenses. And I had a wealth of experience.

True to his word, I spent most of my time running different errands for Mr. Perl and the rest of the staff. When I attended games, most of my time was spent carting hot dogs and beer around the press box rather than doing anything journalistic and there was little time to watch the game. But, as the year went along, I got a few opportunities. First there some rewrites of stories for later editions of the paper. In those days, the paper published multiple issues each day so the stories would have to be updated as more information became available. During the winter, I covered some high school basketball games when the beat reporter was out sick or on vacation. In the spring, I was assigned a feature story on the Mount Washington lacrosse club. I worked at the paper until the day before I left for school. On that last day, Mr. Perl gathered the staff for a small farewell party for me. We stood around the conference room table and ate the sportswriters' delight—buckets of Kentucky fried chicken, fries and Coke.

Mr. Perl requested everyone quiet down for a minute. "I want to offer a few words. Michael. It has been a pleasure to have you as a part of the staff for the last year. Your enthusiasm (he hesitated for a second). Well I think you have reminded all of us why we got in the business in the first place. You worked hard and you earned your money. But you also earned our respect. In fact, because of you, the Gazette has decided to create an annual scholarship for promising journalistic talent. I am glad to announce that you are the first recipient. I think this should come in handy."

As the rest of the staff applauded, he handed me an envelope with a check for $5000, enough to pay my tuition for the first two years which would allow me to use the money I had saved from the two jobs for room and board and books and eliminate any financial pressure. I had planned to get a part time job at school and that, along with summer jobs and the scholarship, would most likely carry me through the next four years.

There was one other thing that Mr. Perl had for me. After the party, he called me in to his office. "I have something I want to give you personally." He handed me a package which I opened to find a portable typewriter. "I expect good things to come from that typewriter. You let me know how things are going. You have the phone number."

Living at the Watkins was equally rewarding. They showed genuine interest in my stories and work at the Gazette. Especially Mr. Watkins. He relished any inside information I had on the Orioles or Colts, telling me that it gave him a leg up on his customers when they talked sports. Because the Watkins were always warm and welcoming to me, living at the house felt comfortable, more than my parents' house had been, and at the holidays the place hummed and bubbled over in joy when Darnell and Celia arrived.

When the time came for me to leave for school, Mr. Watkins said he would drive me up. "We did it for Darnell. We'll do it for you."

I protested but there was no changing the mind of a Watkins. We headed up early on a Sunday. When I stepped from the car, I had two suitcases of clothes and the typewriter Mr. Perl had given me. Other than the memories and experiences of the previous nineteen years, most of what I had in the world was in my two hands. Mr. Watkins handed me an envelope and said, "You take care of business now, Michael, and we'll see you at Thanksgiving. Wait to open that envelope until you get to your room." When I did open the envelope, I saw it held $1500, which came to sixty weeks' worth of rent that I had paid to the Watkins.

My first few weeks at Syracuse were probably similar to what every other freshman experienced in the fall of 1969. Other than registering for classes and attending orientation sessions, I spent most of the first few days drinking beer. New York State had an eighteen year old drinking age at the time and the students took full advantage of it. A keg was virtually a permanent fixture in the common room on my dorm floor. I woke up to a mug of beer and went to sleep with a mug of beer.

But, I still had my ambition. So, after a few days of goofing around, I went to the office of the Daily Orange, the student newspaper. I asked to see the sports editor and was ushered to a desk on the second floor.

"I'm interested in writing for the paper. My name's Michael Sanders. I am a freshman. Just got here."

"We don't need any freshmen writing for the paper."

"Hey look, I have experience. I wrote for the Baltimore Gazette." I pulled out my portfolio and showed him my articles. "I worked for the Gazette for a full year after graduating high school."

"Then what? Did they tell you to go to a journalism school to learn the proper way to write? Hey it's like I said. We don't need any freshmen want-to-be writers. It's a pecking order. People wait to get a chance. There's no way you can short circuit the system. You can leave me your name and contact information. If something comes up, I'll let you know. But don't hold your breath. I suggest you pay attention in class and learn something and wait your turn."

I went back to my dorm and resumed drinking.

For the first month, life was uneventful. I was a bit surprised how many New Yorkers attended the school, though, I suppose one would expect a school in New York State to attract a lot of natives. But it was driven home to me on a daily basis because 1969 had been a rough year for Baltimore sports, all at the hands of New York teams. The Jets upset the Colts in the Super Bowl in January. Behind Joe Namath, the Jets became the first AFL team to claim the title. This upset was followed by the Knicks taking down the Bullets in the NBA playoffs.

For all the harassment I received, you would think that I had something directly to do with the performance of the Baltimore teams. I quickly earned the nickname *Baltimore.* When I ate breakfast in the cafeteria, I would be greeted by "Hey Baltimore, is that the breakfast of non-champions you're eating?" Or some idiot would bump me when I walked down the hallway and say "16-7, over and out." I took it in stride figuring they would eventually tire of the teasing.

But the World Series that year pitted the Orioles against the Mets, another Baltimore versus New York showdown. Prior to the matchup, I was convinced that most of the guys in the dorm were Yankee fans and they never uttered a word acknowledging that the Orioles won the American League over the Yankees, in dominating fashion no less. But, once the Orioles and Mets advanced to the World Series, overnight it seemed those same people turned into Mets fans.

The Series started on October 11 and, for one, day, all was as it was meant to be. Don Buford, the Orioles left fielder, led off the first inning with a home run against Tom Seaver. Mike Cuellar baffled the Mets hitters all day and the Orioles opened with a 4-1 win to take game one. The next day, the Mets earned the win by riding six no-hit innings from Jerry Koosman. The two teams had entered the ninth tied at one. Then the Mets strung together three singles to score a run and hold on for a 2-1 victory. The Series was tied a game apiece and the newly discovered Mets fans, in my midst, were still mild in their boasting. Both games were tightly played and, for all their hope, the Mets fans hardly felt secure that they had the dominating team. Every baseball expert in the country stood behind the Orioles as the probable winner.

After a day off, the Series resumed at Shea Stadium. In the bottom of the first, Tommy Agee homered to give the Mets a lead that they would not relinquish. Gary Gentry and Nolan Ryan shut down the Oriole bats, helped by several outstanding defensive plays from Agee. Game three went to the Mets 5-0. When I went to dinner, that night, I was serenaded by chants of "New York Mets. New York Mets" and pounding on the tables. When I took a bite of chicken, one guy came racing over and said, "Just wanted to make sure you weren't gonna choke on that chicken. You being from Baltimore and all."

For the first three games, I had followed the action on the television in the lounge in my dormitory. Just me and my roommate, Blake, who also was from Baltimore, amongst a sea of Mets fans. But, on the day of game four, October 15, I had other plans that did not include listening to the game. It was the first National Moratorium Day against the Vietnam War and I had planned to participate.

In many cities, around the country, the day was marked by services, rallies and seminars. The largest crowds marched in Boston, where Senator Ted Kennedy spoke to the protestors, and Washington, where Dr. Spock and Pete Seeger were among the speakers. A similar protest at Syracuse began in Walnut Park where thousands of people gathered and marched into the center of the city. The organizers had also opted to sponsor a community outreach program in which students would be shuttled to different areas around the city to speak, person to person, about the reasons for ending the War. I was excited to be a part of it. I was reminded of George Watkins' description of the lunch counter sit-ins and felt this would be my chance to be part of an event that could change the course of history. It would be challenging. After all, the University was an island of liberalism surrounded by endless conservative neighborhoods.

Along with four other students, I went to an area about fifteen minutes north of the city. The farther you traveled from downtown Syracuse, the more conservative it became. We each picked a different street carrying in our arms a stack of information sheets that highlighted the main arguments against the War. I started knocking on doors. No answer at the first house. Then no answer at the next house and the one after that. Not a surprise since many of the people would be at work.

At the fifth house, a man, who I judged to be about seventy years old, opened the door a crack.

"Hi, I'm from Syracuse University and I am talking to your neighbors about the Vietnam War and our goal of convincing the government to end it. Do you have a moment to talk with me?"

He slammed the door shut and I heard him murmur "Commie." I met similar responses at the few houses that opened their doors. I had walked two blocks and knocked on a few dozen doors and I had nothing to show for it. Not one person had let me talk to them.

When I turned the corner, I came across a young woman pushing a child on a swing set in her backyard. I approached the gate and called out to her, "Hi I'm from Syracuse University and I'd like to talk to you about why we should end the war in Vietnam."

"Sure, come on in." It was more than likely that she invited me in just so she had someone to talk to, anxious for anything to break the monotony of pushing a three year old kid on a swing.

I told her about the Moratorium and how we were circulating through neighborhoods to talk to people and drive home the reasons for the government to end the war. I explained why the popular domino theory, a reason that supporters of the War often cited, was a fallacy.

"It's a civil war and we have no right to be there. The people of Vietnam have the right to determine, by themselves, who they want to lead their country. It is not the position of the United States to do this."

The political argument didn't sway her. So, I started talking about the moral aspect. The thousands of deaths to Vietnam citizens. The horrors of war that were being inflicted on young U.S. men, fighting halfway around the globe in a country that held no practical impact on our freedom and life.

"How old is your son, ma'am?" I asked. Without waiting for her to answer, I continued, "What if he was eighteen years old and the government wanted to ship him off to fight in Vietnam. How would you feel about that? Could you support the government if they wanted to do that?"

"I don't think so. My husband says we have to support the government no matter what. But I see the pictures on television every night. It is horrifying. For our boys. For the Vietnam people. I just don't understand why we have to inflict this on anybody. Life shouldn't be ending at eighteen years old. It should be starting and war is no way to start it."

I asked her to sign a petition demanding that the government end the War. She did. I spent another four hours canvassing the neighborhood. In total, fifty doors were slammed in my face. I was cursed at by at least a dozen people. But, I also got two dozen signatures on the petition. And I think I changed a mind or two. Change starts with small steps. With the hopes and commitments of a few. That's what George Watkins told me and look what he accomplished.

It was dark by the time I returned to campus. As soon as I entered my dorm, someone shouted out, "Hey Baltimore, the Mets won today. You're a loser again." I didn't think so. I certainly didn't feel like a loser. I felt I had done something far more important than watching a game or trash talking about the outcome.

But, in fact, the Mets won 2-1 in ten innings that afternoon. Tom Seaver pitched magnificently and Don Clendenon homered in the tenth inning to secure the victory.

With all the harassment that had been directed my way, I was not looking forward to what I might face on October 16. Down three games to one, the momentum was certainly with the Mets and it seemed inevitable that they would defy the odds and capture the World Series. When I returned from class in the afternoon, the game was playing on the television in the main lobby. In those days, no one had their own television. If you wanted to watch something, you went to the lobby and hoped that a consensus would be reached as to what to watch. There was no trouble finding a consensus this day. I estimated over a hundred guys were watching the game—all Mets fans, or at least anti-Michael Sanders agitators. I approached cautiously and stood against the window. It was the top of the sixth inning and the Orioles led 3-0. I exhaled.

Almost immediately, things changed. Had I hit some type of trip wire that had ignited the Mets? Being the superstitious type, I suspected that I was to blame for what happened in the bottom of the sixth. The Mets scored two runs to cut the deficit to one run aided by a questionable call on a ball that may or may not have hit a Mets batter. Gil Hodges, the manager, tricked the umpires into awarding Cleon Jones first base and, regardless of what had actually happened, the Mets went on to score two runs and the game seemed to be slipping away.

In the seventh inning, Al Weis hit a home run to tie the game and that signaled that it was time to head to my room. Maybe the change of scenery would change the course of the game. As a kid, I had always changed rooms when the Orioles were losing, hoping it would change the outcome of the game. At this point, I had to try anything.

I turned on the radio. My roommate, Blake and I listened nervously. The Orioles had failed to score in the top of the eighth. But in the bottom of the inning, the Mets scored two runs and now they led 5-3, putting them three outs from clinching the World Series. In the top of the ninth, the first two Orioles were retired easily. That left it to Davey Johnson to keep the hope alive. He worked the count to 2-1 before lifting a soft fly ball to left field. The ball was caught by Cleon Jones for the final out and the Mets were world champions. Fans charged the field to celebrate but I doubt they had any more enthusiasm than the crowd that stormed my floor within minutes of the final out.

In a rare display of common sense, probably more so out of my disdain for confrontation, I jumped from my bed and locked the door when I heard the oncoming rumble. Whoever led the pack, turned the doorknob and was thwarted. Then the pounding and shouting started. A second group had gathered on the grounds outside my third story window. The taunts started and a few stones were hurled at the window. Blake flashed a middle finger at the crowd.

"I'm going out there," Blake said as he moved toward the door.

"I wouldn't think a confrontation would be in anyone's best interest. Why don't you let them get rid of their energy and let it die down?"

"Fuck it. I'm going to take a piss. Maybe on one of them," and Blake opened the door and waded into the crowd. I moved toward the door but stayed inside the room, propping my foot and body against it. Blake attempted to step through the crowd but his path was blocked and the crowd was unwilling to yield its position. So, Blake pushed the first guy he could get his hands on. It was like watching a physics experiment on wave patterns. The guy fell into the crowd, moving each ensuing line backward until the last guy hit the wall opposite our room. That guy then bounced off the wall and his momentum pushed him forward, moving the very same people, who had fallen backwards, toward Blake until the guy who Blake originally pushed, lost his balance and fell forward into Blake with his arms extended. Blake was thrown back, his head hitting the number plate on the door. A gash opened behind his left ear and, when Blake went to rub the spot, his hand became stained with blood. I pulled the door open, grabbed Blake, as he was readying to retaliate, and collared him into the room.

The crowd loitered outside the room continuing to shout and pound the door for a few more minutes. When it became evident that we had no further intention of confronting them, or even responding to their taunts, they began to lose interest and went back to their rooms. When we left the room for dinner, that night, no one bothered to say a word. We ate in peace.

Later that night, I wrote a story recounting the events of the day, and the entire World Series experience, and took it to the editor of the Daily Orange the next day.

"I thought I told you we aren't interested in any stories from freshmen."

"Just do me a favor and read it." He did.

"Interesting, but we don't run first person stories and we don't do stories about major league sports. The people who read this paper are interested in two things. What happened in last Saturday's football game. And what's going to happen in next Saturday's football game. They could care less about your story. It has no relevance for them."

"Well I thought it was worth a try." I took back the article, crumpled it, tossed it in the trashcan and left. I had no further contact with the Daily Orange, until the spring, when I received a phone call from the sports editor.

"I have an opportunity for you if you're interested."

"Sure. What's up?"

"Are you familiar with George Plimpton?

"Of course. He wrote Paper Lion."

"Well we'd like to do something similar. With the rugby team. If you are willing, all you have to do is show up at the field, behind Manley Fieldhouse, tomorrow night and ask for Bill Franklin. Then write a story about your experience playing the game."

"I thought you didn't do first person articles?"

"Listen either you're interested or you're not."

"Sure, I'll do it. But I don't know the first thing about rugby much less playing it."

"Just show up. Bill will take care of you."

My knowledge of rugby, in fact, was a total void. I went to the library and did some research. It was evident that rugby was one tough game and I immediately questioned my decision to take on the assignment, realizing that I was about to cause major pain to my body. Could it be that this was how the editors on the paper weeded out the competition?

But, I showed up the next night ready to play. I approached the field and stood on the sideline watching the guys loosen up. They were big, much bigger than me. They were fast and they were fearless. I had done little in the way of athletics since high school. I had put on a few pounds in the last two years and my body was far from the shape it had been in when I played basketball. So I could only imagine what was in store for my body once I started running and getting hit.

A few more guys joined me on the sideline, stretching their limbs or running in place to loosen up.

"I'm looking for Bill Franklin." They pointed to a guy standing in the center of the field kicking practice punts with the ball. I strolled out.

"You the guy from the Daily Orange that's gonna try playing rugby with us?" I nodded and he pulled a pen and piece of paper from his pocket. "We're glad to have you. Just need you to list your next of kin and phone number on this paper." When he saw the look of horror on my face, he laughed and said, "Just kidding. You should live to talk about your experience. Or at least write about it. Of course, when you wake up tomorrow you may wish you hadn't lived through it. Sometimes death is the better option."

I grinned. "How 'bout putting me somewhere, on the field, out of the mainstream action?"

"Then you might as well go stand on the sideline and watch. There is no safe harbor on the pitch, which is what we call the field in case you didn't know. But, let's try you at outside center. It's more about speed than strength at that position. I'll put you on my team so go put on a red pinny. You can watch for a while and I'll bring you in when there's a break in the action. Just follow the game and you should be able to understand what to do."

I took my place on the sideline, the touch line as they called it, and stood beside four other substitutes. Next to a keg of beer.

"Here help yourself," one of them offered. "It'll help ease the pain."

That sounded good. I filled a plastic cup and started drinking as the game started. The guys standing with me began explaining the rules and the strategy while I watched.

Bill's team started the game by kicking off. One of the players on the other team caught the ball and began running up the field as our players shifted to thwart the attack and try to take possession of the ball. The play flowed back and forth with each team attempting to move toward the goal line and score. Players tackled opposing players, the ball changing hands as each team tried to foil the attack of the other team.

Up and down the field it went for about fifteen minutes. Finally we broke through and scored the first points when our inside center back crossed the try line and grounded the ball about three meters to the right of the goal posts. That score put us ahead 5-0 and then we converted the kick to add two more points to our total.

As the players moved back to the center of the field to restart play, Bill waved for me to come onto the pitch. I jogged out to my position. The other team kicked off and now I was running, though not exactly sure where to. But at least my legs were churning. As play pushed toward our try line, I reached the half way line, or what we would call mid-field. I felt as if tiny needles were piercing every square inch of my lungs. I slowed to catch my breath. My legs ached and I had been playing for less than two minutes. Seeing me standing still the right wing shouted, "Come on. Get your ass moving and get into the game."

At this point, the other team had gained possession of the ball and was moving toward us. I started backpedaling, something I was certain would make my hamstrings none too happy the next day. I prepared to defend my area though I had no confidence that I would be able to do anything if the ball came my way.

The other team crossed the twenty-two meter line. As one of my teammates advanced to challenge, the opposing ball carrier passed the ball slightly forward which resulted in a penalty and a stoppage of play. Out of the ensuing scrum, our halfback gained control and started running forward. Automatically, I started running forward as well. A tackler approached our halfback who then passed the ball to the inside center back. In the next instant, he threw the ball towards me. I caught it and began running forward.

Good sense would have dictated that I pass the ball to an open teammate. Instead I continued to run forward. But, lacking any quality evasive moves, I was quickly and harshly tackled. I landed with the ball pressed against my chest and my right arm cradling the ball. As the other players converged to contest my possession, the ball trickled out and rolled a few feet away. Fortunately, we maintained possession and began our push up the field. Good sense, again, would have dictated that I feign an injury or somehow crawl off the field. My body felt like it had been run over by a steamroller, my lungs burned and my stomach had this strange hollow feeling. Somehow, I mustered the strength and determination and lifted myself off the ground and started running again.

In the end, I played about twelve minutes before our team scored again. With a break in the action, Bill excused me from the field and brought in an experienced player. By my calculations, I lasted about eleven minutes longer than any sane person in my condition should have. Those twelve minutes, however, had given me a good feel for the intensity and fierceness of the game. I carried the ball, I passed the ball, I was tackled, and I made tackles. I even made a kick while on the run. And that was enough to form the basics of my story. I was more than glad to watch the rest of the game from the sideline.

Once the game ended, all the players gathered around the keg. We drank for about an hour until the keg was drained. From the neck up, I felt great. Proud that I had survived. From the neck down, it was another story. I was tired. The night air had turned chilly. It was April 30 but there was definitely a hint of approaching snow. As my body cooled off, in the chill, I could feel my muscles tightening. But, for now, the beer made everything feel okay and tomorrow was a few hours away.

Tomorrow came way too soon though. My alarm rang at eight o'clock. I went to move my arm to shut it off. Nothing. I knew my arm hadn't fallen off because I could feel every aching muscle. But I couldn't lift it off the bed. Blake popped out of bed and turned off the alarm. I didn't budge. Just stared at the ceiling. I felt like the scarecrow in the Wizard of Oz after he had been torn apart by the flying monkeys. There would be no going to classes today. Fortunately, it was Friday and I had a light schedule. Which left me to ponder how I would get to the bathroom to empty my bladder.

Another two hours passed and dealing with my bladder became paramount. The urge was strong so I summoned whatever strength remained and raised my torso from the bed. I twisted and managed to get my feet to hit the floor and stood up. It took several minutes to cover the distance to the bathroom and then stand in front of the urinal. I returned to my bed and Blake brought me a sandwich from the cafeteria and some ibuprofen and I spent the rest of the day nursing my broken body and sleeping.

Lying in bed, oblivious to everything other than my aching body, I was totally unaware that trouble was brewing in Ohio, at Kent State, that day. A demonstration against the war had turned turbulent after President Nixon had announced that the United States had invaded Cambodian the day before. It was the latest in a series of events that had galvanized the anti-war movement.

Previously, in November, word of the My Lai massacre had surfaced and American citizens were alarmed and disturbed when they heard about the atrocity. Then, a month later, the government held its first draft lottery. All men born between January 1, 1944 and December 31, 1950 drew numbers. September one pulled the number one draft position but I was far luckier. My birthdate drew number two hundred twenty-one. Of course, I had my student deferment so there was nothing to worry about. The government would end up calling up draftees through number one hundred ninety-five over the following year.

When President Nixon announced the Cambodian invasion, it was a clear indication that the war effort in Southeast Asia was expanding. Nixon had run for election, in 1968, under a plan calling for the Vietnamization of the war, whereby the US would gradually turn over the war effort against the Communists to the Vietnamese people. So this latest development, a clear escalation, inflamed anti-war protestors. At Kent State, the demonstration spilled into the center of town that night. Looting and vandalism followed. The police were called in and the Mayor declared a state of emergency.

The following day, as I continued to recover, the situation at Kent State intensified. Due to the continuing turmoil, the mayor requested National Guard troops be deployed. Governor Rhodes of Ohio complied and troops began arriving at ten o'clock Saturday night. By that time, the students had staged further demonstrations and burned the ROTC building. As they battled the blaze, rocks were thrown at the firemen and the police responded with tear gas to disperse the crowd. Many were arrested.

By Sunday, I was up and moving around, with plenty of residual soreness. As I improved, things were getting worse as campuses, across the country, started to react to the Kent State situation. Meanwhile, the Kent State students had organized another rally for eight o'clock on Sunday night. A curfew had been put in effect and by 8:45 pm, police were using tear gas again to disperse the crowd. But, the students reassembled and began a sit-in. The National Guard responded around eleven by enforcing the curfew and chasing the students. Across the country, anti-war leaders, on campuses, began meeting to determine what to do in support of the Kent State students and to protest against the latest war action.

At noon, on May 4, approximately two thousand students gathered for a noontime protest at Kent State. The National Guard companies moved in to disperse the crowd, lobbing tear gas canisters into their midst. The students retaliated, throwing rocks at the guardsmen before retreating up a nearby hill. The guardsman pursued the protestors with bayonets affixed. But they went the wrong way. Instead of following the students, who had turned left at the top of Blanket Hill, they continued straight ahead, ultimately reaching a dead end.

While the Guardsman had managed to disperse most of the crowd from the Commons area, some protestors remained and continued to throw rocks and tear gas canisters at the guardsmen. The troops were forced to retrace their steps down the hill, moving back toward the Commons. A few minutes later, at 12:24pm, twenty-nine of the guardsman began firing their rifles at the students without cause and without justification. In the end, four students were killed and nine wounded. Two of the dead were simply walking from class and were not even part of the protest.

Reactions were swift across the country's campuses. Our student government had organized a rally on the Quad for two o'clock that day. I was among three thousand people who showed up. At that time, the leaders of the rally informed the crowd of the deaths at Kent State and called for a student strike. They also announced that a meeting would be held at eight p.m. that night, at Hendricks Chapel, to finalize plans as to what should be done.

At the evening meeting, it was decided that the student body should go on strike and peacefully shut down all regular campus activity. But the mood soon turned ugly. Some students ran through campus, smashing windows. The student bookstore was firebombed. Barricades were erected along all of the entry points to the main campus. We moved jersey walls to block access and then piled anything we could find on top. Trashcans and large tree branches. Furniture was carried out of the dorms and placed on the pile. Desks from the classrooms. Rolling blackboards. Anything we could put our hands on. We even managed to carry a telephone pole and place it on the barricade.

We stood vigilant around the clock. I stood at a spot near Archbold gym which was located down the hill from my dorm. We waited for the police but when they came they offered no interference. I spent most of that Monday night at the barricade, returning to my room to get some sleep in the late morning of the next day. I was back at the barricade that evening and spent the night again. Chancellor Corbally had cancelled classes through the next day. Early the following morning, the snow began falling. We stood around a bonfire to warm our hands, passing joints around the circle. It was May 6. It was cold and snowing. And Syracuse University was shut down.

Exhausted, I returned to the dorm. When I reached my room, Blake, who had never been politically active, was sitting at the desk. "Some guy named Perl called for you while you were out. Said to call him back first chance you got."

There was a phone booth by the elevator on my floor. I gathered my quarters, went down the hall and placed a called to the Gazette. "Mr. Perl. Its' Michael Sanders. You left a message to call."

"Yeah Michael. How are you? Hope you're keeping your ass out of trouble. I see things are getting bad on most of the campuses. How's it going up there?"

"Probably no different than what's happening everywhere else. The campus is shut down. Classes have been canceled. We've erected barricades to block entry."

"Well I hope you stay safe. Be smart. But I called for another reason. I learned that the Associated Press is looking for a stringer to cover the football team at Syracuse next fall. I recommended you. The job is yours if you want it." The idea sounded great to me. "I'd love to do it."

"They'll pay you fifty dollars for each story. You'll be responsible for filing an article on each home game and pre-season reports starting in August. Here's the name of the guy to contact."

I thanked Mr. Perl and ended the call. Up to now, I had assumed that I would return to Baltimore for the summer though I hadn't secured a job yet. But, with this new opportunity, it would be better to find a job and an apartment in Syracuse. Fortunately, there was plenty of money in my savings account. I figured I had a few weeks before school would be over, which would give me plenty of time to find a place and a summer job.

But the strike continued on and the campus remained shut down. Early the following week, the last for classes prior to finals, the campus reopened under a threat from Chancellor Corbally that the entire spring semester would not count if we didn't return and let regular activities resume. The barricades remained in place but no serious effort was made to prevent the coming and going of all parties.

Each academic college was allowed to determine how they would complete the semester and grade the students. Most decided that there would be no formal classes for the final week. In my case, all of my professors eliminated finals as well. By the middle of the week, students began leaving campus, returning home for the summer. Having to vacate the dorm but not having secured an apartment yet, I took my two suitcases of clothes and my typewriter and moved into a Holiday Inn in downtown Syracuse.

Days later, when two people were killed by police during demonstrations at Jackson State University, a black college, most of the students were gone from campus. As a result, there was no outrage like what accompanied the Kent State shootings. "Par for the course" would be how Celia would later describe it. "Kill a few white kids and the whole country is up in arms. But kill a few black kids and it's business as usual."

The following week, I found a job and was hired at minimum wage by a record store on South Crouse Avenue, a few blocks from campus. A few days after that, I found an apartment nearby as well. It had a small kitchen with an eating area and a tiny living room. One bathroom. But three bedrooms so I figured I could find roommates down the road. The apartment was fairly shabby and in desperate need of painting. But it was fully furnished which convinced me to take it. I moved out of the Holiday Inn the next day and into my apartment. With all that had happened, my rugby story never made it to print—at the time, there were far more important things for the paper to cover and sports wasn't one of them. And then, in a snap, the semester was over. I settled into my apartment, began working at the record store and started preparing myself for the upcoming football season

# CHAPTER TEN

Syracuse University football was steeped in a rich history dating back into the nineteenth century. Through the years, the program had its share of success culminating in a national championship in 1959. And the program had a long list of legendary players. Jim Brown. Ernie Davis, who won the Heisman trophy in 1961. Floyd Little. Larry Csonka. Heck, I had been as anxious to attend Syracuse because of its football program as I was to enroll in the journalism program. But by the time I arrived on campus, in 1969, the team had sunk into mediocrity. By 1970, the program was beginning to signal that, perhaps, it was falling behind the times, failing to recognize the shifting paradigm of college sports and the players participating.

To prepare for the Associated Press assignment, I plunged into extensive research about the team, poring over the statistics from the 1969 season. I familiarized myself with the players on the team and studied the coach, Ben Schwartzwalder. As I was soon to witness, the season quickly went off the tracks as a racial divide enveloped the team.

The problems had begun almost two years prior when a white football player beat up a black student. When Coach Schwartzwalder addressed the team about the problem, rather than unite the team, it resulted in a schism between the white and black players. The black players began pressing the school to hire a black assistant coach, someone they felt would be more attuned to their needs and feelings. Schwartzwalder made several hollow promises to do so. At the start of the 1969 season, there were five black starters and no black assistant coach. By the end of the season, all five were on the bench, without any reason given for their demotion. And there was no black assistant coach on the horizon.

Schwartzwalder had instilled a military-like culture ever since his hiring in 1949. He had his successes, including the 1959 national championship. But, by 1969, his approach certainly rankled the minority athletes. He expected everyone to act a certain way and to follow what he considered proper dress and appearance. So, when several of the black players refused to stand for the national anthem, at a December basketball game, and raised clenched fists, the coach was furious. His subsequent meeting with the players only heightened the tensions. The players again called for the hiring of a black coach. Schwartzwalder took no action and the players chose to boycott spring football practice. Despite multiple attempts at a solution and reconciliation, mediated by Chancellor Corbally, fall football practice began with the continued boycott by the black players.

And that was the situation that I walked into when I went to interview Coach Schwartzwalder prior to the official start of practice on August 27. I had called for an appointment and was told to come at one o'clock. I gathered my pad and the tape recorder that I had recently purchased. I intended to focus on his outlook for the season but I also decided not to shy away from asking about the boycott. As I walked to the football offices at the fieldhouse, I could hear Celia whispering in my ear, "Now don't mess this up this time. Last time you dealt with black athletes, look what happened to them."

When I arrived, a few of the assistant coaches were standing in the main office.

"I'm Michael Sanders, from the AP, and I'm here to talk with Coach Schwartzwalder," I announced.

One of them looked at me and said, "Aren't you kind of girly to be talking football with the Coach?"

"Excuse me?"

"I mean with your ponytail (I had not cut my hair from the time I arrived as a freshman and I had recently taken to wearing it in a ponytail) and girly bell bottoms. You just don't look like someone who knows anything about football. I wouldn't want to be the one to tell the coach the kind of person waiting to interview him."

"Then why don't you just tell him the guy from the Associated Press is here for the one o'clock appointment."

A few minutes later, I was ushered into Schwartzwalder's office. I introduced myself and held out my hand. Schwartzwalder just looked at me for a minute and then said, "Your parents let you go around like that. It's a disgrace."

"Coach, I didn't come here to talk about my appearance. Or what my parents think about it. I came to ask you a few questions about the team."

"Look kid. I have my rules. And one of them is that I don't do interviews with people that look like you."

"Ok Coach. I'll tell you what. I'm going to turn on my tape recorder and I'm going to ask you a few questions. If you don't answer, I'll write my story without your input."

I turned on the tape recorder and asked my first question. About the plans for the offense that year. He didn't respond. So, I moved onto the next question. Still no response. I ran through all my questions and then came the final question about the situation with the black players. His steely eyes locked onto my eyes, his mouth tightened. He looked ready to bite my head off. But, he refrained from answering. I stood up from my chair, "Thanks for the insight, Coach. I think you gave me exactly what I was looking for."

I wrote a brief story highlighting the returning players and the expectations for the coming year. At the same time, I called the New York bureau chief and advised him of the lack of cooperation from the coaching staff. He contacted Schwartzwalder but had no more luck than I did. So, I continued to track things as best as I could. I went to the open practices and observed. I talked with the boycotting black players and followed the efforts of the administration to resolve the problems. And I filed stories, some of which were picked up by area newspapers.

Finally, under pressure from the administration to neutralize the bad press that the school was receiving on a daily basis, Schwartzwalder relented and agreed to an interview with me prior to the first game on the schedule, an away game against Houston.

The interview went smoothly and Schwartzwalder answered questions about the outlook for the season, the key players on offense and defense and his own expectations. Then I asked about the situation with the black players.

"Coach, as you know, the team has had its share of headlines regarding the black player boycott. Is there anything you would like to say about the situation?"

"We were never conscious of racism. Our white players didn't feel this thing existed. They feel it is a matter of groupism versus individualism."

"But Jim Brown came to the campus as a mediator. When he investigated, he found that there were numerous cases of name calling, poor medical treatment for the black players and a double standard for them in regard to winning positions on the team."

"Jim Brown says I'm old and stubborn. I don't feel old. It's still a lot of fun to work with young men."

"Do you feel these players are mistaken in their claims? Do you feel you have treated them fairly?"

"Well I always felt the Negro player needed a little more

consideration. Most of these young men we have, have had a tough financial background. Our policy over the years is that we try never to lift our voice, to be more gentle with these boys because they are more sensitive."

I was stunned by his patronizing and condescending tone. Celia would have probably said something like that's just the white establishment acting the way it's always done toward blacks. But, it was surprising to actually hear the Coach say something so obviously racist, knowing it was likely to be published in newspapers across the country. I thanked him for the interview and left.

When my story was published, I ran into a lot of unexpected negative feedback. Too many people felt I had shown a bias in favor of the boycotting players. "This is not a sports story. It's an op-ed piece. I think you should keep your opinions to yourself," a friend told me.

On September 18, the team played the University of Houston, on the road. By halftime, Houston led 35-7, ending in a 42-15 victory. The following week, against Kansas at home, things were not much better as Kansas prevailed 31-14. When I arrived at the stadium that day, picketers marched outside, carrying signs protesting Schwartzwalder and the football program. Shortly after the game started, the demonstrators moved down to Marshall Street, an off-campus retail area, and the protests turned violent. Students blocked the street and threw rocks at the police, leading to some looting and arrests.

The team was back on the road the following week but the results were no better. Illinois won 27-0. Yet somehow the team turned it around, winning six of their final seven games to end with a winning record for the year. They even upset Penn State. Schwartzwalder was named Eastern Coach of the year. The black players never returned that season.

# CHAPTER ELEVEN

Football season ended on November 21 and I looked forward to going home for Thanksgiving. I had been busy for months, between school and my reporting assignment. So, the idea of just relaxing for a few days was appealing. But, my boss at the record store had a different idea. He demanded that all of the employees work through the holiday to handle the planned sale. And, since the Christmas season was the critical selling season, we were all expected to work as much as possible through Christmas. So, it was not until December 25 that I was able to head back to Baltimore.

I hopped a late evening Greyhound bus out of Syracuse. With stops in Binghamton, Scranton and Harrisburg, the bus did not arrive into Baltimore until early the next morning. After grabbing an egg sandwich at the snack bar at the Greyhound terminal, I decided it would be quickest and easiest, and certainly a lot less expensive, to take a cab to my father's store rather than head out to my suburban home.

The cab pulled onto Fulton and, when it approached Mount Street, I asked the driver to let me off at the corner. I wanted to walk the last two blocks to have a final chance to gather my thoughts and my confidence. As I neared the store, I saw Mr. Watkins sweeping the street in front of the barbershop. So, I crossed over.

"Mr. Watkins, it's great to see you." We embraced.

"Ain't you a sight? Ponytail and all. But you look healthy. How you doing?"

I told him about my time at school. It had been over a year since I had been home. So, there was a lot to tell. I asked about Darnell and the rest of the family.

"He's home for vacation. So is Celia. They'd love to see you. Can you come over the house one night?"

"I think I should be able to. But, first I have to go home and visit with my parents."

"Well I saw your Dad this morning. He talks about you all the time. I know he'll be happy to see you."

"To tell you the truth, I'm kind of nervous. It's been a while."

"Nothing to be nervous about. He's your dad."

"You, more than most people know that it hasn't been too smooth between us. Last time I was in Baltimore, it was rough. Back when I stayed with you, my father and I certainly weren't seeing eye to eye then."

"Look you're family. You wouldn't be where you are today without him. You wouldn't be the person you are."

"I would think I am the person I am despite him. I did it all without him, without his support."

"Listen Michael. My father was a crusty man. Not a bad man. But he was detached. He didn't interact well with his family. I always felt distant from him. And I always felt that I had disappointed him. Then Celia was born. I never even recognized that he bonded with her. I probably was so blinded by my perspective of him that I didn't pay attention. It wasn't until he passed away and Celia gave a eulogy at the funeral that I realized how close they were. She had given him another chance to show the type of man he could be. She gave him a chance to peel away all the layers that life's trials had built around him. She didn't judge. She didn't have expectations. She just gave him the chance to love again and be loved. She gave him that second chance. That's what you have to do. You have to give your father his second chance. If things don't work out, if they don't get better, it can't be because you gave up on him."

Infused with the spirit of Mr. Watkins' story, I crossed the street and entered the grocery store. To my surprise, my father, who was standing by the cash register, stepped out, smiled, and extended his hand but I went for a hug instead.

"When did you get in?"

"I took the overnight bus and got in about an hour ago. When I got out of the cab, I saw Mr. Watkins so I stopped to say hello to him."

"You must be tired."

"I am. I think that bus stopped in every town between here and Syracuse."

"I know your mother will be anxious to see you. Why don't you take my car and drive home. You can come back and pick me up tonight."

Our conversation was short but at least it was not contentious, for a change. I headed home and spent the day talking with my mother and resting. Later, I returned to pick up my father and the three of us went out for dinner. All in all, the first day went smoothly. In fact, the entire visit went smoothly. For the first time, in a long time, I had nothing to do. No classes. No papers or tests. No reporting. No work. I just relaxed.

On the third night, my father came home after work and told me that Mr. Watkins had stopped in the store and suggested I come by for dinner the next night.

"I hope you don't mind but I accepted for you. I know how much you want to see them. If you drop me at work, in the morning, you can use the car for the day. You won't have to figure out how to get to the Watkins."

"How will you get home?"

"I think I can convince your mother to come get me. I'll take her out to dinner."

The next morning, after dropping my father at the store, I headed down to the Gazette to visit Mr. Perl and my friends on the staff. In the time that I had been away, I had talked with Mr. Perl a few times. He liked to keep track of my progress as a student and as a writer. But I had only seen him once since I left for school in September 1969. It was at the second home football game of 1970. A game against the University of Maryland that turned out to be the first win of the season for the troubled Syracuse football team. He had come to Syracuse to cover the game for the Gazette, which also gave him a chance to check up on me. We spoke briefly in the press box but he was sitting with Arnie Burdick of the Syracuse Herald American, so there was only time for a quick exchange. We both had a job to do.

The receptionist, at the main desk, recognized me and told me to head up.

"No need for an escort. You're still a staff member, as far as I'm concerned."

When I stepped off the elevator, the full staff was sitting around the conference table, discussing the assignments for the day. I circled the table and shook hands with everyone. Mr. Perl then suggested I wait for him in his office.

"I was hoping you might stop by one of these days. It's not often we get to see someone who's determined to redo the canons of the profession. What was the first lesson I taught you."

"Just report the facts?"

"And what did you do? You put yourself into the story on the black players boycott. You tilted the story. You wrote it in a way that it no longer just reported the facts. That's why they had to chop it up. If you want my advice, just be a journalist when you report. Leave the other stuff to your creative writing."

"I might have gotten carried away a bit. But there were things that needed to be said and I wanted to make sure the reader got the point."

"Then you should be writing on the op-ed page. It's your job to report the story. That's all. The reader will reach his own conclusion. And you know, the reader doesn't have to agree with you. There are plenty of people who think those black players were wrong."

"I had a platform and I felt a responsibility. I reported a story about unfairness. A systemic unfairness. If the story seems biased, then it was because I was writing about bias."

"Look, what's the first piece of writing that I saw from you. A letter to the editor about an opinion column I had written. My column wasn't a news story. And your response wasn't a news story. That's why it was printed in the opinion section. My column and your letter were not paraded in front of the readership as news. It was presented as opinion. All I'm saying is that, if you want to be in this profession, you have to follow the rules."

"What if the rules need to be changed? What if we have a higher responsibility than just reporting the news?"

"Sounds a bit autocratic to me. You're saying that you have to tell the reader how to think? You need to give them more credit."

"What I'm saying is that there is more to reporting than just recapping the facts as they are presented. I want to capture the ambience of the situation. How did the person look? Was he nervous? Was he looking at me or averting my eyes? How steady was his voice? His body language. After all, he's selectively telling me what he wants me to hear. Isn't he giving me his interpretation of the facts? When I add all those other elements, that's what makes the story come out. That's what gives the reader all the information."

"Is that what they teach you these days in journalism school? Because, if so, I disagree and I think you'll find a lot of editors who disagree. And, on another point, what do they teach you about story structure and style? Whatever happened to starting with the lead?"

"It's there."

"Buried about six sentences into the story. Look, if I'm writing the story, I'm going to start with something like *Eight black players are boycotting the Syracuse football team.* You started with some melodramatic hogwash. Don't get me wrong. Your writing is captivating. But it belongs as the opening of some movie script, with a voice-over announcer. Not as a news story."

I knew it was useless to continue the argument. Perl was not about to back down. So, I changed the subject and we talked for another hour. I was anxious to hear his take on the Orioles' prospects for the coming season and Perl was more than happy to fill me in. I thanked him for his time and help. Then I left and headed to the Watkins' house.

I took the story with me, knowing that the Watkins family would ask about my writing. I hoped the story would repair any lingering damage to my relationship with Celia. After all, the last time I saw her we argued about my pursuit of Hicks and Jones for my story for the Gazette. But, I quickly found that there was no issue between Celia and me. I should have known better. I knew Celia too well to think she would hold anything against me. She greeted me with a hug and a kiss as soon as I entered the living room. She was bubbling over in her enthusiasm at seeing me. I felt the same attraction that I had always felt. For a moment, I wondered if I would have the courage to do something about it. But it was 1970. The same fear that had struck me in seventh grade, when I had dismissed my friendship with Darnell, paralyzed me now. And, so, I did nothing.

"So, Celia, I see you still have that crush on me," I joked as we continued to embrace. Everyone laughed. She leaned in and whispered in my ear, "It's about time you noticed. I'm still waiting to take another shower with you." I wasn't sure whether she had bested me again or was truly serious. Either way, she had stopped me in my tracks again. And I knew I would, again, do nothing about it.

We gathered around the dining room table, which was filled with platters of fried chicken and sides of mashed potatoes, string beans, biscuits and coleslaw. When everyone was served, Mr. Watkins struck up the conversation by telling me about George, who had moved to Atlanta to work with Reverend Abernathy and the Southern Christian Leadership Conference. "He only gets home once or twice a year. But we've been down to see him in Atlanta."

"The neighborhood's changed a bit in the last year as well. A few of the old timers passed on. You remember Mrs. Brown. You used to carry her groceries home. Died of cancer during the summer. And Mrs. Williams. Her daughter moved her up to New York so she could take care of her. Diabetes and all. And that's the best of the changes. A lot's gotten worse. Guys hanging out on the corners selling drugs. Getting scarier out there. Business is good but it's changing too. Guys wearing those Afros. Had to learn some new styling techniques."

"Who's helping you out in the shop?" I asked.

"Got a few kids that are helping me out. One comes in three days a week and the other helps out on Saturdays. The rest of the time, I make do as best as I can. Glad to have you back if you want the work."

'I appreciate the offer but I think I better see this college thing through." I turned to Darnell, who was sitting at my left side. "How's everything going with you?"

"Pretty good. Harvard keeps you hopping. But I'm doing ok."

"I think he's being a bit modest," Mrs. Watkins chimed in. "He's pulling straight A's."

"Me and about fifty percent of the rest of the school. Hard to imagine there can be a more competitive environment. "

"I'm sure you'll hold your own. You still living in a dorm?"

"Yeah but I'm moving into an apartment when I go back after break. I'm going to stay during the summer and work at a law firm up there. If all goes well, I plan to apply to Harvard Law."

"I can't imagine you'll have too much trouble getting in. Any particular type of law?"

"Probably look to do something with discrimination issues. But, I'll see how it goes." There was no one better suited to tackle those issues than Darnell.

I asked about his social life. Darnell said Boston was the best place to be, always lots going on. He had a girlfriend for one semester but they broke up after sophomore year. We talked about the anti-war protests and Harvard-Yale football games.

And then it was time to catch up with Celia, who now sported a large Afro, ala Angela Davis. Her face was still angelic and she looked more like a model than a revolutionary. After graduating from Princeton, she immediately moved down to Alabama for a year to work on voter registration. Just as she had promised. Now she was in her second year at the University of Maryland Medical School. Not Hopkins as she had said a few years ago.

"You know I'm a West side girl. I didn't feel comfortable over there on the east side of town. Besides the financial package was better."

She had rented an apartment on Paca Street, which she shared with three other students. Made for a quick walk to school every day. "All I do is go to class and study as it is. Thought living close would make life easier."

"No boyfriend?" I asked

"You know I've been waiting for you." Everyone chuckled.

"There's no time for boyfriends now. I told you that all I do is go to class and study. And come here, once a week, for dinner. And what about you?"

I told them about freshman year—participating in the Vietnam

Moratorium, classes, the spring strike, my rugby story that never made it. Then getting the AP stringer job, getting an apartment and staying the summer in Syracuse, working at the music store. And then I pulled the story about the black boycott of the football team from my shirt pocket. As I unfolded the paper, I filled them in on the background. "I thought you might like to read it," and handed the story to Celia.

*When the Syracuse football team takes the field this Saturday against Houston, there will be eight players missing from the action. It won't be because of injuries or illness. Or academics. Or some kind of eligibility issue. It won't be because they are inconsequential players, left to ride the bench, or worse, left home from the traveling squad. It will be because they are black. And it will be because they are boycotting the team.*

*It has been a long simmering dispute between the players and the coaching staff, stretching as far back as two years ago when a white football player beat up a black student. When that student filed discrimination charges with the Human Rights Commission, the University ordered Coach Ben Schwartzwalder to talk to the team about racism. Schwartzwalder is a fireplug shaped man, short and muscular with a face that screams, "There are two ways to do things—my way and my way." His environment is one that knows only of discipline with stern reminders that there are certain ways to look and certain ways to behave. Asking this man to assume the delicate task of addressing his players on a sensitive issue—well, just say it's not something that's in his wheelhouse.*

*Which leads to the only point of agreement, between the two sides, that Schwartzwalder's talk served only to separate the team into two groups—the white players versus the black players. Shortly thereafter, when two vacancies opened up on the coaching staff, the black players pressed for the hiring of a black coach. Ask the black players and they will tell you a promise was made to hire a black coach. Ask Schwartzwalder and he will tell you no such promise was ever made. Guess who prevailed? When the 1969 season started, there were five starting black players and no black coaches. By the end of a mediocre season, all five players were on the bench. There were no explanations. And there was still no black coach on the horizon.*

*The players pressed their concerns but only found that Schwartzwalder continued to ignore their grievances. Maybe it was the Coach's background. A paratrooper in World War II. A decorated combatant. Tough. Patriotic to the nth degree. You did your duty. You followed orders. You didn't question authority. Then or now. You didn't challenge Schwartzwalder.*

*But it's a changing world. Citizens now questioning the government over an unpopular war. Marching. Burning draft cards. So, why shouldn't black players question their treatment especially when there were clear hints of racism throughout the football program? With a head coach with both feet embedded in a different time, a different lifestyle. Lacking any clue how to deal with young black men. So how did Schwartzwalder look to fix the situation when he couldn't bend the players? He brought in Floyd Little as a temporary coach for the spring season. Floyd Little. Black. Famed running back. He would put the house back in order.*

*The experiment lasted all of three days when Little departed, throwing his support behind the coaching staff and against the players. The players weren't fooled. A token gesture at best. At worst, a "good" black to straighten out the wayward souls. No real commitment. No real change. So, what do you do when you are disrespected as black men? Do you put it aside and just return to being football players. No, you boycott the spring practice.*

*Now, mix in an administration attempting to mediate the dispute. Chancellor Corbally ordered Schwartzwalder to hire a black coach and Schwartzwalder did, finding Carlmon Jones, a recent graduate of Florida A&M. And then Schwartzwalder tells seven of the black players that they are no longer on the team. Hire a coach, fire the players. Greg Allen, following his conscience, stands by his group and quits the team. The eight file a complaint with the Human Rights commission. The administration, motivated by expediency, tells Schwartzwalder to propose a set of terms for the reinstatement of the boycotting players.*

*But the administration finds that the alumni aren't happy. Not with his handling of the student strike in the spring of 1970 when he closed school early and eliminated finals for graduating seniors. And now they aren't happy with his attempt to find a way to settle the boycott and avoid further embarrassment for the university. But the alumni wield a lot of power. Power in the form of money, which Corbally realized when contributions tailed off during the summer. So, what do you do if you are Chancellor of a school facing a moral dilemma and a possible rebuke from the Human Rights Commission? You side with the money and suspend the players for the season.*

*And so the situation drags on for eight black men. And for a university and its storied football team. With two feet stuck in the past.*

*And a lot of eyes staring at a questionable future.*

Celia looked up, "Wow. Is this what they printed?"

"Well, not exactly. It is what I wrote. But they said it was too biased and was an opinion piece not a news story. So, they edited it. But I think the final story was pretty sympathetic to the players. I thought you might want to see the original."

"I'm impressed. I think you may have gotten it right this time." Mr. Watkins and Darnell read the story next.

"The damn shame of it all is that, for all the turmoil, the team had a successful season. Schwartzwalder even earned Eastern Coach of the year honors. Who knows what will happen to the black players in the long run? Who knows if they will ever play football again?"

"All you can do is report on what you see. You shined a light on questionable behavior in the football program and at the school. Things will work out. There are powers greater than the Coach and even the Chancellor of Syracuse University. They have the Human Rights Commission looking at them. And, thanks to you, they have thousands of ordinary citizens that know they didn't do right by the black players."

"Yeah but I remember what you told me when I wrote my article about Hicks and Jones. You said nothing ever happens to the white establishment. And that's what's happened here. Nothing changed. The Coach is still there. Hell he even was honored for what he did during the season when he should have been run out of town. It doesn't seem fair. The only ones who lost anything were the black players."

"They lost the chance to play in a few football games," Mr. Watkins offered. "That's a small price to pay for keeping one's dignity. A small price for doing what's right. The changes that are happening, in the country, didn't happen with one newspaper article or one boycott. It has to accumulate. It has to overwhelm before change happens."

"Look at the war. You participated in the Moratorium. You and thousands of others went on strike. You marched. You shut down college campuses. Kids were killed and yet the war still goes on. Were your efforts wasted? I don't think so. You can feel a change coming in the political climate. People are opening their eyes and they are disenchanted. The War will eventually be shut down. And the injustices that occur, like what those black football players experienced, will change too."

The five of us talked for hours more before I finally had to excuse myself to head home. Celia asked how much longer I planned to be in town.

"You could hang out with us on New Year's Eve. I'm having a party at my apartment. Darnell's coming down. You'd probably like hanging out with all these future doctors."

But I had intended to stay only one more day because I wanted a few days to get organized and back to work before the second semester started.

"I appreciate the invitation and I wish I could hang with you guys. But I have to get back to school. I'm actually leaving on Sunday morning."

"Then you have to promise, at the very least, to come visit me in Boston during spring break or at next summer," Darnell proposed.

"I think I can do that," I answered.

We hugged and said our goodbyes. As I drove home, I thought about the evening. It had been a year and a half since I had last seen the Watkins family. In the few hours we spent together, I was reminded how much I missed seeing them, just sitting around and talking. Sharing. I promised myself to do a better job staying in touch with Darnell and Celia. But it would be another year and a half before I would see either of them again.

# CHAPTER TWELVE

There was one surprise awaiting me before I headed back to Syracuse. After spending the last day at home with my parents, enjoying one final family dinner together, I asked my father if he could drop me at the bus station the next morning.

"What time's the bus you want to catch?"

"There's one at ten. So we should leave around eight thirty."

"I'll be ready."

I awoke the next morning around seven. After taking a shower, I packed my clothes and bounded down the stairs for a quick breakfast. Both my parents were already sitting at the kitchen table with cups of coffee and bagels.

"Did you sleep ok?" my mother asked and I nodded affirmatively. "How about an egg and bagel sandwich?" Again I nodded okay.

"I guess you must be anxious to get back to Syracuse," my father chimed in. "How long's the bus ride?"

"I think it's probably only five to six hours of actual driving. But, with all the stops, it takes closer to eight hours. I probably won't get back to my apartment until close to seven tonight."

"Well maybe this will help make the trip go quicker," my father said as he handed me a sealed envelope. I tore it open to find a set of car keys.

"Your mother and I thought you might be able to use a car," and he pushed away from the table and walked to the front door. I followed him and when he opened the door, there it was. Sitting in the driveway was a new red Ford Pinto.

"You're kidding me. This is unbelievable. I can't believe you guys did this."

"Consider it a belated high school graduation gift. We thought it would help you get around between work and classes and all. Plus we thought it might help you get home a little bit more often."

Maybe Mr. Watkins was on to something with my father. It wasn't as if I was looking for anything material-wise from my parents. Never had and never would. But this certainly was a huge gesture on their part and perhaps an acknowledgment, maybe even an acceptance that I was moving on my own path. I wasn't ready to put aside everything that had gone before. But, at least now, a door to a renewed relationship with my parents had opened and it would be incumbent upon me to meet them halfway.

We said our good-byes and I pulled my new Pinto onto the street and headed off to Syracuse. Four and one half hours later, I walked through the back door of my apartment. About four and one half hours sooner than I would have arrived on the Greyhound.

"Hey man, welcome back. Are my eyes seeing right? You bought a car while you were in Baltimore," my roommate, Danny, asked.

I had met Danny at the record store. He was a few years older than me and had started working at the store a few weeks after me. Danny had never been much of a student and had no interest in attending college, opting instead for a construction job out of high school. But the work didn't suit him, he was not one that tolerated the extremes of the weather he was required to work in. So, he moved back in with his parents where he lazed around for months until they kicked him out after catching him screwing the housekeeper on the kitchen table. Desperate for an income, he got a job at the record store and when he arrived on his first day with a suitcase in hand and no place to stay, I offered him one of the rooms in my apartment. Which he accepted at $150 per month.

"No, my parents gave it to me. So you off today?"

"Nah, I worked four hours this morning. Just hanging out now until Doug gets off work and then we're driving down to Ithaca. James Gang's playing. You want to come along? I'm sure Doug has an extra ticket."

Doug was my other roommate and assistant manager of the record store. He had also moved into the apartment over the summer. Doug was the one who controlled the concert tickets that the promoters usually comped to the store. Since the store manager was only into classical music, Doug was given all the tickets to the rock concerts, which meant the three of us went to all the shows we wanted.

To be honest, the James Gang was not one of the groups I preferred. I found Joe Walsh's voice to be too grating for my ear. But their music was ok and I had nothing else to do that night.

"Yeah I'm in. What time are we leaving?"

"Probably about five. Concert's at eight. You know Doug. He wants to check out the scene first. Probably hit a bar once we get there."

A few hours later, we loaded into Doug's Econoline van—which was well equipped for road trips having a wood plank, attached to each side to serve as seating in the cargo area, a mattress lining the floor of the van and a refrigerator set behind the driver's seat—and hit the road for the hour drive down to Ithaca.

It being the tail end of the Christmas vacation, the bars we initially tried were mostly empty so after a few beers, we headed to the concert. The parking lot was crowded but we were able to find a spot. The aroma of marijuana was heavy in the air and we lit a joint that we shared as we walked toward the gym.

Once inside, as we passed through the turnstiles, there were two girls standing and talking in front of the lavatories off to the left. Moments later a third girl emerged from the restroom and joined the other two. As we passed by, both Danny and Doug stopped and greeted the girls, none of whom I recognized.

"Hey, you should have told me you were coming tonight. I coulda got you freebies. You know, the salesmen from the record companies always make sure we get plenty of tickets to the concerts in the area," Doug said, addressing the dark-haired, skinny girl, who was wearing a Danskin black stretch top under an unbuttoned flannel shirt and faded bellbottoms.

"Yeah, it was kind of a last minute decision to come but I'll keep that in mind for the next time we want to go to a concert," she replied. And then the girls stepped away and I followed the dark-haired girl as if my eyes were tied to her waist by a leash.

I turned to Doug and Danny, "How do you know those girls?" I asked as we hurdled over people spread out on the floor until we found a spot dead center about fifty feet from the stage.

"I only know the one I spoke to. Didn't Danny tell you? Barry hired the one girl as a cashier last week. The skinny one with the dark hair. Ginny quit so we needed someone."

"Oh man, I forgot to tell you. I knew she'd be your type. Her name's Becky."

"Well, at least Barry's taste is getting better," I blurted.

Over the years, Barry, the owner of College Records, had a precise method for hiring employees. Half would be gay like Barry and the other half of the employees would be straight, generally guys that Barry found attractive. And then he always made sure there was one woman on staff to avoid any gender complaints. It made for an interesting dynamic. When work was slow, the gay guys would line up on one side of the store eyeing the male customers. Giggling. Making passes. Doug, Danny and I would stand, on the opposite wall, checking out the women who came into the store, doing the very same thing. And the one woman employee would be stationed at the front register laughing at all of us.

Doug and Danny sat down spreading their legs out directly in front of them and placing their arms, in easel-like fashion, behind them to make sure we had enough space. I continued to stand and scan the floor looking for Becky and her two friends. In a room filled with hundreds of dark haired girls, many dressed in flannel shirts and most in jeans, if not bellbottoms, it was difficult to pick out anyone. But I was determined to locate her. Finally I caught sight of her over to the right of the stage. As the lights were dimming, I stepped away.

"I gotta go. I'll meet you at the van after the show."

I stumbled towards the rear and then circled around to the right, guiding myself along the wall of the gym. The stage lights came on and as the James Gang took their spots, there was enough light for me to wend my way towards Becky and her friends. I stepped over a few people and finally reached their spot on the floor.

Becky twisted her head and looked up with a quizzical expression— one that said *who the fuck are you and where are you going?* A look that showed no hint of recognition from our brief encounter at the entrance.

"Becky?" I squeaked in a voice that undermined any confidence I had that this was a good move.

"Yeah?"

"I'm Michael. I'm with Danny and Doug from the record store. They said you just started working there. I work there too. Thought I'd come over and introduce myself."

"Oh, the writer. I heard a bit about you. They said that you're always busy with writing and working and school. Not a lot of time for play."

"I guess that's me. Mind if I sit down?"

"It's a free world, the spot's all yours" she replied and turned her head back towards the stage as the first chords of "Funk48" streamed from the amps.

I sat down not sure if she had actually invited me to sit there or whether she was only acknowledging that there was open space and I was welcome to occupy it. The loudness of the music and the fact that her back was towards me would keep me from finding out at least for a few minutes. So, I sat, my folded knees resting just a few inches from her right hip.

The band finished the first song and immediately launched into a second one. My gaze shifted from the stage to her shoulder and then back to the stage. Each time I looked at her, I checked out another feature. Her hair, her ears, her legs, my eyes always returning to the stage so as not to linger too long.

Suddenly, she bent her head back and motioned me forward with her hand. Her mouth moved next to my ear, "If you are going to stare at me all night, why don't you slide over and let me lean against you."

I complied with her request. There was nothing that I could imagine that would be better. I nudged myself a little to the left, pulled up my knees and spread them apart. I placed my hands to the side for support. As if drawn by an invisible magnetic force, Becky slid back, her ass connecting with my groin, her shoulders nestling into my chest. She leaned back, handed me a joint and said, "That's better. It does make the music much more enjoyable don't you think."

After finishing the second song, Joe Walsh, the lead guitarist, introduced the next song. "Here's a new song. One from our next album. Called *Walk Away*."

Given a brief reprieve from the music, I started to speak. Becky pressed back and put her finger to my lips, "Just relax and enjoy the feeling. No need to talk."

She squirmed a bit and grabbed hold of my forearms moving them across her chest. She dropped a light kiss on my neck. After about fifteen minutes, her hands locked on to my arms and pulled them down to her knees and up her thighs and then back to her chest. And then she did it again. At that point, I was not sure how much more of the concert I paid attention to, my mind locked onto Becky's presence.

But, at some point, the music stopped, the concert was over and the lights came on. Becky lurched forward and stood. I followed her lead.

"So, I guess I'll see you at the store then," she smiled.

"Well maybe we could hang out tonight."

"Aren't you driving back to Syracuse tonight?"

"Of course, but maybe we could meet up later?"

"Maybe you shouldn't press your luck. Let's leave things where they are for now. "

So, I drove back to Syracuse with Doug and Danny with my head still reeling, as much from thoughts of Becky as from the effects of the several joints we had smoked during the concert. Although I was not scheduled to work the next day, I still went down to the store early in the morning in hopes of seeing her. But she was off that day as well. And, with the following day being New Year's Day, the store was closed so it was not until the following day that I saw Becky. When I arrived at work, Doug greeted me with a wink and a smile, "You can thank me for the work schedule later."

As it turned out both Becky and I were working the noon to nine shift that day. She was sitting in the back room when I arrived. After clocking in, I walked with her to the front counter chatting about the concert and how we each spent New Year's Eve. Later, as our lunch hour approached, I invited her to join me for pizza at Cosmo's, which was next door to the store, and she accepted.

"You seem to be showing an awful lot of interest in me," Becky said before taking a bite of her pizza.

"Probably has something to do with the fact that I think you're great looking. Just thought we could hang out a bit and get to know each other better." She reminded me of Celia in her confidence, directness and candor.

"We can. But you should know that I have a boyfriend. I don't want to give you the wrong idea."

Although she did have a boyfriend, that boyfriend was not living in Syracuse at the moment, which left the door open a crack. He had left in November to move to a beach house in Jamaica and Becky, without the funds to travel, stayed behind hoping to save enough money from her job to join him in a few months. Since she had graduated the previous spring, most of her friends had also left Syracuse which meant she was glad to have someone to hang out with. We began spending a lot of time together as best my schedule allowed. Much to my disappointment, it was purely platonic.

One night, as I was closing the store, things took an unexpected turn. Although I had told Becky that I needed to work on a paper that night, she lingered while I prepared the deposit.

"You don't have to hang around. It'll take a few minutes to count all the money and prepare the bank slip. You should head home."

"Well, I thought you might like to smoke this joint with me."

Although it was probably not the wisest choice given the school work I needed to do, I was more than glad to oblige so we went to the basement and smoked. After that, it didn't take a whole lot of convincing to get me to accept her invitation to go back to her apartment. We stopped at the bank, dropped off the deposit and then drove the few blocks to her place and, once there, she put on a Billie Holiday album and we sat on the floor in bean bag chairs with a few cinnamon scented pillar candles burning and drank a bottle of wine. So much for the schoolwork. As we mellowed out, she snuggled in against me and began rubbing my chest. Before long, we were in her bed making love. And within days after that first encounter, I began spending most nights at Becky's apartment.

And that's where Doug found me one snowy February night when he called on the phone.

"I figured you were there. I hate to interrupt but I need your help. There's been a break-in at the store. Can you meet Danny and me and help clean up?"

"Of course."

Rather than drive my car on the unplowed streets, I decided to walk the few blocks to the store and I arrived at the same time that Doug and Danny were pulling onto the lot in Doug's van.

"Man, I don't mind being dragged out in the middle of the night. But if someone broke into the store and stole a bunch of records, I just hope they did us all a favor and took all the Carpenters records. That would make all of this worthwhile," Danny said.

"Doesn't seem likely that a burglar would fit the profile of a Carpenters' fan," I offered.

We entered through the back door, turned on the lights and inspected the damage. Most of the front display window had been knocked out. The bins of records and racks of tapes appeared to be untouched but, the section of the store that held the stereo equipment, was a mess. Speakers, amps and record players were strewn across the floor. After a quick appraisal of the situation, it appeared certain that several units were missing. Moments later, the police arrived and filed a report and then we set about cleaning up the place and covering the open window.

Doug asked us to check the basement for a sheet of plywood that he thought he had seen down there leaning against the back wall. Danny and I brought the sheet upstairs and carried it outside, braced it against the window frame and Doug started to hammer nails into place.

As I stood in the cold, holding one side of the board, things just didn't seem exactly right to me. I noticed shards of glass scattered along the pavement in front of the store. I was no detective, beyond my experience tracking Coach McCaskill and his players, but the entire scene seemed odd.

"Doug. This is kind of strange. The sidewalk is covered with glass," I said.

"What's strange about that?" Danny asked.

"Well, if the store was broken into, wouldn't most of the glass be inside the store. The force would make the glass fly away from the object that broke it. This looks like the window was broken from the inside. There's virtually no glass in the store. And, besides, how did you know there was a sheet of plywood in the basement? Why would we even have a sheet of plywood in the basement especially one that exactly fits this window? Did Barry think that there might be a broken window in the future and decided to stock up on plywood just in case? Is there something going on Doug? It all seems too coincidental. It looks like this has been staged."

"I can't say for sure but I also can't disagree with you. I heard Barry on the phone the other day and it sounded like he was planning something. Something to cover his ass. And you know the rumors."

"What rumors?" Danny asked.

"The stories about Barry and certain members of the football team, about him servicing a bunch of the players over the years. The other day, I overhead his phone conversation and it sounded like the person on the other end was asking for stereo equipment as a payback. I'm guessing that he staged the break-in to pay off the players and still be able to put in an insurance claim. It's his store and his problem so, beyond getting this place back in order, I don't really give a shit about what went down."

"Hmm. Sounds exactly like the type of thing you'd be interested in," Danny suggested, looking in my direction. "You know, maybe you could do another one of your investigative stories. Or maybe take a new approach and do another participatory story like when you tried rugby. You know, let Barry service you and see where it leads."

"You have a warped mind, Danny. I couldn't be less interested in pursuing any angle here."

The fact of the matter was that I had shown very little interest in my writing, both creative and journalistic, ever since I began staying at Becky's and ignoring my responsibilities. Months later, I would wonder how I ever managed to get through the semester at all since I skipped most of my classes and was late on most of the assignments all because nights at Becky's were fueled by a steady stream of drugs—pot and Quaaludes mostly. There was even a night of smoking opium which I hoped would propel me into a burst of creative energy. But, like most nights, it only led to a long night of lovemaking. We'd sleep away most days until late morning and then rise and go work at the store. Doug was always accommodating by assigning the two of us the late afternoon or evening shift.

In late February, we broke from our normal routine and drove to Buffalo to attend a Pink Floyd concert and it marked my first time trying

LSD. There was a remarkable light show, although I am not sure if the rest of the audience witnessed the same show I did. When the concert ended, I was too high to drive and so was Becky. Instead, we walked the streets for hours on a bitter cold night with the wind whipping off Lake Erie until we sobered up. On the ride back, racked with hunger, we stopped at an all-night gas station to find something to eat. Both of us wanted something more substantial than chips or cookies or candy. We finally settled on a package of Oscar Meyer hot dogs even though we had no way to cook them.

"Are you sure this is a good idea?" she asked.

"Yeah. It'll be like eating bologna. You don't have to cook bologna and you don't have to cook hot dogs. It's the same shit in both."

So our hunger won out and we purchased the hot dogs. When we had climbed back into the car, I ripped open the package with my teeth and we both began eating the raw hot dogs. No bun. No condiments. Together, we finished half of the package.

By the time we arrived home, the hot dogs were already doing a number on my stomach. On Becky's as well. I let her hit the toilet first. I puked for the next six hours. Just sat myself down on the floor and rested my head on the toilet seat. Six hours later, I picked myself off the floor and walked toward the bedroom. Becky was laying diagonally across the bed with her head hanging over the edge. A trash can directly underneath, filled with the churned remains of the hot dogs she had eaten. The room reeked but I soon passed out on the bed.

Somehow, we both managed to drag ourselves to work that afternoon.

"Just like bologna huh?" she lashed out at me.

"So, I was wrong." Whether it was the dumb idea of eating uncooked hot dogs, or eating far more than we should have, or it was the effects of the LSD or a combination of all of it, I swore off food for the next two days.

I recovered just in time to head off to another concert at the War Memorial Coliseum in downtown Syracuse. Derek and the Dominoes were the headliners. And some guy named Elton John as the opening act. The place rocked. But Becky was passed out on her seat. She had taken two Quaaludes and fell asleep, missing the entire concert. I lugged her to the car and back to her apartment and then headed home to my place.

At the end of March, we saw Bonnie Raitt at Jabberwocky, a small venue on the Syracuse campus, for a mellow evening of folk and blues.

Even more mellow for Becky who again had taken Quaaludes before the show. It had become her habit to take a few every night after work. More often than not, I found myself dragging her back to her apartment and then returning to my place to spend the night. Which turned out to be a blessing in disguise because, earlier in March, one of my professors had sent a message via one of my classmates. An ultimatum. Show up for class or be prepared to fail, no matter my test results (although I skipped classes, I went for the tests and, much to the professor's dismay, always scored high on the exams). I obeyed and began attending all my classes. I was in salvage mode. I made it through the semester, still finding time to work at the store and spending a little time with Becky.

Once the semester ended, it was summer break and I was freed from any school obligations. I went back to working full time at the store and spending the nights with Becky. Early in the summer, we attended a few concerts. Santana and then the Byrds. But Becky was losing interest. All she did was go to work, take her evening Quaaludes and then sleep away the morning. And I soon followed suit, falling into the same pattern. I figured the summer was my vacation so wasting away the time seemed to be no big deal.

Even though I was getting high on a nightly basis, I was able to pull it together when my junior year began. I went to classes but lagged on doing any work outside of what was minimally required. I continued in my position as a stringer covering the football team, filing a few stories leading up to the start of the season but with little interest beyond cashing the checks that came my way. Then my lifestyle caught up with me. On September 18, the football team opened up at home against Wisconsin with a noon start time and I was expected to cover the game and write a story. Instead, I was fast asleep in Becky's bed.

Around three o'clock, I awoke and soon realized that I had missed the game. Without cleaning up or taking a shower, I threw on my clothes and started jogging up to campus. The crowds were streaming toward me, heading back to their cars. I finally reached the press gate on the far side of the stadium.

"Hey Michael. Running a bit late aren't you," Paul, one of the security guards, remarked.

"Yeah. Wasn't feeling too good this morning. Touch of flu."

"Looks to me you have a touch of something. But I would bet it's not the flu."

"Great. Thanks for the diagnosis. Can you let me in?"

"Sorry Michael. Cannot do."

"Come on Paul. I need to get my story."

"I'm sorry Michael. No one gets in. I think the interviews are just about over anyhow."

"Well. Who won?" I was thinking I might be able to piece together enough facts to file a story.

"It was a 20-20 tie." Paul motioned me away. There would be no story to file.

Monday morning, I received a call from my boss at the Associated Press.

"What's going on, Michael. What happened to your story?"

"I'm sorry, Mr. Bowen. I was under the weather. I overslept. I promise it won't happen again."

"It better not. I got dozens of guys praying for the chance to take your spot. You got one more chance."

Three weeks later, I blew that chance.

# CHAPTER 13

After the season opener at home against Wisconsin, the Syracuse football team played the next three Saturdays on the road—at Northwestern, at Indiana and at Maryland. That led up to October 16 when Penn State was slated to play at Archbold Stadium. Clearly the biggest game of the year for the Syracuse faithful. In the previous three weeks, I had been especially diligent in attending practices and filing stories. But, the night before the Penn State game, the Grateful Dead were playing at Cornell. An event I could not miss.

Doug was in command again. He had three tickets. As usual, Becky didn't want to go. Her interest had waned on all things other than drugs. She had become a shut-in except for the days she had to go to work, a job which she now hated but kept at because she needed the money if she was to make it to Jamaica. Work. Drugs. Sleep. That became the extent of her life.

So, Danny and I (guilt-free for leaving Becky behind) took the tickets and joined Doug for the ride to Ithaca. I rode shotgun and Danny was sprawled out on the mattress in the back.

"I got something else for us. Check out the glove compartment," Doug suggested.

I opened the glove compartment to find a small tin foil package. I unwrapped it and there were three tabs of LSD.

"Should make for the perfect night," Doug said as I inspected the contents. Shortly after parking the van, Doug and Danny dropped the acid. I declined.

"What gives?" Danny asked.

I had sworn off acid after the incident where I puked my guts out for hours after the Pink Floyd concert in Buffalo. Though I was sure the raw hot dogs were the culprit, I had decided to avoid anything that was ingested that night. To be on the safe side, that meant no more acid.

"Just can't do it," I said lamely.

But, before the concert had even started, there were plenty of other drugs available. As quickly as I was given a joint, took a hit and passed it along, another joint was in my hands.

Soon the lights dimmed. My eyes opened wide.

*Ladies and Gentlemen. The Grateful Dead.* And the notes from Jerry

Garcia's guitar began floating from the stage. *Casey Jones.* I felt I was in one of those commercials where the aroma from the frying pan on top of the stove wiggles through the air in a cloud toward someone's waiting nose in the next room. I could see the notes. They danced around my nose and crept up the side of my face to my ears. I opened my mouth and tasted the music.

Like most Dead concerts, the music seemed to last forever. This night they played for over four hours. It was after midnight when we stumbled out of the arena. As we made our way to the van, Doug bumped into a group of guys that worked at our sister store in Ithaca.

"Marty, what's going on?"

"My man, Doug. How ya doing?"

"I'm doing great Marty. What could be better than a night with the Dead?"

"Amen. Hey we're going to grab something to eat and then head back to Stan's house. Gonna keep the party going. Care to join us?"

It sounded good to all three of us. So, we hopped in the van and followed Marty's car to an IHOP a few miles down the road. I drove since Doug and Dan were still tripping.

Truth be told, IHOP had become my favorite place to go when I was high. Not because the food was anything special. But the menu was so colorful. Heaps of vanilla ice cream, covered with strawberry syrup, sitting on top of a Belgian waffle. Or a stack of pancakes with butter oozing out the top and maple syrup dripping down the edges. Plus, late at night, the food would always go down easy. The only place I found that rivaled an IHOP was a donut shop where the sheer number of choices intrigued me. Chocolate Frosted. Cream filled. Custard. Always indecisive, I would take a dozen assorted and eat two or three bites out of each donut until I had satisfied my cravings.

After the meal, we followed Marty's car back to Stan's house, an old Victorian, and entered a large front room that was littered with beer bottles. A dark brown sofa, stained with who knows what sat against one wall. The cushions were battered, looking like they had just finished a fifteen round bout. A few bean bag chairs were spaced around the floor, which was made of oak planks. A small table held a lava lamp and a few ashtrays with the remnants of cigarettes and joints. Navy blue sheets were tacked to the wall to cover the windows. A single floor lamp stood in the corner and provided the only light in the room, shining up towards the ceiling. A stereo system sat opposite the sofa with wires leading to the speakers which had been hung on the wall. A peace symbol poster was above the sofa and a Jane Fonda Barbarella poster to the right of the doorway.

Marty took a seat at one end of the sofa and Stan took the other end after first turning on the stereo. Jefferson Airplane. *Surrealistic Pillow.* Doug, Dan and I each plopped into beanbag chairs. Jenny, who appeared to be Marty's girlfriend, lit up a joint and handed it to him. As he took a hit, Jenny stood over him and directed the rising trail of smoke to her nose.

"Why don't you see if anybody else is up," Marty asked Jenny. "If not, wake them up. Tell them we got a party going on."

He passed the joint to Stan, pulled a second joint from his shirt pocket, lit it, took a hit and passed it to Doug.

In the meantime, Jenny had climbed the stairwell and, after a few minutes, she returned.

"I think the others will be down once they get themselves together."

She positioned herself on the sofa with her head resting in Marty's lap and her now bare feet bridged across Stan's thighs. The joints continued to make their journey from mouth to mouth. As one finished, another was lit.

More footsteps could be heard coming down the steps. And in short order, three more women joined the party. Sara. Liz. And, to my astonishment, Ellen Wagner from my third grade class.

I had not seen her for years, ever since my mother had forced my family out to Baltimore County. Back in third grade, Ellen was the tallest girl in the class with a pleasant face that was spotted with a few light brown freckles across the bridge of her nose. By junior high, I thought she was really cute but I was shy and thought she was out of my league. It had been over eight years since I had last seen her. Those eight years had done well by her. She was now about five foot eight with auburn hair, somewhat frizzy and shoulder length. The freckles had disappeared. She now stood in front of me, her long legs seemingly only covered by a flannel shirt that went to mid-thigh and flopped open exposing the top of her breasts.

"Ellen," I stammered.

"Holy Shit. Michael? Michael Sanders. What the fuck are you doing here?"

She turned to Marty, "I went to fucking elementary school with this guy. Can you fucking believe it?"

I told her how we met up with Marty and Stan after the Dead concert and how they invited us back to party.

"Shit. I mean. Jesus Christ, Michael. What the fuck are you up to? Besides going to a Dead concert."

"I'm at Syracuse. What about you?"

"Cornell. I'm at Cornell."

That hardly surprised me. Ellen had always been the smartest girl in the class. An Ivy League school. Pretty much what would be expected for her.

"I mean. Holy fuck. How many years has it been since I saw you? "

"I think it's been since seventh grade or so."

"What the fuck happened to you? I remember hearing some story about you getting beat up and then. And then you were gone."

"Yeah a bunch of guys got me pretty good in the stairway during summer school one day. My mother kinda freaked and moved us out to the county."

"Yeah.Yeah.I fucking remember. You and that black kid. What the fuck was his name?"

"Darnell," I answered.

"Yeah. Yeah. Darnell. They said a bunch of racist guys cornered him in the stairwell and that you tried to help him out."

"I don't know how much I helped him. We both got beat up pretty bad. He was my friend. I was just trying to do whatever I could. Which turned out not to be very much."

"The rumor was that they heard you were at Gwynn Oak the day of that demonstration to integrate the park."

"I was but just as an onlooker. Same with Darnell. I think those guys at summer school were just looking for an excuse to go after someone. It just turned out to be Darnell. And me."

"Whatever. I think seeing you calls for a celebration. I mean I am fucking excited to see you."

With that, Ellen left the room and returned with a bottle of Tequila. Half empty. She knelt in front of me. The flannel shirt slid up her thighs.

"To old friends" and she took a swig from the bottle, passed it to me and I did the same.

The bottle made its way around the room. Between the grass and the Tequila, everyone was soon wasted. And now it was Dylan and Highway 61 Revisited playing on the stereo.

Gradually, everyone else in the room passed out. Ellen and I talked on.

"So how are you coming with your plans to be the first woman President of the United States?" I asked.

"When did I ever say I wanted to be President?"

"Back in third grade. Mrs. Garrett's class. She asked us what we wanted to be and you said you would become the first woman President."

"Christ, I was so pompous back then. President. What the fuck was I thinking?"

"So, you changed your mind?"

"Well let's just say I'm not on that track. I'll be happy to finish up my undergrad work and get into law school. That's about as focused as I can be these days. And what about you? What was it that you wanted to become?"

"A writer."

"And how's that coming for you?"

"I'm making some progress. I did some writing for the Baltimore Gazette, after high school, while I was trying to save enough money to go to college. And I've been writing for the AP, covering the football team, the last two years."

"A journalist then?"

"In truth, I wanted to do creative writing but figured I needed to purse the journalism as a way to make a living."

"So did you give up on the creative writing?"

"It seems to be on the back burner. On the back, back burner. Never seem to have the time beyond taking the courses in school and even that's a struggle. I just can't turn it on and write on cue. We get assignments to write a poem or a short story. I sit at the desk and I stare at the paper. For hours. It just seems so unnatural. And then, when the professors return the stories, their comments are *your writing is too detached. It's like reading a diary or you need to open up and write with more heart.* It used to be fun and something I could do for hours, but now I can't get it going and, when I do, none of it is any good anyway. I think I would be happy just to write something that's bad. But I can't even do that."

"Well you shouldn't give up. I mean if you're still passionate about writing then figure out what it takes. You gotta find that energy that got you started in the first place. Besides I think you would make a great writer."

"Really. What would ever give you that idea?"

"I don't know. It just seems like being a writer fits. You seemed to take everything in and didn't just jump into the water. In that way, you were a little different than the other boys in class. You didn't seem to have the need to constantly be making a fool of yourself."

"I think I made a fool of myself plenty of times."

"Look everyone did. But you were more laid back. The other boys were show-offs, they always had to be the center of attention. You stayed in the background, almost like you were acting as the storyteller rather than the actor. I don't know if it was that you were surer of yourself or what. Plus you seemed to get along with everyone."

"Believe me, I think you are mistaking my lack of confidence for a more noteworthy attribute."

"No Michael. I think you're the one who's shortchanging himself. You had qualities that the other boys didn't. It was almost like you let your feminine side show through. You seemed to care about things. And people. I remember thinking that about you when we were in junior high. Fuck. I think I even had a little crush on you."

"Hey I'm flattered but you had plenty of guys hanging around you."

"Which is why I probably had that crush on you. But you were also kind of shy. You never showed any interest in me."

"I was probably intimidated. You were the smartest girl in the class. And good looking. I figured I never had much of a chance."

"And now here we are. Eight years later. Do you think your chances have improved?"

Although I had long ago lost any shyness around women, I still was somewhat ungraceful making a move. I needed to be Cary Grant. Clark Gable. Rhett Butler. Grab her in my arms, lift her up and carry her up the stairs to her bed. Instead, I was still Michael Sanders. But Ellen took care of any moves that needed to be made. She leaned forward and her hands reached for my pony tail and pulled off the rubber band. She spread her fingers and stroked them through my hair and then lightly kissed my lips.

"I. I. I think so," I stuttered.

"I think your chances might be a little better if you come with me to my bedroom."

I followed her up the stairs looking at her beautiful ass as her shirt rode up with each step she took. We passed a bunch of other rooms. Ellen's bedroom was at the end of the hall. The mattress and box spring sat directly on the floor and a three drawer dresser was in one corner. Everything in the room was flowery. Purples and lavenders and blueberry and dusty rose. The curtains. The walls. The posters. The candles. She turned on her record player. Neil Young.

I started to take off my shirt.

"No. Let me."

She gracefully slid each button through its opening and parted my shirt. Her tongue pecked at my stomach and then traced loops from one hip to the other. She leaned back and raked her hair behind her shoulders then moved back toward me and placed her finger on the zipper on my jeans. Her finger lightly ran up and down the zipper. Over and over. Until she finally clutched it and pulled the zipper down. She unbuttoned my pants and slid them off. And then my boxers. She placed her hands on my lower back and pushed me onto the bed. Rolled me over and climbed on top and pulled off her shirt. My head was spinning. We made love and then I passed out.

When I awoke, the next morning, Ellen still had her legs wrapped around my hips. We were chest to chest and her face was nestled into my neck.

"Shit. Ellen. Wake up. What time is it?"

She lifted her head, looked at the clock and said, "Eleven. But it's Saturday. Go back to sleep."

"Shit. I'm supposed to be at the football game. Fuck. Fuck. Fuck."

"A football game. You're gonna fucking leave me for a fucking football game."

"Well. Not anymore. I'm too late already. Look, I gotta make a call. Is there a phone in the house?"

"Downstairs in the kitchen."

I slipped on my jeans and ran down the steps to call my boss at the AP. I got him on the line.

"Mr. Bowen. It's Michael Sanders. I screwed up. I'm stuck out of town and couldn't get back in time for the game."

"Don't worry about it. Everything's taken care of. Johnny Robbins is covering the game."

"What?"

"Backup plan you know. I had this feeling that I couldn't count on you so I assigned him to the game. Had to make sure. He'll be covering the team from now on. You're finished."

Knowing there was no chance to convince him otherwise, I apologized, "I'm sorry I let you down Mr. Bowen."

"You let yourself down kid."

I hung up the phone and went back to Ellen's bed. She did her best to sooth my disappointment. But I was pissed. When we finally got up, no one else was in the house. Doug and Danny had gone back to Syracuse earlier in the morning. "I peeked in the room and you didn't look like you wanted to be disturbed. You looked pretty content," was how Danny put it when I asked him, later that day, why they left me behind.

"I better get back. I already fucked up today."

"Okay. Okay. I know you have to go. But look. I meant what I said. I was really excited to see you. I was really glad we spent the night together."

"Me too."

"Will you call me then? Will you come back down?"

"Of course."

I chose not to say anything about Becky and, given Ellen's enthusiastic and unconditional invitation, I assumed she had no ongoing relationship that would interfere. Though it was doubtful that I would return to Ithaca, I wasn't ready to hurt her feelings by brushing her off.

I left Stan's house and walked for fifteen minutes until I reached the Interstate. I held out my thumb and almost instantly a car stopped and picked me up. As the car sped up the highway to Syracuse, the disappointment in losing my job was all consuming. But, at the same time, the one thing I was not feeling was any guilt over what happened the night before with Ellen. Without question, my relationship with Becky was nearing the end. We spent less and less time together. And when we did, she was always high and out of it. On the few occasions that we had sex, she showed no passion or interest. And she certainly showed no interest or passion about anything else other than her Quaaludes. From the beginning she had planned to join her boyfriend at some point so I had always been on borrowed time.

When the car reached the exit for downtown Syracuse, I jumped out and walked the thirty minutes back to my apartment. It was quiet. Doug and Danny were at work. I grabbed a beer from the refrigerator and headed to my bedroom. All I could think about was taking a shower and going to sleep. Nearing the bedroom, I was surprised to see the door closed. And there was a note tacked to it.

A note folded in half. *Michael* handwritten on the front. I pulled out the tack and grabbed the note. I stared at my name, for what seemed like minutes, carefully examining the note to see that it was really my name written on the front. And then I unfolded the note. *Gone to Jamaica. See ya*

# CHAPTER FOURTEEN

It wasn't the fact that Becky had suddenly left for Jamaica that surprised me. She had made her intentions known from our first day together. And it wasn't the fact that she hadn't said goodbye that surprised me either. Though I certainly deserved a more fitting farewell, our relationship had been deteriorating to a point that any behavior she showed would not have been a shock. No, the true surprise was that she had managed to pull it off at all. Managed to find enough clear moments, during her nightly drug filled haze, to call the airline and book a flight. To pack her things and get to the airport. To wrap up whatever there was to her life in Syracuse. To finally get her shit together.

Nor was I upset or disheartened by her leaving. In fact, though I would certainly miss her, her leaving was a relief. In retrospect, there had not been much to our relationship over the last few months anyway. Very little sex. Even less conversation and companionship. Maybe she had been pushing me away to make the break easier for both of us. Whether or not this was her intent, I shrugged off the news, tossed out the note and set about carrying on with my life, which certainly needed a lot of attention. After all, I had screwed up my job with the AP that day. I was still struggling in my creative writing classes. Maybe Becky's departure would give me a kick in the ass and get me focused again. Besides, Ellen was now a more distinct option though I was uncertain if I was ready for any type of relationship. I was soon to find out.

When Doug returned home from work that night he immediately remarked, "Hey man, you don't waste any time do you?"

"What are you talking about?"

"Becky up and leaves and you already have Ellen ready to take her place."

"Hey I didn't know Becky was leaving. And Ellen. Well, she was something I fell into last night."

"Well you certainly fell into the right pile of shit, amigo. Ellen is one fine chick. And she must have the hots for you. She called the store looking for you this afternoon. Told me to have you call her. Here's her number."

I knew Ellen was aggressive and she apparently had me in her sights.

Without question, Ellen was highly attractive, both physically and intellectually, but I still wasn't sure I was ready to get involved emotionally. But I owed her a phone call.

"Hey I just wanted to make sure you made it back to Syracuse ok. I didn't have your number so I thought I could reach you by calling the store."

"Yeah I made it back ok."

"Look Michael, I meant what I said. I'd really like to see you again."

"I'm sure that can be arranged."

"You don't sound very convincing. Is something wrong? I thought you had a good time."

"I did. I did. It's just that I got some news when I got back and it rattled me a bit."

"What kind of news?"

"Oh nothing earth shattering. Just that my girlfriend suddenly left town yesterday."

"What? You have a girlfriend. You fucked me and you have a girlfriend. Don't you think you should have mentioned that little detail?"

"It didn't cross my mind in the heat of the moment. I didn't think it would matter to you. It's not like you asked."

"It does matter and, just because I didn't ask doesn't mean that I wouldn't care. Why would I even think to ask? I don't do background checks before I go to bed with a guy. I assume there is some integrity there and that you would be decent enough to tell me."

"You're right. I should have said something. But it's really not what you think it is."

"Then, what is it."

"She's just a girl. She had, she has a boyfriend in Jamaica and she had always planned to move there at some point. And I guess that's what she's done. She let me know her plans from the start. So whatever we had was nothing more than a temporary thing. We hung out. We had sex. But it was pretty much over and done by the time I saw you. So there's really nothing that you should be upset about."

"Are you upset that she's gone?"

"No. No, I'm just surprised that she left without saying good-bye. But it's probably all for the best."

"But no closure?"

"I guess not. But I'm ok with it. We really hadn't been together much over the last few weeks. She spent most of her time spaced out. I stayed away from her most days."

"So, where's that leave us?"

"I told you I'm cool spending time with you and seeing where things go. But we live fifty miles apart so I can't be running down to Ithaca every day. And I work most weekends so I can't get there as much as I might like or you might like."

"So then let's take it as it comes."

But Ellen could never take life as it comes. Instead, she was the type who had to force the action. Had to go after what she wanted. It was no surprise, then, when on the following Friday night she walked into the record store just before closing time, toting a backpack full of books and clothes.

"Hey, Michael. Got any plans tonight?"

Before I could answer, she said, "Thought I would take a chance and hitchhike up here. Thought we might be able to reprise last weekend."

That sounded like a good idea and it certainly turned out that way. As soon as we returned to my apartment and reached the bedroom, Ellen wrapped her arms around my waist, pushed me onto the bed and began pulling off my clothes. Just as she did the first time.

For the next month, Ellen hitchhiked to Syracuse every Friday afternoon and spent the weekend with me. Each Sunday night, I would drive her back to Ithaca.

As each week passed, I became more and more enamored with Ellen and, apparently, she became more enamored with me as well. I marveled at her focus and energy. She brought an intensity to whatever she was doing at the time. Whether it was studying, making love, or just sitting around and talking, she was animated and compelling to watch. She didn't do anything half way and she stayed committed to what she wanted. I envied her for her drive because it was the very thing that I lacked, as I had proven over and over again. I had always juggled a lot of balls—school, work, writing—but I had never been able to stay focused on any one thing while I was doing it. My mind would wander, thinking what other things I needed to take care of. By the time Ellen started spending time with me, another lethargy had taken hold. I had trouble getting motivated to tackle my classwork or my writing. While Ellen spent the day studying when we were together, I would just sit around if I wasn't at work. Just staring out the window at the snow covering the trees and thinking about the things I was avoiding until I would drift off.

"What's wrong with you?" she asked one weekend.

"What do you mean?"

"You don't do anything. If you're not at work, or sleeping with me, you just sit there and stare into space. You must have something to do. Reading. Studying. Something. I know you like writing. But I never see you doing any of those things."

"I can't get motivated. I feel like I'm spinning my wheels. When I lost the AP job, I think I lost the desire to write. Maybe I'm not cut out for what I thought I was."

"What a crock of shit. You just need to find what you had. You have to get back to what worked for you before. Stop overthinking things."

"I know. But it's so unnatural now. I can't get any flow. Maybe I have writer's block."

"That would imply that you were making an effort. You can't have writer's block if you don't even try. Besides what about the other courses you take? I never see you doing any work for them."

"I keep up during the week so I have plenty of time to spend with you."

"Bullshit. So it's just the writing courses that you ignore?"

"I told you I don't have the feel for writing these days."

"What did you do when you had the feel?"

"I sat down and just started writing. Something popped into my head and that's all it took. Now I just draw a blank. Last week, in class, the professor passed around a bag and we each had to reach in, pull out an item and write a story using the item as the focal point. I pulled a set of car keys. Now what the fuck was I supposed to say about car keys?"

"So what did you do?"

'I managed to put some words down on the paper. But it wasn't very good. It was hardly worthy."

Ellen was not sympathetic at all.

"I can't understand why you don't try harder. It's not like you haven't done it before. You always tell me about your days playing basketball. I imagine your skills didn't improve by not practicing. It's the same for your writing."

Because she had always been highly motivated and things came naturally for her, Ellen did not have a lot of understanding for my situation. Nevertheless, she did have a suggestion.

"Look Michael, next week is the start of Christmas break. Why don't you come down to Baltimore with me? We can go to my parents' beach house in Ocean City. Get away from everything. Clear your mind. All you've been doing for the last two years is going to school and going to work. How 'bout taking some time for yourself. I think if you relax for a week, you might be able to break down whatever barriers are keeping you from writing."

Ellen was right. Other than a few brief visits home, I had taken little down time since graduating from high school. A week in Ocean City might help get me back on track.

"I'm in."

The following Friday, I packed up my car, picked up Ellen in Ithaca and headed south to Baltimore for two days with my parents and then a week in Ocean City. Ellen was supportive and accommodating, letting me dictate the pace for once.

Her family's condo was on the tenth floor with a balcony that looked out on the ocean. The weather was cold but the condo felt summery with décor that was light in color and warm and cozy in its nature. We took daily walks along the deserted beach walking arm in arm as the strong winds whipped the sand into our faces. Every other day, we walked the boardwalk and stopped in the few shops that were open for customers. We skipped the restaurants, opting to bring in carry-out food each day and then watched television until midnight. But most of the time we just hung out. Ellen spent much of the time reading and doing classwork at the kitchen table. I spent most of my time sitting around doing nothing. But, while the time in Ocean City was fun and relaxing, when all was said and done, my mind no more ready to tackle the challenges. At no time during the week did I feel ready to write. I remained unmotivated and uninspired.

I had spent a lot of alone time sitting on the balcony, wrapped in a blanket, drinking coffee and looking out on the swirling waves. Instead of worrying about my failures in the classroom, or my lost AP job, I instead thought about my other failures. Like the people I had continued to neglect and disappoint. My parents, who gave me a car in the hope that I would visit more often only to find that another year had passed by the time I came home again, and then for a mere two days. And Darnell who had asked me to visit him in Boston. I hadn't followed through and hadn't contacted him since we parted the previous Christmas. Plus I didn't make time to visit him and the Watkins family during this brief Christmas visit to Baltimore. And Celia. That relationship was still confusing and, now, with Ellen in the picture, even more so. In every case, I had reneged on my promises and stayed away.

On New Year's Day, no more focused than before, we headed back to school.

Ellen had given me the space but now was anxious to learn if the week of relaxation had achieved what she hoped. After skirting the issue for the first two hours of the drive, she peppered me with questions as we reached northern Pennsylvania on the interstate.

"I'm afraid it didn't help. I had a good time. But, there's still nothing there. There's two weeks left in the semester. I am afraid what's going to happen because I have to turn in a short story and I still don't have a clue what to write about."

"Well, that's certainly not good. But I tell you what. Can you pull off at the next exit?"

"You need to take a leak?"

"No."

"Hungry."

"No."

"It's Mahanoy City. What in the world would make you want to stop in Mahanoy City at this time of day? There won't be anything open."

"I just need to stretch my legs."

As I steered the car onto the exit ramp, it was cold and snowing lightly. The town was deserted. Every shop and restaurant was closed for the night. The citizens of Mahanoy City were bundled up in their homes. A few cars, coated with a thin layer of snow, stood in an unlit gas station on one corner. A gray streaked cat scampered across a lawn and into an alley, the only sign of life.

"Where do you want to go?" I asked.

"Just keep driving."

We turned onto East Center Street.

"There. Pull over there."

I pulled the car to the curb. In front of a small park at the corner of East Center and Fifth Streets. Ellen climbed out of the car and I followed. There was almost total silence. Other than the hum of the yellowed street light. And the crunch of our feet on the fresh snow. Ellen walked across the small patch of ground towards three benches, two of which faced the park's tennis court and the other which faced the street. She brushed the snow from the one facing the street and motioned me toward her.

"Sit down. Right here."

The cold, from the bench, pierced my jeans and the breeze caused a few tears to trickle down my cheeks. I blinked a few times and with a quick sniffle, I wiped them away.

"Now what?"

"Sshh. Don't talk. Slide forward a little."

As I begin to move, Ellen placed her hands behind my knees and pulled forward until my shoulders were against the back of the bench, my butt barely catching the edge of the seat and my legs now extended out a good few feet. Ellen pulled her jeans down around her ankles and climbed atop my legs. She pulled the zipper of my jeans down and reached her hand in.

"Wow. Do you think this is a good idea? I mean we're sitting right in the middle of town."

"Sshh. There's no one around."

I put my hands on her hips and Ellen glided up and down. With great fervor. The snowflakes glistened as they fell on her hair and her breath shot out in layers of fog that parted against my face. We both climaxed, in a few minutes, muffling our voices in the others' coat. Ellen rested her head against my chest, for another minute, and then stood and pulled up her jeans. She grabbed my hand, wrapped my arm around her waist and led me back to the car.

As I pulled the car back onto the interstate, Ellen turned and smiled, "Now, maybe you have something to write about."

And that's exactly happened. I used the experience to inspire a story that was not a great work of art but good enough to submit.

A few weeks later, when I received my grade, I called Ellen.

"I owe you one. I got a "B" in my creative writing class."

"Hey that's great. "

"So, I have to ask. Did we stop in Mahanoy City because you wanted to do something crazy or because you thought it would help me?"

"A little of both. You needed something to break the logjam in your mind. I thought it might help. Plus it was fun. I mean. Who else fucks on a park bench in the middle of town at night of New Year's Day?"

Ellen's idea for a kick start did more than get me through my course. It got me going again. There was no other reason to explain why my creative juices returned, so I gave her little escapade full credit. I was able to tackle the writing exercises in the next semester's creative writing class with greater ease and was doing a little writing on my own as well. And I took an investigative journalism course that was right up my alley. Things were good all around, with school and with Ellen as well. We continued to see each other every weekend.

In early March, Ellen got the good news she had been hoping for. Acceptance to Harvard Law School. When she called to tell me the news, she broached her latest idea.

"How about moving to Boston with me? We can get an apartment together."

"Hey I would love to. But you know that I have another year to go."

"Transfer. Finish up at one of the Boston schools."

"I don't know. I'm just getting back in the groove. I'm not sure it's a good idea."

"Well think about it. We have time to figure it out."

Ellen did not press the issue. But, when we spent time together on the weekends, she would drop gentle reminders. Like encouraging me to send off applications. Which I did. By April, I had been accepted at several schools, but none that I thought was as good as what Syracuse offered. But there was still time. There was no rush to make a decision.

In the spring, I began researching a story on the treatment of minorities on campus for my investigative journalism class. I spoke with leaders of the Black Student Union and a loose organization of Puerto Rican students. The final interview I had set up was an interview was with the Women's Collective, a group of students focused on women's issues on campus. I attended their weekly meeting on May 8 to listen to their concerns. After two hours the meeting broke up and I approached the President of the group.

"Can I ask you a few questions?"

"Sure."

We moved to another room and sat on opposite sides of her desk. A television, sitting in one corner, was on and as we sat down and I prepared to ask my first question, President Nixon began an address to the country. He announced that the US Navy would immediately begin an aerial mining of Haiphong harbor, the major port for North Vietnam. The aim was to cut off the flow of supplies into the North. Accompanied by a renewal of bombing in Hanoi and other targets in the North, a strategy that President Johnson had suspended in 1968, the President had set a course of action that clearly was yet another escalation of the war effort.

By the next day, the student government had called for a meeting at Hendricks Chapel to discuss a response to the President's actions. After a series of speeches denouncing the latest military plan, it was decided that we would assemble at noon the next day in Walnut Park and then march into downtown Syracuse in protest. It was déjà vu for me, having participated in my share of marches over the years. The student government leaders also encouraged us to contact Congress to express our concerns. They set up tables in the chapel lobby where students could send telegrams. I sent one off—*May Richard Nixon sail on his ship of folly into Haiphong Harbor.* I milled around for a bit, talking with a few familiar faces. People who I recognized from previous demonstrations but who were otherwise nameless. We spouted our usual outrage. But no one seemed to have the fervor that invigorated us in the past.

Around two o'clock, I headed back to my apartment, planning to do some work on my article about campus minorities. I spread my notes on the table and began organizing them into common piles. The phone rang and I rocked back on my chair to grab it. It was my mother.

"Michael. Your father's had a stroke. You need to come home as quick as you can."

# CHAPTER FIFTEEN

"How is he?"

"He's asleep now. The doctors don't know anything yet. "

I took a quick shower, packed a bag and was on the road to Baltimore in twenty minutes. As I passed the Ithaca exit, I thought about calling Ellen to let her know the situation. But there was no time. When I passed Mahanoy City, I thought about her again and promised myself to call her as soon as I arrived in Baltimore. I drove straight to Sinai hospital arriving around seven o'clock. The same Sinai Hospital where I had been born and then, years later, where I was taken after getting beat up with Darnell back in the summer of 1963.

My mother was sitting in the waiting area outside ICU. In the time it had taken to reach the hospital, my father was awake and was now resting. But his condition was serious. The movement on his left side had deteriorated and his speech was affected. The doctors were unsure about the long term prognosis but it was apparent he would be facing months of rehabilitation.

"You can go in and visit him at seven for a few minutes. That's when they let us into the ICU unit. Then I need you to go home and get some rest. Because tomorrow you need to go and open the store. And then run it for your father."

The next morning, I left the house at six and went to the store. I opened the door, turned on the lights and looked around the familiar surroundings. Around seven, the employees arrived. Since my last time at the store, my father had hired a full-time security guard because of the surging crime in the neighborhood. There were now two full-time stock boys and a butcher that worked the new meat counter. The other employees were holdovers from the days that I worked at the store. Emma was the morning cashier, Janice handled the books and Paul ran the receiving department. My father still did the ordering, supervised the floor and took over as cashier when Emma left at three. I would be his fill-in for the day.

"Hi. I'm Charlie. How's your dad doing?"

Charlie was the new security guard and, in his previous career, had been a policeman who had retired three years earlier from the force. He had the body of a middle linebacker. But with a benign face that seemed perpetually in a smile. He lived in the neighborhood and began stopping by the store every day during his retirement complaining that he had nothing to do. Soon my father hired him. Because his body said he meant business but his face and his manner put people at ease.

"Don't know anything yet. Doctors are still evaluating his condition."

A few minutes later, Mr. Watkins came through the front door.

"Michael, how's your dad doing? I saw the ambulance take him away yesterday."

"I don't know yet, Mr. Watkins. He has some paralysis on his left side and can't talk. We know he'll go to rehab in a few days but the doctors haven't told us what to expect long term."

"Well, I'll have him in my prayers. I'm glad that you're here. You let me know if there's anything I can do. You know where to find me."

After Mr. Watkins left, I introduced myself to the new employees.

"Let's just carry on as if my Dad was here. Do what he would expect you to do. Let me know what you need and I'll do my best to take care of it. I'll need your help to get through this."

The day went smoothly. Paul took care of the two delivery trucks that arrived and then took over supervising the stock boys. Janice prepared the deposit as usual, wrote the checks for payment and offered to do the ordering. She suggested letting Ralph, the butcher, order the meats.

"He's been pining to do it for months anyhow. Now would be a good time to give him a chance."

I took her advice and told Ralph to take over the ordering of the fresh meats. He was thrilled.

"Thanks, Michael. I'll put the list together and show it to you before I do anything."

With the employees pitching in, I was free to roam the aisles and think about what might need to happen over the ensuing months as my father recovered. At three, I took over the register when Emma left.

After closing at six, I drove to the hospital. My father had been moved to a regular room earlier in the day. He was awake and alert when I went in. But no movement had returned to his left side and he was still unable to speak. The doctors decided that, if his condition remained stable, he would be moved across the street to a rehab center by the end of the week.

My mother asked how the day went at the store because my father would want to know. Though he couldn't talk or move, his hearing was fine.

"Everything was normal. "

"How did the employees take to you?"

"No problems. Wanted to know when Dad would be back. They all pitched in. I let Ralph order the meats and he was so excited."

I sat with my father until visiting hours were over. My mother suggested we stop at the Suburban House for dinner, before heading home. I ordered my favorite, a corned beef reuben, and my mother had a tuna salad sandwich. While we waited for the food, my mother brought up the subject that had been on my mind all day. A subject that I knew would not leave me with much of a choice.

"Michael, let me get right to it. I'm going to need you to take over for your father and tend to the store."

"I can absolutely help out for a few more days. But then I have to get back to school. It's only three weeks to finals. Plus I have a job. I need to get back as soon as possible."

"I know what I am asking is a lot. It will upend your life and it will be a huge sacrifice. But we depend on the store for our income."

"I'm not sure that the store can't run by itself, Mom. Janice already handles the bookkeeping and she can take over the ordering. Emma has the register until three. Paul knows the store better than me. He supervises the stock boys and can watch the floor. Paul can close too. He's responsible and he cares. We can make him store manager."

"No one cares like family, Michael. I'm sure Paul and Emma and Janice can take care of things for a few days. But, your father is not likely to return anytime soon. Someone in the family has to take over. And that has to be you because I'll have my hands full caring for your father."

"And what am I supposed to do about school?"

"Take a leave of absence. The university will understand and accommodate you. Didn't they do that for you before? Then we'll figure it out as we go."

As upset as I was about the prospect of taking over my father's store, I realized that it was the only viable option for my family. But what did that option mean for me?

Over the last four years, I had made my own way. Made my own decisions. Supported myself. Chose the path I wanted to follow. I had no responsibility to anyone other than myself. And I felt no responsibility to my parents over those four years. After all, they had shown no support for my plans. And yet, despite that, I knew stepping up and taking over the store was something that I had to do. It was the right thing to do. At least, for the time being. Besides, seeing my plans disrupted was not a new experience for me.

"OK Mom. I'll do it."

I had not put up much resistance when my mother asked me to take over. And once I had agreed to do it, it was time to break the news to Ellen.

# CHAPTER SIXTEEN

It had only been a few days since I last spoke to Ellen. On the ride back to Ithaca on Sunday, she had become a bit more anxious about our situation. She had been low key up to then, not pressing me to make a decision about moving to Boston. But, with graduation looming a few weeks away, she pushed me for an answer. She wanted to make the move to Boston immediately after graduation so she would have time to find a place, get set up and be settled in when school opened for the fall. I had gone so far as to say I would go with her to look things over. But I knew she wanted a firmer commitment than that. She would not welcome the news I was about to tell her.

Soon after she answered the phone, she was on the offensive.

"Michael, have you thought anymore about moving to Boston?"

"Well that's what I called to talk about. Things have changed. I'm actually down in Baltimore. My father had a stroke the other day."

"Oh my God, is he okay?"

"Not great. He has no movement on his left side and he can't talk. He'll be moving to rehab in a few days. It looks like it's going to be a long recovery. If at all."

"I'm so sorry. How's your mother holding up? How are you doing?"

"We're both fine. I had to manage my father's store today. And that's what I have to discuss with you. My mother asked me tonight to stick around and run the store until my father's ready to return to work. I said I would."

"What the fuck does that mean?"

"I'm not sure. But I would think that it will be at least six months before he's ready to resume running the store."

"But what about your life. Your plans. What are you going to do about all of that?"

"I'm going to call school tomorrow and ask to take incompletes in my courses and hope they give me some time to finish the work over the summer. Under the circumstances, I hope they'll be considerate. But I don't see any way that I can move to Boston in the fall."

"I understand that you have to help your family. But how can you put your life on hold. You've got to figure something out. Fuck. You've got to come with me."

"Look let's see how it plays out."

That remark would never be one that Ellen could accept. Though she had offered a similar sentiment after we slept together the first time, she never meant what she said. *Let's take it as it comes.* But Ellen Wagner could never take it as it came. She always had to force the action.

For the next few weeks, she would call nightly to see how things were going. She sounded understanding but there was an impatience in her voice. A distance was growing between us. She would talk about her last days at Cornell. The parties. The goodbyes. Packing for the trip to Boston. How excited she was about what lay ahead. I talked about the mess from the package of eggs that a customer dropped on the floor that morning. The delivery truck that arrived two hours late causing us to run out of milk. The freezer that went up. She talked about hope. About fulfilling dreams. I talked about routine and responsibility.

Before long the calls were less frequent. The conversations more strained. And then they stopped completely. Ellen was in Boston. At Harvard Law. On the path to her dreams. I was in hell.

# CHAPTER SEVENTEEN

Working at the store, six days a week, afforded little time to do anything else. Not that there was anything else to do. Or anyplace to go. I had no friends left in town. Lenny had moved to San Francisco. Darnell was in Boston. I had lost touch with everyone else. There was no chance of meeting anyone at the store and I was too lazy and too tired to engage in new pursuits outside of work.

For the first few months, wrapping up my college courses kept me occupied when I wasn't at the store. I completed my article about minorities on campus. I finished my other term papers and arranged to take finals at Towson State, proctored by an administrator, who was the brother of the rehab nurse caring for my father. Though it stretched out until mid-summer, I was able to complete my junior year and take a leave of absence in good standing. But, once I had completed the course work, there was a void in my life and nothing to fill the hours when I wasn't working at the store.

My one respite was spending time with Mr. Watkins. We met, every morning at a diner around the corner for coffee. We talked politics. Sports. The changes in the neighborhood. He kept me updated on Celia, who was beginning her residency at New York Presbyterian Hospital and Darnell who was entering his first year of law school at Harvard.

In early October, my father had improved to the point that he was able to return home. He continued his rehab, three times a week, as an outpatient. Some feeling had returned to his left side and he had regained his speech, though it was often difficult to understand him. With his return home, it gave me the opportunity to break away and get my own apartment. It had been difficult living in my parents' house after being on my own for the previous four years. No matter how much free rein I was given, it was difficult to live under someone else's roof and someone else's rules. Moving into my own apartment gave me a feeling of reclaiming a part of myself.

In the six months since I had taken over my father's store, business was thriving. The older people in the neighborhood had been accustomed to shopping there for years and they remained loyal. The younger ones, with no other options in the immediate area, also did all their shopping at the store. There was little for me to worry about beyond keeping the shelves stocked with the right merchandise and paying the bills.

Whereas my father had remained an island, I decided to get involved in the Baltimore Chamber of Commerce and the Maryland Grocers Association. In both cases, the evening meetings gave me an alternative to going home. It was a chance to do something at night around other people. And although most of the members of both organizations were much older than me, they welcomed a fresh face and soon I had been elected a vice president of the Grocers Association.

It was a challenging time. Many of the other store owners, in Baltimore City, were facing a similar situation to what I was experiencing. Their neighborhoods were deteriorating. Crime was rising. Guys were taking over street corners to sell drugs. Hanging around. Creating a threatening environment. Iron bars were going up on windows. Extra precautions were being taken upon opening or closing the stores. More security guards were hired.

I found this new reality especially distressing after having spent so much time in the neighborhood, both at my father's store and at the Watkins house. I had felt safe on the streets. Safe to play in the alleys. Safe to go to the rec center. To the Watkins house. Now, that was no longer the case. When Mrs. Williams, one of my long time customers, was mugged one evening on her way back from the store, we all felt a sense of urgency to address the situation. Within days, we formed a community group made up of the area businesses and concerned neighbors as a first step. Then, using Mr. Watkins' connections, we applied pressure on the city and we were able to persuade the Baltimore Police Department to increase the frequency of the foot patrols, though it did little to curtail the changes.

None of the store owners had experienced any direct problems to date but the fear was there. At the same time that we were taking these extra precautions, we as business owners were also feeling less welcome. It took Mr. Watkins to explain why? Other than him, the rest of us were all white and we escaped to our cozy suburban homes every night. The residents in the neighborhood, who were predominately all black now, were not afforded the same luxury. For them, confronting the persistent problems went on twenty-four hours a day. We had become interlopers. Most of these businesses had been established by individuals who were born, raised and lived on these same streets, a time not so distant when the owners were fully engaged members of the neighborhood. But not anymore. Now we took our money and we ran.

It was under these conditions that Charlie, our security guard, approached me one morning with an idea.

"Hey Michael, I been giving some thought about how things have been going downhill in the neighborhood. Like we been talking about. And I got an idea."

"What do you have in mind, Charlie?"

"Well it's like I always say. We got to find a positive approach. We got to show folks the good things and we got to do it in a united way. Halloween's coming end of the month. What would you say to organizing a trick or treat day at all the stores? If you'd be willing, we could hand out candy to all the shops and have the neighborhood kids go from one to the next and collect the goodies. Try to generate some community togetherness."

That sounded like a good idea to me. And there was absolutely nothing to lose.

"Seems like a good idea, Charlie. I'll see if the other stores would be willing to join in."

The owners all agreed to participate so I distributed candy, free-of-charge, to all the stores in our area and put up notices announcing that kids should dress up and trick-or-treat at the stores. Emma decorated the store, wrapping orange and black crepe paper around the register area, hanging honeycomb spiders and witches from the ceiling and putting paper cutouts in the windows. Few came however and of those who did none bothered to put on a costume.

"At least we tried," Mr. Watkins sympathized at breakfast the next morning. "But the needs of this community go well beyond passing out candy for a day."

Charlie was not ready to give up yet. After a few days, he suggested we sponsor a food give-away for the holidays, another solid idea since there were many in the neighborhood who struggled to put food on the table. A few weeks before Thanksgiving, I contacted the pastor of the Fulton Baptist Church on North Avenue with the idea. Would he be receptive to overseeing a program to distribute food to needy families in the area at Christmas? He agreed to organize the effort. I planned to give fifty percent of my profits for the month and convinced the Grocers Association to donate one thousand dollars to the program. The rest of my suppliers also chipped in. The other businesses did the same. On December 20, we gathered at the Church. Each store owner showed up with their families. We handed out food to the families the pastor had selected, reaching over one hundred families.

As rewarding as the program proved to be, it had not changed a thing on the streets. Our efforts were just drips in the bucket and that bucket had a huge hole in the bottom of it. Years of neglect by the city, by the fleeing white populace and by the systemic bias in housing, education and jobs had taken its toll. By seven, each night, the drug dealers controlled the street corners and their business was brisk. The houses gradually became more run down. The older ladies continued to sweep their doorsteps and the pavements in front of their houses. But the younger people did far less. Weeds popped up along the facades of the buildings and along the front steps. Trash accumulated in the alleys. Paint chips hung from the shutters, window frames and doorways as houses went unpainted. Leaves, from the few trees that dotted the streets, would accumulate in the gutters, leaving unseemly brown stains. Even I understood why all this was happening. People were struggling to survive and that's where they had to put their focus. And the fact was that we store owners were no better. We no longer made improvements to our property. We let things decay and failed to re-invest our money.

It came as no surprise that my long-time customers were complaining more frequently, afraid to send their kids and grandkids out into the street, especially at night. If only the well intentioned people could gain control. Chase away the drug dealers. Keep the streets the way they remembered them. And wanted them to be. But that would take more than good intentions. It would take money and power, both of which were sorely lacking in the community. The changes in the neighborhood had not happened overnight and the solutions would not materialize overnight either.

Charlie and I continued talking about what could be done to improve the situation. One afternoon, I was telling him about how, when I was a kid and first stated working at the store, I used to carry home the groceries for the customers and how they would refuse to let me leave their home until I ate something. As I finished the story, Charlie's face lit up.

"Hey boss, that gives me an idea. It seems to me that we got to get the people who live here more invested in the neighborhood. I listen to them all the time. They're frustrated and they think there's nothing they can do to fix things. And that makes them fade into the background waiting on the police or the city or the store owners to take some kind of action. What if these people could be mobilized? Help them start a business that would put its proceeds back into the community. If those women you talked about were willing to bake their special pies and cakes, it could be the very thing to get things moving. If you would be willing, you could provide free ingredients—flour, butter, fruits, eggs, chocolate, whatever was needed—at least at the beginning to help it get off the ground. Let them bring the desserts to the store and with the proceeds from the sales, give half to them and half to the rec center to build after-school and summer programs. Maybe you could use your connections to get other stores around the city to sell the cakes as well. If the people here saw how their efforts were plowing money back into the community, it would do nothing but increase their pride. They'd have ownership, something that ain't there right now."

Again, it sounded like Charlie had hit upon a good idea. Although there would be a lot of planning that would be required to make this happen.

I began spending a portion of each day putting together a business plan. One day, shortly after Christmas, I was sitting in my office, busily mapping out the plans for this new venture, when one of the stock boys came to the door.

"There's someone here to see you, Michael."

I walked to the front register. It was Darnell. We embraced and then I led him back to my office.

"My dad said I would find you here. I'm so sorry to hear about your father. How's he doing?"

"Improving a little each day. But he has a long way to go. When did you get in?"

"Last week. I wanted to come see you right away once my father told me what had happened. But he said you were busy with a food drive. I was impressed to hear what you did."

"It really wasn't much. And it wasn't me. It was the community that pulled it off."

"That's not what I meant. I think that was great too. But, I meant taking over for your father."

"Yeah. Great. So, I became the very thing I hated. A grocery store owner. Not exactly what I intended. My plans to be a writer are certainly in the toilet."

"Hey, you did what you had to do. You know sometimes you get to choose what to do with your life. And sometimes life chooses for you. Sometimes you're just along for the ride. These other things you want to do, there's plenty of time to do them."

"If that's what you think Darnell, then you're sadly mistaken. I don't think I'll be getting out of this place any time soon."

"Maybe so. But maybe you shouldn't look at this as a setback. Maybe it was meant to happen. I was thinking how Mark Twain was a riverboat pilot before he stated writing. Steinbeck worked in a fish hatchery. Dickens had to go to work in a shoe polish factory because his father went to debtors' prison. And then he was a law clerk. There was no time limit that prevented them from becoming writers and they used those very experiences in their writing."

"Yeah well I am hardly on a level with those guys."

"Hey I'm just saying that there is nothing preventing you from a writing career, whenever you want to give it a try. There's nothing keeping you from doing it now."

Before I could reply, Ray, the other stock boy, was at the door.

"Michael, Emma needs your help at the register."

"Well I better go see what's going on. But how 'bout meeting me after work? We can grab dinner and then hang out at my apartment."

"Sounds good to me. I'll come back around six."

After Darnell left and I had taken care of Emma's issue, I returned to my desk, stacked high with order forms, receipts, inventory charts and invoices, and began thinking about my conversation with Darnell. If it was only as simple as Darnell implied. It would be great to think that working at the grocery store was only a brief detour from my intended path. But I was hardly Twain or Dickens or Steinbeck. And rather than my work experience becoming a reservoir of ideas, like it had been for them, it had the exact opposite effect, zapping me of any creativity. Didn't Darnell understand that? You had to have the desire to write and you had to have something to write about. I had neither.

At six, Darnell returned and we went to dinner. When Darnell asked about the food drive, I told him about the new business idea Charlie had come up with. For the first ten or fifteen minutes, I was doing all the talking. I finally took a breath and said, "So, I didn't have the chance to ask you about law school. How's it going?"

"About what I expected. Plenty of work. Plenty of competition. "

"I'm sure you won't have any problems. You have a pretty good track record."

"I hope you're right. You know I've been studying with a friend of yours."

"Let me guess. Ellen Wagner. Small world. Did she remember you?"

"Not until I told her who I was. Oh yeah, she says, the guy who got beat up with Michael Sanders. Never remembered we were in the same classes together for all those years. But we started to study together. And hang out a bit. She asked if I was in touch with you. You should give her a call. She's home for the holiday."

"I think I'll leave well enough alone. She wasn't too pleased that I didn't follow her to Boston. "

"That's what she said. She was disappointed but she said she understood your decision."

"Right. But she had to move on. Couldn't let a grocery store manager derail a budding legal career."

"You sound bitter."

"Not really. I wouldn't have gone to Boston under any circumstances. I always wanted to finish up at Syracuse. But it was hard finding a way to tell her. My father's stroke probably gave me a way out. I was ok with the way it went. I guess it's more that I'm disappointed with where my life is at now. Maybe I wasn't meant to get the thing I wanted. Maybe I wasn't meant to be a writer."

"Maybe you were meant to do other things and be a writer. Besides, I don't see where one precludes the other. You seem to be doing a lot of good things now. What with the food drive and now this new business idea."

"Just making the best of an unfortunate situation. Working at the stores brings me little satisfaction. The community things. Well it makes things a bit more meaningful."

"And those are the good things. Important things. I know you wanted to be a writer. But you also wanted to make a difference. And you're doing that. Like I said before, there's a lot of years left to try other things. You know Michael, sometimes the shortest distance to realizing your true dream is not a straight line."

"I know. I know. I tell myself that all the time. That I'll get the chance. But, I feel like there's a huge hole in my life and that the longer things keep going the way they are, the bigger the hole will get. The longer I don't write, the more I don't feel like writing."

"Then do it now. What are you afraid of?"

"Nothing. I just don't have the time. I'm not in the right frame of mind."

"Bullshit. You got off track long before your father's stroke. Ellen filled me in about losing your job with AP. And spending more time stoned than writing. I think you're afraid. Afraid what people might think."

"Fuck you. You've got a lot of nerve. I don't give a fuck what people think."

"You do. You always have. All the other stuff. The excuses. Well it's just a smokescreen."

"I didn't choose to be where I am."

"Yeah and you can choose to change things if you want. You've had your fair share of luck over the years Michael. Like hooking up with the Gazette. Getting the AP job. You never complained that things were unfair then. Now that the tide is against you, you're giving up."

"Fuck you."

"Look, Michael. I don't know what all's going on in your mind. I think you've got issues and you need to resolve those issues.

"What issues do I have?"

"I think you know what issues."

I had no idea what issues Darrell was talking about. Just like the time Celia accused me of being in the dark. Was this a signature trait of the Watkins family? To hint at some hidden shortcoming of mine.

"I just think there are things clouding your mind. Things you have to come to grips with. That's what's keeping you from writing or doing what you want. It's not the store."

"You know Darnell. I don't give a shit. Think what you want. All I know is that I have to be up early tomorrow for work. I'm heading home."

With that I stood up, threw twenty dollars on the table, and headed out. No handshake. No goodbye.

I didn't see Darnell the remainder of his time in Baltimore. Or Ellen. I didn't call her either though I was tempted. But in the end, I didn't call. It wasn't worth the trouble.

# CHAPTER EIGHTEEN

A few months after the dinner with Darnell, Mount Street Cakes and Pies was up and running. The response from the women, in the community, and the retail outlets I approached, was far greater than anyone expected.

After mapping out the plans, during the first few weeks of 1973, I began posting flyers around the neighborhood and casually mentioning it to my customers. Mr. Watkins, who strongly supported the idea, offered his barbershop for the initial meeting.

"It's got a lot more open space than your store. It'll be easier to talk."

He also recruited his wife to head up the group of women. Two dozen attended the first meeting and all agreed to participate.

Almost immediately, Mrs. Watkins nixed my idea of having each woman bake in her own home.

"I think we can accomplish a lot more if we can find a place where we can all work together. It'll be more fun too."

She approached Fulton Baptist Church, the same church I had enlisted for the food drive. The church had a large kitchen that sat unused most days. The pastor was glad to accommodate us and we agreed to give the Church ten percent of the profits for use of the facility.

Mrs. Watkins proved right about using the church's kitchen. She realized the group had far bolder plans than Charlie or I had imagined. I thought two dozen desserts each day would be a modest way to start. They felt that, with twenty-four people working together, they could produce at least fifty cakes and pies per day.

"If you can sell them, we'll get 'em made," Mrs. Watkins told me.

Initially, I had planned to tap my friends in the grocers' association to carry the products. But, again the women had other ideas.

"Can't we take a stall at Lexington Market? We could sell whole pies and cakes. And we could do slices to sell at lunchtime. We'll take turns manning the stall."

Though the cost would eventually come out of the revenues, I agreed to front the money for the rent along with display cases, one refrigeration unit, a sign board and a cash register.

At the beginning of the last week of April, Mrs. Watkins presented me with the shopping list for the supplies that would be needed. Fixings for sweet potato pie. Chocolate cake. Cherry pie. And a dozen others. I purchased the goods and delivered the supplies to the Church in the used van I had purchased for the business. The women started baking and, on May 1, they opened for business.

It was as if Baltimore was waiting for these desserts. Within a month, the women were making and selling over one hundred cakes and pies per day. Besides selling the products at the market, we had expanded to other retail outlets around the city. Two months in, the cash flow had turned positive. After holding back enough money to fund the operations, I handed a sizeable check to the women. The group then went to the rec center and presented a one thousand dollar check, the first of many.

As my one year anniversary working at the store passed, everything, on the business side, was excellent. The store continued to turn record profits. Mount Street Cakes and Pies was running smoothly. On the other hand, nothing had changed in my personal life. Whereas I was taking satisfaction in what I had accomplished at the store, there was no light at the end of the tunnel for my social life or my writing. I had made no attempts to improve either.

During the year, my father had slowly progressed to the point that his speaking was only minimally slurred. He had taken to walking with a cane. He was able to fend for himself in most cases. But he could not drive, had difficulty walking up and down steps, and continued to go to rehab three days a week. Then he decided it was time to return to work and implored me to take him on his non-rehab days. It was a request I did not relish but, the sooner he became capable of resuming his role, the sooner I could resume my life.

I picked him up on the first Tuesday in May and brought him to work early. He strolled up and down the aisles. Nothing had changed. Same products. Same displays. He had no complaints. He chatted with Ralph, the butcher, and when the first delivery showed up, he walked out to the dock to watch Paul unload the truck. By nine, when the first customers began to arrive, he was getting fatigued. I set up a chair at the register and had him sit down. He reveled in the attention.

"Mr. Al. It's so good to see you. How you coming along?"

"Welcome back Mr. Al. You looking good."

He talked with each customer, recapping his condition and the year of rehabbing.

Before long, Emma came back to my office.

"Is he going to sit there all day? He's slowing up the line, talking with everyone."

"Give him a minute to figure out what to do with him."

After another half-hour, I walked to the front.

"Dad, why don't we go say hello to Mr. Watkins. I'm sure he's looking forward to seeing you."

That visit killed off thirty minutes.

"You look tired, Dad. Why don't we head back to your house, grab some lunch on the way and after that you can rest."

For the next few months, that was our routine every Tuesday and Thursday.

On the first Tuesday in early August, I picked up my father at six as usual. When we arrived at the store, Paul, who had taken over opening the store each morning, met me in front of my office.

"We have a problem. There's a guy sleeping on the back dock. Can't get him to budge. You want me to call the cops?"

"No, let me go talk to him. Just keep my father occupied in the store."

Had Paul not clued me in, I may have walked right past the sleeping visitor. He had blended into the gray cinder block wall. Snuggled against it. As comfortable as was possible. With discarded boxes serving as bed and blanket. And an empty potato sack stuffed with waste paper for a pillow.

I bent down and could hear him breathing. Knotted clumps of hair stuck out from a tattered baseball cap that read *Mooney's Trucking.* He wore a blue patterned flannel shirt, much too warm for a day in August, even early in the morning. A frayed undershirt underneath. Gray pants stained in an assortment of colors. No socks. And sneakers that had no laces and were cut away, in the back, so that he wore them like sandals.

"Sir. You have to wake up."

There was still no movement. He was on his side so I grabbed his shoulder and shook him. An empty whiskey bottled tumbled from his hands.

"Sir. Wake up. Or I'll have to call the cops."

"What da hell?"

He opened his eyes and rolled onto his back.

"Just leave me be. It's too damn early."

"Sorry I can't do that sir. This is a place of business. There will be trucks showing up any moment. I can't have you laying out here."

"I need my sleep. I ain't bother'n nobody."

"Sir. I'll tell you what. How bout I help you into our washroom. You can wash your face. Take care of any business. Then I'll give you five dollars and you can go buy yourself a nice breakfast down the street."

After a few more minutes of coaxing, I was able to get him on his feet and into the washroom. I handed him a five dollar bill and sent him on his way. But, as I guided him out the back door, my father was standing nearby.

"I tried to keep him away," Paul whispered. "But he insisted."

"Who was that guy?"

"Oh just some guy. Needed to use the washroom."

"Paul said he caught him sleeping on the dock. You running a bed and breakfast now?"

"No. Just a fluke. Probably got drunk in the alley and fell asleep. It's taken care of now."

But I was wrong. The next morning, we again found the guy sleeping on the back dock. I nudged him awake and let him use the washroom.

"What's your name?" I asked.

"Jimmy. Jimmy Hightower."

"Jimmy. Don't you have another place you can sleep?"

"Ain't got no place to go. I'm homeless, man. Got kicked out of my apartment a longs time ago. Ain't got no home. No job neither. My family's they's all down south and I ain't got no way to git there."

"Well you've got to figure out something 'cause you can't continue to sleep back here. You know there are shelters in the city you can stay at. Go try to get help from social services. Maybe you can go ask Pastor Brown, up at Fulton Baptist, for help."

"Ain't nobody interested in helping Jimmy. Been down dat road."

"Look, you've got to do something to help yourself."

I led him to the back door and handed him another five dollars.

"Now you promise me that you're gonna go look for help."

He grunted and walked away.

"He's gonna be like a stray dog," Paul said after Jimmy had turned the corner. "You feed a stray dog. He comes back the next day. And keeps coming back."

"If he does come back, you make sure he's out of here before I show up with my father tomorrow. Here's five dollars to give him, just in case."

"You know he ain't spending this money on food, like you think. Just pissin it away on drugs or liquor."

As Paul had predicted, Jimmy was back the next morning. But Paul took care of getting him out before I arrived with my father.

"I told you that guy would be back. You gotta call the cops."

"And then what. They haul him away. He'll still be back in a few days. Maybe we can find another way."

When Jimmy was back in his spot, the next morning, I woke him and led him, as usual, to the washroom. But then I took him to my office and sat him down.

"Jimmy, you gotta change. This can't go on. I can't have you sleeping on my dock. And you can't go on living this way."

"I makes do. What choice I got anyway? I ain't got no money. "

"Suppose you come to work for me Jimmy. Earn some money. Get a place to stay. You think you can do that?"

Jimmy looked at me with a quizzical expression.

"Now why you want to be helpin' me out?"

"Let's just say I'd like to see you turn your life around. You've already gone a long way down the wrong path."

Jimmy sat silent for a minute.

"I ain't sure I got much work left in me. But what da hell. Whatcha got in mind?"

"We'll get you cleaned up first. Then you can help unload trucks. Do some cleaning around the store. Maybe help the customers carry their packages home."

I took Jimmy over to Mr. Watkins and paid for a haircut and shave. Then we walked around the corner where there was a third floor apartment for rent. It was small but clean. Some minimal furnishings—a bed, a kitchen table with two chairs and a ragged sofa. I told the owner that we'd take it. That I would be responsible for the rent and security deposit. That Jimmy would live there. I would send him back in ten minutes with three hundred dollars for the rent and security deposit.

Once we were back at the store, I wrote out a check for the three hundred dollars. I handed Jimmy an extra hundred dollars.

"Jimmy. Go take a shower. Get cleaned up. Then go up the street and buy yourself a clean shirt and pants. A decent pair of shoes. Throw away what you have. Then you come to work at seven tomorrow. Ok?"

"Yeah boss."

The next morning, Jimmy didn't show up at the store. But, at least, he wasn't sleeping on the back dock. I went around the corner to the apartment but he wasn't there either. He didn't show the following week. I continued to check for him at the apartment. If he was there, he didn't answer. No one had seen him since that first day. Or, if they had, they weren't talking.

"Well I guess we got rid of Jimmy," I told Paul when I returned the store.

"Probably just took your money and went out drinkin' and whorin'," Paul said.

Trying to be optimistic, I suggested, "Maybe he bought a bus ticket and went back to his family."

Two more weeks passed and I had not seen or heard from Jimmy. So I skipped writing a check for the rent on the apartment and figured I would just forfeit the deposit. At least it would be the last money I would have to spend on Jimmy's behalf. I'd wasted a few hundred dollars but it was easy to accept. It had been worth the try.

# CHAPTER NINETEEN

With Labor Day approaching, I decided to close the store for the first time for a holiday other than Thanksgiving, Christmas Day and New Year's Day. I felt the employees deserved it. I knew I could use the day off to rest.

Since the next day was a Tuesday, I brought my father to work and Paul opened the store. The three of us were standing on the loading dock when one of the regular delivery men came running up the alley. As he approached the property, he began waving and motioning us to follow him.

"What's wrong Stan?" Paul shouted

"There's a body lying in the alley. Blocking the way. I think the person's dead."

My father remained on the dock while Paul and I followed Stan up the alley. Running. As we neared the body, I recognized the gray stained pants. The blue plaid shirt. The baseball cap that said *Mooney's Trucking*. It was Jimmy. Lying face down. Lifeless. Much like when I would find him sleeping on the loading dock. I figured he had passed out in the alley, never making it to his intended destination, which was probably my loading dock.

I knelt beside him and shook his shoulder. No response.

"C'mon Jimmy. Time to move."

His usual stink was worse than ever. I rolled him over and fell back. Stunned. A large red spot covered his shirt and a dried puddle of blood was spread across the pavement. I felt for a pulse. There was none.

"Paul. Run back to the store and call the cops. Then stay there and watch the store for me."

Stan and I waited by the body. I kept rubbing my hands against my pants. Though none of Jimmy's blood had transferred onto my hands, I felt soiled.

The cops showed five minutes later. The two foot patrolman and then three cars, one after the other, with sirens blaring and lights flashing. They pulled in the alley, closing off access. Sandwiching Stan's truck between the police cars and Jimmy's body.

The first patrolman approached, looking at Stan and me.

"Someone called about a dead body?" He took notice of Jimmy lying on the pavement and said, "One of you run over this guy with your truck?"

"No, officer. He was already lying in the alley when I pulled in."

"Officer, we found him. Right where he's lying. Well next to where he was lying. I rolled him over."

"Why'd you want to do that?"

"I kinda knew the guy. Found him sleeping on my loading dock, a few times, weeks ago. But he hasn't been around for some time now. When I saw him lying there, I rolled him over to see if he was ok."

Another officer bent down to examine the body.

"Looks like your friend took a knife to his chest and bled out."

"We're gonna need to ask both of you some more questions."

"I have to get back to my store."

"And I have to make my deliveries. Can I get my truck out of here?"

Right then, an ambulance pulled up to the top of the alley.

"Ok, look, we have to move our cars to let the ambulance in. You can pull your truck out. Go on and make your delivery at his store (pointing to me). I'll be down in a few minutes. It won't take long. I need to get your statement and then you can be on your way."

As I walked back to the store, I kept turning my head, watching as they lifted Jimmy into the ambulance. Many in the neighborhood had gathered, taking in the crime scene from their yards or back doors. Women in their housedresses or still in their nightgowns. Kids stopping off, on their way to the first day of school, to take a peek.

A few minutes after I was back at the store, the first officer pulled up. Stan had pulled his truck in and Paul had begun unloading.

"Why don't you talk to Stan first so he can be on his way?"

The officer asked Stan to recount what he saw.

"I pulled into the alley. The body was just lying there."

"Did you see anyone around? Anything out of the ordinary."

"No."

"So what happened next?"

"I got out of the truck and walked up to the body. I just shouted at the guy. Told him to move. Never got closer than five feet. I assumed he was dead. At least he looked dead so I ran down to the store to get help."

Since Stan didn't have anything else to offer, the officer told him he would be in touch if he had any further questions. And then he turned to me, "So you say you know this guy?"

"Only that we found him sleeping on the back dock a few weeks ago, like I said." I pointed to the wall where Jimmy had made his bedroom. "Slept over there. But I haven't seen him for weeks."

"You know his name."

"He said it was Jimmy Hightower."

"You ever see him around the neighborhood. Before he showed up on your loading dock."

"No. Never. I never asked him where he had lived. He told me he was homeless. That he had family somewhere down South but didn't have any money to get back."

"So, you chased him away?"

"Kind of. I gave him five bucks and told him to go get something to eat. Next day, he was back and I gave him another five bucks. After a week or so, I offered him a job. Helped him get a place. Get cleaned up. But he never showed for work and I haven't seen him since."

"Did you give him any more money?"

"Yeah a hundred bucks to go get some new clothes. Told him to go to the apartment, around the corner. And that's the last I saw him."

The officer asked for the address of the apartment and I gave it to him. He handed me a card.

"If you think of anything else, you give me a call."

Within minutes of the police leaving, my father was on my case.

"Some good you did that guy."

"Hey all I did was try to help the guy."

"You should've stayed out of it. It wasn't any of your business. You should have just called the cops. Let them handle it. Let them get rid of him. Instead you gave the guy money."

"I just gave him a chance."

"He didn't want a chance. He used you. Took your money. Probably used it for drugs or liquor, like Paul said he would. That money probably got him in more trouble than he could handle."

"Well, it's over now."

I turned and walked away. I didn't want to feel guilty but I wondered if my father was right. If Paul was right. Maybe all I did was hasten the guy's demise. Maybe he would have been better off if I hadn't intervened. Maybe he would still be alive.

For the next few days, Jimmy's death was the talk on the streets. It was the first time there had been a murder in the neighborhood. At least as far as Mr. Watkins could remember and he had lived there longer than most. It was as if a seal had been broken and people feared a surge of bad things coming. They knew crime had increased. There had been numerous muggings. Drugs were being sold in the open with no shortage of customers. But a murder. That was new territory. That was something that happened in other parts of the city but not here. So they talked about it. But for all the talk, no one knew what had happened. No one knew why Jimmy Hightower was found dead, stabbed in the chest.

For some reason that even eluded me, I felt an obligation to follow through on Jimmy's behalf. As shallow and brief as our relationship had been, I was probably the only one who had shown any concern for him in the last weeks of his life. When I spotted the police on foot patrol, a few days later, I asked if there were any leads or suspects in Jimmy's murder.

"We're not at liberty to talk about it. But, off the record, I can tell you everything leads to a dead end."

The police had canvassed the neighborhood but no one saw anything or knew anything. They never found the murder weapon.

"What happened to his body?"

"Just sitting in the morgue for now. Waiting for someone to claim it. If no one does, they'll cremate him next week."

"No one will. Claim him, that is. There is no family."

I felt bad about this. Though Jimmy was surely not my responsibility, I felt obliged to see that he had a proper burial. So, at the end of the week, when time had run out for someone to claim the body, I went to the central police headquarters and offered to take the body and arrange a funeral. I had Jimmy transported to the Joseph H. Sloane funeral home and asked Pastor Brown, from Fulton Baptist Church to preside. I had no idea if Jimmy was Baptist. But I doubted he would have cared. The next day we held the funeral. Only Mr. Watkins and I attended.

The new normalcy quickly returned to the neighborhood though you could sense that Jimmy's death had shook its core. For weeks, there were no developments and no reason given for Jimmy's murder. Then word slowly began to leak out on the street. Jimmy's death had been meant as a message. One of the drug dealers, a guy named Willie Boyd who controlled the business along Mount Street, had retaliated for Jimmy's failure to pay his debt. Boyd had kept it under wraps until the police lost interest in solving the case. But now, he wanted people to know exactly what had happened.

Jimmy had always been a small time user. A nickel bag here. A snort's worth there. Panhandling to earn whatever he could for drugs and alcohol. At the liquor store, you had to pay to get what you wanted. But Willie Boyd was only too glad to offer credit, once he knew you. And knew where to find you. Jimmy kept his debt low enough to avoid any trouble. From time to time, he would run errands for Boyd to help work off his debt.

But then Jimmy showed up one day with a hundred dollars in his pocket. And a check made out to some realty company for an apartment he never took possession of. Enough to pay his debt in full. And then some. Jimmy took advantage of his situation. The money allowed him to get high more often. To go up to the whore house on Monroe Street and spend five bucks for a ten minute fuck. Ply himself and some new found friends with some weed and whiskey.

And then the money ran out. And he began running up a tab again. Told Willie he could get more money from the same place the first pile came from. Some guy he could tap. A white guy who felt sorry for him. A guy who would pay him to stay off of his loading dock. Only Jimmy never went back and got more money. And the tab only grew deeper. With the drug dealer. With the whorehouse that Boyd also owned. Until the debt grew too big and they came asking for payment. Boyd's henchmen beat him up the first time and gave him a few days to make things right. He went off and hid but they caught up with him. They didn't give him a second chance. There had to be consequences. The other customers needed to know that you didn't cross Willie Boyd. Not in any way or for any reason. But especially not when it came to his business. He ruled the drug trade ruthlessly. Same with his whore house. And he was looking to branch out. He had big plans. Numbers games. Money lending. And more. He had his mind set on getting into the protection game and forcing the businesses in the area to pony up monthly payments. But he met resistance from the owners. So it became paramount to send a message. Reputation mattered.

There were already stories circulating about how Willie was taking control of the streets. How he whacked a guy who accidentally bumped into his mother as she came out of her house. The guy laughed and made no apology as she dropped her pocketbook. The guy was only too glad to make the apology after Willie took a baseball bat to his leg. There was another story about a guy who made a joke at Willie's expense and word got back to Willie. When the guy stopped to make a purchase, Willie slapped him repeatedly in front of the man's kids until he cried and begged for him to stop. And now there was the story about Jimmy's death to add to Willie's growing legend.

I was shaken. Over the threat that Willie Boyd posed and over Jimmy's story. How had my good intentions gone so far astray? In a way, I had become an accomplice to Jimmy's murder. I was convinced that, without my involvement, Jimmy would still be alive. And what if the police were to find out what had occurred? Would they be asking why I had given him the money? What was it that I had hoped to accomplish? Save a lost soul? Fat chance. People don't change. At least not ones like Jimmy Hightower.

But no one came asking. No one cared. Jimmy's life had meant nothing to anyone. Maybe it meant something to some long forgotten relatives living in the south. But no one in Baltimore cared. Until he died. Then he became a cautionary tale for the others on the street. Don't let what happened to Jimmy Hightower happen to you.

As for me, I got past it. Whatever it was that I had done. To Jimmy. Yes, it had caused me to think about what happened. Had I imposed my idea of the right way to live on Jimmy? Had I tried to change the nature of things when it wasn't my place? To interfere where I didn't belong. But, as I said, I got past it. It was easy to push it aside. There were no reminders.

As rattled as everyone had been when they learned the story behind Jimmy's death, it was nothing compared to the next death to hit the neighborhood.

# CHAPTER TWENTY

That next death to hit Mount Street was my father's. Albert Sanders. It didn't raise the fears and level of concern among the residents that Jimmy Hightower's death had. But it had a huge impact nonetheless.

After all, Albert Sanders had been part of the fabric of Mount Street for some fifty years. From the time his mother first carried him up the stairs to the second level that served as their living quarters above his father's grocery store. To the games of stickball and tag, played in the streets, during his youth. To the excitement of shooting craps in the alley and Saturday night encounters with numerous young ladies, in the empty schoolhouse, during his teenage years. It was those fond memories he recalled while hunkering down in the trenches in Italy during World War Two. And the silent promise that he made to himself to return to Mount Street while bullets soared above his head, shaking his confidence in that very promise. To the hours upon hours spent in that grocery store during his adulthood. That he cared about Mount Street, and its people, was the best thing to be said about Albert Sanders. And it was also the worst. Mount Street was his true family, the one to whom he gave his loyalty, his time and his emotions.

Whereas Jimmy Hightower's death signaled the beginning of a new reality on the street and the foreshadowing of many similar events to come, my father's death marked the end of a way of life to a community that had seen too many changes already. To a very small degree, the neighborhood had remained racially mixed. Although most of the old Jewish population had moved out years before, a few still remained. The bigger change was to the sense of caring and camaraderie evident in his youth that had disappeared. Sweeping the sidewalks. Sitting on the front stoops on hot summer nights, sharing stories. Looking after a neighbor's child. All that had been displaced by the drug-dealing thugs now taking control of the streets.

In a way, I saw the impact of these changes surface in the eyes of my father during his recovery from the stroke. There was a noticeable difference in his attitude about people, a certain resignation, a certain discomfort. There were evident changes in his behavior, in the way he spoke to and about people. I first detected it when he would refer to his physical therapist as the *schvartzer taskmaster* (schvartzer being the

Yiddish word for black). I had never heard him use the term before. Never during all the years living in his house. Or working in the store. I wondered if, had his therapist been white, he would have simply referred to him as his taskmaster. Or would he need to describe him as his veiser (Yiddish for white) taskmaster. I doubted it.

Did the fact that he felt the need to describe the therapist as *schvartzer* reveal a newly surfaced prejudice on his part? A prejudice that either did not previously exist or, at the least, he kept hidden. I had never seen him treat a black person different than anyone else. But had the stroke exposed a deep seated prejudice? I knew he was bitter over what his condition had robbed him of. Maybe that caused him to lash out indiscriminately at people in the basest manner. Whether it was dealing with the therapist, or my mother, or me, his manner had certainly become brusque and odd.

When he returned to the store, on that first Tuesday in May, he quietly scanned the streets. There was a certain look of defeat on his face. Once in the store, he slowly inspected the shelves, the office and the loading docks before taking a seat by the register. To the customers, who expressed genuine pleasure in seeing him, he appeared the same. He basked in their good wishes.

But he had changed and evidence of that change began to surface. Over time, when he took his position at the register, it was as much to keep an eye on Emma and to watch the customers as it was to greet people.

Somehow, in his mind, he had determined that Emma was stealing so he closely followed her every move. After she would count out the change, he would demand to be the one to hand it back to the customer. And he would count it out again as he placed the money in the customer's hand. He emptied the till more often, determined to limit her access to the money.

It was worse with the customers. He watched them like a hawk, certain that they were stuffing packages into their handbags or coat pockets.

Emma soon complained and when I asked my father on the ride home one night, he snapped, "That schvartzer's been robbing me blind for years."

"I have to tell you, Dad, I think you're off base with Emma. And I have to ask you to stop using that term around me. Especially around the store. People can hear."

"What term?"

"Schvartzer. It's degrading and prejudiced."

"It means nothing. It's just a term. You think you are so much better."

He continued to use the term, with even more delight now that he knew it irritated me. And his sudden distrust spilled over to other areas. One day, I found him out on the loading dock sifting through the trash.

"Dad, what's going on?"

"I got a feeling Paul's been stashing fresh cases of food in the trash and then grabbing it after we close."

"Where in hell did you get that idea? Of all the people to accuse. Paul? As long as he's been working here. As great as he's been to you over the years."

"You don't know these schvartzers like I do. You've been around a year. I spent my whole life here. I know their ways."

The argument continued to escalate. My father went on a tirade. Criticizing everything from my management style to his "thieving" customers and employees. He was paying me too much money. Only to watch me make the wrong decisions. Taking money out of his pocket. When he finally had run out of things to scream about, he grabbed his hat and said, "I'm going to see Watkins."

He stormed out the front door and walked briskly. Much faster than he was accustomed to. As he stepped off the curb onto the street, his cane wobbled, his hand slipped and he tumbled to the pavement. He fell face first and his forehead took the full brunt of the fall. Emma saw my father go down and screamed out, "Michael. Hurry!"

The alarm in her voice sent me tearing from the storage area. Charlie, the security guard, also took off running and reached the front of the store first and ran out the door. I followed. We reached my father within seconds of his fall but it was too late. Whether he had suffered another stroke or simply had taken a wrong step, he was unconscious and unresponsive. By the time the ambulance arrived, he was gone.

I accompanied the ambulance to the hospital and, upon arriving, called my mother to break the news. Word spread quickly along Mount Street. I asked Paul to manage the store the rest of the day. A bit of irony considering it was his new found distrust of Paul that led to my father's death. Later in the day, I called Paul and told him the store would be closed the next day so that the employees could attend the funeral. He posted a sign in the window, *Due to the untimely death of Albert Sanders, the store will be closed tomorrow so that our employees may pay their respects. Rest in peace, Mr. Al.*

As was the tradition in the Jewish religion, the funeral was held the next day. All twenty-four women from the Mount Street Cakes and Pies attended. Each of the employees came. Mr. Watkins and his wife. And Pastor Brown from Fulton Baptist Church. And dozens of others that I recognized but did not know by name. All of them remembered him for the man he was and not the man he had become in the last year of his life. I was surprised by their fondness for him. But, I quickly learned why when one of the women from the area told me, "You know. Mr. Al took care of us. When we was having tough times, he never let me and my family go hungry. He made sure we had somethin' to eat and never asked to be repaid." Hearing these stories made it that much sadder for me when I thought about how he looked upon these people in that last year of his life. And that much more confusing.

My parents had never been religious but my mother decided we should sit *shiva* for the usual one week. Services were held each morning and evening in her house. Neighbors came to express their condolences. Business acquaintances. Friends. Family. I stayed around the clock, sleeping in my old bedroom. In the meantime, Paul reopened the store the following day.

When the Watkins family came to pay their respects, I told Mr. Watkins that I had been troubled by my father's recent behavior.

"He didn't seem any different to me. Other than his speech being slow. What is it that you saw?"

I explained the comments he had made about Emma, Paul and his customers.

"He used a derogatory term, a Yiddish word, whenever he referred to them and I thought it was offensive. When I told him that, he made sure to use it that much more. Then the day he died, I found him searching through the trash. When I asked what he was doing, he told me that he was sure Paul was stealing product and hiding it in the dumpster to collect later. We argued and then he stormed out and that's when he fell and hit his head. He was coming to see you. Do you think he was prejudiced his entire life and we only came to see it these last few months? Like the stroke rattled his brain and made him speak his true feelings."

"I don't know, Michael. People are complicated. You shouldn't think less of him. We are all walking contradictions."

"That sounds like Celia talking. I remember her saying something very similar to me years ago at your dinner table."

"Well she did learn about life sitting at my knee and hearing my stories."

"What do you think she would have said about my father? About the way he acted at the end."

"Probably that he's no different than the rest of us. And that goes for you, me and Celia. We all judge and those judgments are often based on false notions. Maybe your father grew up hearing his parents spout things about other people. Or maybe he was the victim of other people's contempt himself. Or maybe he heard it on the streets or when he ate dinner at a restaurant with friends. Maybe he had some experience and that led to some misguided generalization about people. There is no shortage of that kind of stuff going around and it just seems to seep into folks. So, if you're asking me, I think your father was just afraid about his own inadequacies and that made him feel insecure and look to blame it on others. You know, Michael, I believe that we all come in to this world with a clean slate. Put a white toddler and a black toddler in a room and they'll play together and get along just fine. But then we grow up and, right or wrong, we start looking at differences instead of similarities. Looking for reasons why things are never right with the world. I think we look for scapegoats, someone we can assign all the bad things to. It always struck me funny that the people who spew hatred are the first people to find refuge in the Bible and they always find some minor verse to back up what they believe. I ain't saying we should ignore bad behavior. I just feel like we could all do with a little less worrying about other people's shortcomings and spend more time working on our own."

Listening to Mr. Watkins talk always led me to reflect about my own life and behavior. I was no better than my father in that regard. Maybe worse. While he may have suppressed those thoughts, I had let them get the better of me time and again.

On the third day at my mother's house, Mr. Perl came by.

"I was so sorry to hear about your father, Michael. I hope you are doing ok."

I introduced him to my mother and then, since she was busy talking with her friends, we headed to the empty den. On the way, we passed through the dining room where there was a table filled with trays of cookies and pastries, sent in by neighbors and friends for the mourning period. Knowing that Mr. Perl had a sweet tooth almost as unrestrained as his love for a bottle of beer, I offered him a plate and he was only too glad to fill it up with one of every type on the platters.

"I've been wondering what happened to you," he said in between bites of a chocolate cookie. "It's been two years, I think, since I heard anything about you. And the last I heard was not good."

Of course, he was referring to my dismissal as the AP stringer.

I explained that my father had suffered a stroke and that I had dropped out of college to take over the store. And that's what I had been doing for the last year and a half. There was nothing else. If I had been reporting the story, the lead would have been simple. *Michael Sanders dropped out of college to manage his father's grocery store after his father suffered a stroke. There is nothing else going on in his life. Nothing else to report.* I think Mr. Perl would have been impressed with the brevity and conciseness of the story.

"So does that mean you've given up on your writing career?" He took a bite out of a square piece of chocolate ribbon cake. "This is delicious."

"Let's just say I put it aside to help out my parents."

"And now what? "

In the hectic days following my father's death, I had not taken any time to think about what was to come. I assumed nothing would change and that I would be managing the grocery store until further notice.

"Are you still interested in writing?" he asked while downing a piece of ruggalah.

"I think about it sometimes. But it has been so long since I tried. I don't know if I have the ability anymore. I don't know if I have the same desire as before. I've lost my momentum."

"Would you want to give it a try again if you had a chance?"

"Do you have something in mind?"

Recently, two of the reporters had left to take jobs at other newspapers and another had been promoted to columnist. Perl had three positions to fill at the Gazette. He offered me one of the jobs.

"It's yours if you want it. You know the paper. You have the experience. You can write. Take a week or two. You have other things to worry about and to take care of. After you have a chance to clear your mind, think it over. If it is something you can do, and want to do, give me a call."

The offer was enticing. I thought about it a lot over the next few days. When my father had suffered his stroke a year and a half ago, I had suggested to my mother that the store could run itself. Nothing had changed in my thinking. The employees knew their jobs. I had promoted Paul to general manager and he had done well in the position and was certainly capable of handling the store day in and day out. My mother would continue to receive the income she needed and, if necessary, I would agree to spend my days off checking up on things. All of that would give us time to try to sell the business. It was a plan. One that would allow me to take the job with the Gazette, restart my career while not deserting my mother and ignoring her needs.

Two weeks passed after Perl made the offer. I had not said anything to my mother. But I had made up my mind. I called Perl and accepted the job and asked for another two weeks to clean up matters with the store. Later that day, I talked to Paul and told him my plans. He was on board, thanking me for the opportunity and assuring me that things would continue as they had. That left my mother.

I called her later in the day.

"Mom how about I come over for dinner tonight? I'd like to talk to you about the store. I have some ideas."

"That's great. I've been meaning to ask you to come over and talk. There are things that have been on my mind as well."

Before I had a chance to tell her my plans, my mother opened the discussion.

"Michael, I've been thinking a lot about the store the last few days. When your father set things up years ago, he made me co-owner. And he never got around to updating his will. So, as it stands, I inherit his interest in the store also. I already called the lawyers and asked them to draw up new documents to give you a forty-nine percent share as well as my share comes when I die."

"That's more than fair Mom."

"But there's more. Your father had certain concerns and reservations about things you were doing. He didn't like the cake business you started. Or how you handled the situation with that guy who died in the alley. Or even the responsibilities that you passed off to Paul and Ralph."

"I know that. He didn't hold anything back."

"So, I want to propose something. I want to be more involved in the business. We can run things together. Divide up the responsibilities. I have an interest to protect and I want to do that."

Never good with a poker face, I could tell by my mother's expression that my expression must have shown my astonishment. I was irate. There was no way that I would answer to my mother. I had been entrusted to run the store when my father had his stroke. During that time, the store had turned its highest profits ever. As a result, my parents saw more money in their pockets. I was not about to take a step back and answer to someone who didn't have the first clue about the business.

I began to argue my case. It was absurd that my mother, with no experience, would become involved in the store. It was unfair. It totally disregarded my sacrifice. As I ranted, a thought entered my mind. *What the hell am I doing? Isn't this exactly what I want? A way out of the store.*

It dawned on me that rather than departing because of my new opportunity at the Gazette, I could blame it on my mother's new intent. If she was planning to be involved to that extent, then the store would have a family member overseeing the operation and free me to pursue my own goals. I took a deep breath.

"You know Mom. You have every right to get involved. You're invested. Your life. Your income. So go ahead. Take over. You are more than capable of handling it and you have a group of employees more than capable of backing you up. But it's going to be without me because you won't need me. I'll give you two more weeks. Then I'm gone."

Over the next few days, my mother attempted to revisit the situation with me. But my mind was made up and I was unwilling to engage her in any further discussion. By the end of the week, she began coming to the store every day to get the lay of the land. But she would not show until mid-day. According to Paul, it was the first time she had set foot in the store in over ten years. But she still knew all of the old time employees, greeted them by name and chatted with them as if it had only been days since their last conversation.

Since it was mid-November and we were headed into the busiest time of the year, I finally agreed to delay my departure until the first of the year. Perl agreed to push back my start date at the paper. I concentrated on tying up the loose ends in the business. I spent the mornings doing my normal activities and worked on preparing Mount Street Cakes and Pies for my departure. The women would have to operate independently going forward. When my mother arrived, I would spend the afternoons familiarizing her with the ordering process and the vendors. Janice reviewed the books and explained the payroll and the bank deposits. Paul and Ralph showed her the store operations and Emma taught her the register. My mother easily grasped everything. But then it wasn't exactly rocket science.

As Christmas approached, business was brisk. Mount Street Cakes and Pies had received an extraordinary number of holiday orders along with their regular daily business. We were delivering supplies twice a day to the church to keep up with the demand. The store was equally busy. More deliveries, both incoming and outgoing. More effort needed to keep the shelves stocked. Both Emma and my mother operated registers to minimize the check-out time. All of us were running on fumes and anxiously counting the days until Christmas Eve when the store would close at noon.

We opened two hours early that day to accommodate the last minute shoppers. By eleven the store started to empty. I let Emma, Ralph and the stock boys leave early to give them an early jump on the holiday. Paul offered to close the store but I told him to leave as well.

"You'll have your hands full in another week. Go home."

Before they left, we followed a tradition that my father had started years ago. A toast to the holiday with a shot of Scotch. We gathered at the front register. There were no customers in the store at the time. We raised our glasses and, in unison, said "Merry Christmas" and downed the liquor. Paul, Ralph, Charlie and I followed up with a second shot. And then everyone left except Charlie and me.

A customer or two straggled into the store during the final hour. A few minutes before noon, I announced that the store would be closing momentarily. There were only two customers in the store at the time. Margaret Jackson, who lived a block away, stood at the register and a young guy, who I did not recognize, was still filling a basket with products. Charlie went to the back to check that the shipping area was buttoned up. I rang up Margaret's purchases and, after she left, secured the front door, leaving the keys in the lock. One customer to go. My last Christmas Eve at the store.

"Wrap it up. We're closing in two minutes," I informed the last customer.

He finally walked to the front register and removed his items from the basket and placed them on the conveyor belt. I rang up the first item, a bag of white potatoes.

"Are you new around here?" I asked.

"Yeah. I just moved in. Round the corner. "

"Well welcome to the neighborhood."

I finished ringing up and bagging the order. "That'll be twenty dollars and fifty-two cents."

He handed me a twenty and a five dollar bill. I hit the register and the till opened. As I started to pull the change from the drawer, he pulled a gun, reached across the counter and placed it against my head.

"Put all the money in the bag."

I froze. He tapped the barrel of the gun against my head.

"Give me the money. NOW."

"What?"

He quickly lost his patience and hurdled over the counter and pushed me against the wall. He reached into the drawer and began pulling the bills.

"Think about what you're doing."

My voice was as meek as it was that day that I found Darnell surrounded by four attackers.

Then a sound. A door opening and closing. The squeaking of the soles of shoes against the floor. And the whistling of Silent Night. And, in the next instant, Charlie shouted, "All locked up in the back, Michael" and began walking toward the front.

The robber took a step back. To size up the situation. To figure out his next move. And then he swung his arm. With full force. Toward my head. The barrel of the gun smacked me above the temple on the right side. My head bounced back and banged against the wall. As I crumbled to the floor, I could see Blake, my freshman roommate at Syracuse. I saw his head. Banging against the door of our dorm room. Blood flowing. And me. Grabbing him and pulling him into the room to avoid any further violence. But there was no one there to catch me and pull me to safety.

I hit the floor. And then there was another sound. A pop. And then another. But more muffled then the first one. And then another. And that was the last thing I would remember.

# CHAPTER TWENTY-ONE

Mr. Watkins sat in his barber's chair and read the newspaper as he usually did on Christmas Eve day. It was a luxury he rarely experienced. Most days he was busy from morning till closing. But on Christmas Eve day there were no customers. Never was. But he still opened the shop. In case someone decided at the last minute to get a haircut. He had the radio tuned to a station playing Christmas carols. It was peaceful and quiet as the music blocked the noise from the street. As he turned the page, he peeked above the newspaper and looked out the front window.

He saw the front door closing at the grocery store across the street. Just a split second sooner and he would have seen someone dash out and run down the street. But all was quiet now. Still, it was peculiar how violently the door swung shut, he thought. Since there was nothing else to do, he decided to head home. But first he would stop at the grocery store as he had done for over thirty years. To wish everyone Merry Christmas.

As he approached, the lights were on but there was no movement inside. He opened the door, the keys dangling in the lock, and walked in. No one was in sight.

"Michael!"

No answer. He moved toward the front counter. Still no one appeared. The register was open. And empty. Panic began to set in.

"Michael!!"

He ran around the counter.

"Oh my God."

And that's where he found me. Sprawled on the floor.

Mr. Watkins knelt down and lifted my head in his hands. I woke up. My head felt like it was in a vise.

"Just lay here. I'm going to call for help."

"Where's, where's Charlie? Find Charlie!"

"Ok. Let me look."

Mr. Watkins stood up and began walking toward the rear of the store. He spotted a body on the floor just down the far aisle. It was Charlie. From where he stood, Mr. Watkins could tell he was dead. There was too much blood for him to be anything but dead. Mr.

Watkins reversed course, picked up the phone behind the front counter and called the police.

"There's been a shooting at the grocery store at 1500 Mount Street. Hurry. Call for an ambulance."

He then sat down beside me and cradled my head in his lap. "Just lay still."

Moments later, the two foot patrolmen who walked the neighborhood arrived with guns drawn. They had been in the store only a few hours earlier to pick up their Christmas gifts—a little something that I handed out in appreciation for their work. How quickly things had changed.

"Over here," Mr. Watkins shouted, "and there's a body in the far aisle."

The first policeman moved behind the counter and knelt down beside me.

"Is he hit?"

"I don't think so. But he was out cold when I got here."

"Mr. Sanders, where does it hurt?"

"My head. Both sides. And my arm."

"You've got a pretty good gash on the side of your head. Just lay here until the ambulance arrives. Can you tell me what happened?"

"We were getting ready to close. There was one customer left in the store. I didn't recognize him. I had just rung up his purchase and he pointed a gun at me and asked for the money in the register. Then he hit me on the side of the head and I fell. I heard gun shots before I passed out."

"Can't this wait until he gets checked out?"

"Of course."

The second policeman was by the register now.

"How is he?"

Assured that I was alive, he told the first officer that Charlie was dead. Two bullets, one to the neck and one to the chest. Never had the chance to draw his gun.

"I need to contact his family. Do you have a number for him?"

"There's a file in the back, next to the desk in my office, with the employee names and numbers."

Mr. Watkins volunteered to find the number.

"Mr. Watkins, can you also call my mother?"

Soon more police arrived. Followed by the ambulance. The medics checked my pulse and blood pressure and applied a bandage to the wound on my head.

"You're banged up but you're going to be all right."

It had been ten years since I felt the way I did today. I was far luckier that time. A black eye and some bruises. This time I had a nasty gash on one side of my head. A concussion. And a broken arm. And a memory that would haunt me for the rest of my life.

But I was far luckier than Charlie, who didn't know what hit him. Didn't know who snatched his life. When the police came to see me at the hospital two days later, they said that Charlie never saw it coming. He had come down the far aisle and as he turned the corner, the gunman had fired. The first bullet entered his neck on the right side. The second bullet missed. The third one hit his chest and tore through his heart.

"I'm sorry to have to ask you these questions but we need to get you to recall anything you can. Do you feel up to talking?"

"Yeah. Now's as good as any time."

"Ok, walk me through it. As much as you can remember."

I told the officers that it was around noon, the time we had planned to close. Normal practice for Christmas Eve. The other employees had been sent home about an hour earlier. Only Charlie and I were left.

"Margaret Jackson. She lives on Gilmore Street, I think. She and this guy were the only other two people left in the store. She brought her purchases to the counter and I rang her up. The other guy was still filling his basket. When she left the store, I called out that we were closing in two minutes."

I explained that Charlie had gone to the back room to lock up. The last customer finally came up to the counter.

"I asked him if he was new to the neighborhood because I didn't recognize him. He said he had just moved in around the corner. Handed me the money. A twenty and a five. I hit the register to get him his change. As soon as I did, I felt a gun on the side of my head."

"Did he say anything?"

"Yeah. *Give me the money*. Told me to put it in the shopping bag. I froze."

"Then what?"

"I think he asked for the money again. When I didn't move he jumped over the counter and pushed me against the wall. He started pulling the money from the drawer. I told him to think about what he was doing. And then the back door opened and closed and Charlie shouted that he had finished locking up the back. It startled the guy. "

"Did he still have the gun pointed at you?"

"I'm not sure. Let me think. No. No I think he had it in his right hand but he was using both hands to grab the money. Then he stopped for a second when he heard Charlie shout."

And then it dawned on me. There had been a few seconds when I could have done something. Grab the gun. Jump the guy. Shout out a warning for Charlie at the very least. Maybe if I had acted, Charlie would still be alive. The officer could sense that something was wrong.

"Mr. Sanders, are you ok? Do you want to take a break?"

"I'm ok. It's just that I should have done something. I just stood there."

"No, you did the right thing. If you had tried to do something, you probably would have ended up shot. Like Charlie. The man had a gun. You didn't. He had the upper hand and he was determined to get his way. You were right not to try anything stupid."

But we both knew that the situation cried out for action. It was moments like these that spawned heroes.

"Thanks. Anyhow, when he heard Charlie coming, he stopped for that split second. And then he swung the gun and caught me on the side of the head. I remember falling and hitting the floor. I heard three shots before I blacked out."

"Can you remember anything about him?"

"I can't remember much. To tell you the truth, we had a holiday toast before the other employees left. But I'm sure he was about my height, maybe a bit more. Six foot. Six one. Black but light skinned. Skinny. Maybe a hundred fifty or sixty pounds."

"How about his face. Did he have a beard? Eyes. Shape of his nose. Hair style?

"I can't remember."

"Any distinguishing marks that you can recall? "

"I'm sorry. I just can't remember."

"Do you remember what he was wearing?"

"I didn't take notice."

"Anything else you remember?"

"I'm sorry. I wish I could be more help. But I just don't remember. It's still a blur."

"Well when you're feeling better, you may remember more. We'll send in a sketch artist. See what we can come up with. In the meantime, we're canvassing the neighborhood to see if anybody saw anything."

"What about the store?"

"It'll have to stay closed for now. It's a crime scene. After the New Year, we'll be finished and you can think about reopening."

He hesitated for a second. "We'll get this guy, Mr. Sanders."

I went home from the hospital the next day. My mother wanted me to stay at her house but I wasn't up to it. I went to my apartment and stayed there until Charlie's funeral on January 4. Other than a visit to the police station on New Year's Eve day, it would be the first time I ventured outside since the hold-up.

The police had given the okay to reopen the store after New Year's Day but we remained closed for a few additional days. At the funeral, I told Paul that we would go in on the seventh to clean up. There would be food to be tossed out. Restocking to be done. Blood to be cleaned off the floor. As if the stains could ever be removed.

# CHAPTER TWENTY-TWO

When Jimmy Hightower was stabbed to death, the police only made a half-hearted attempt to investigate. There were no leads. No witnesses. No one was talking. There was no family pressing for answers. The trail was cold from the start and within a week, the police ceased their efforts. Jimmy was a homeless man. A druggie. A drunk. A black man. The police felt they had more important things to do. Better places to spend their time.

But with Charlie's murder, the response was different. The neighborhood was worried. The people living there were unaccustomed to such violence. It rocked their foundation. While there had been minor incidents over the years, there had been nothing to the degree of these recent events. A drunk husband or boyfriend beating up his wife or girlfriend and being hauled off to jail for the night. Some teenagers arguing over some inconsequential issue and resorting to a fist fight. But, all of these incidents were fleeting. A normalcy always returned.

There had been a few muggings and then Jimmy's murder but now there had been a robbery and another murder at a store that they all frequented on a daily basis. And a killing of one of their own. Charlie. Someone who was there to protect the peace. Piled on top of Jimmy's murder and the threat from the drug dealers running the streets, the residents were concerned that a trend was emerging. And so were the police. They responded quickly, intent to restore the community's confidence.

After talking with me that day in the hospital, the police went out and found Margaret Jackson and asked her if she had seen a suspicious man while she was shopping?

"Yes sir, I did take some notice of him. He was kinda nervous and all. Peeking up and down the aisles. Peering at the front counter. Ain't never seen him before that day, though."

She was far more helpful in her description of the robber than I had been. She also described him as six foot tall and light complexioned.

"Had him some pockmarks on his face and his cheeks were awful sunken in and all. Some whiskers growing on his chin and upper lip. But sparse. Nothin' else I took notice of."

From her description, the police were able to create a sketch of the guy. When they showed the picture to me, I said he sort of looked like what I remembered. So, the police hit the streets, canvassing the neighborhood to see if anyone knew the guy. No one claimed they did. Nor had anyone seen anything out of the ordinary that day.

A few nights later, the police decided to rouse the drug sellers on the corner of Mount and Fulton. Shake things up and see what might fall out. Three cars pulled up and six cops jumped out. At the time, there were three men standing on the corner. Willie Boyd was the leader and also the kingpin of the drug dealing trio.

"Ok boys. Do you suppose we might find something illegal if we check your pockets? But let's say you boys are smart and want to save us that effort and save yourselves some trouble. That is, if you had anything you might want to tell us about that murder and robbery at the grocery store."

Willie spoke first. He was only too glad to help because there was a motive behind his willingness to help. Before the robbery and murder went down, he had sent his men into the various stores seeking protection money. But the owners had all ignored his demand. But now there was an opportunity. The owners might now be scared and more willing to pay for his protection. If he helped the police nail the guilty party, he might be able to parlay that into gaining their confidence. And then he had another reason to cooperate. A grudge that he held against a guy in the neighborhood. By snitching to the police, he intended to settle that score.

"I don't know nothin' 'bout it myself. But I think Smiley here knows somethin' 'bout it."

He turned to Smiley, "Go on. Tell them what you know. It's alright."

"I was standing over there on the other corner and I seen this tall boy running out of the grocery store that day. He was real tall. And dark skinned. Wearing a jacket that said *Lions Basketball.* A few days later, I jes heard some things on the street 'bout who done the hold-up. But it jes may be a rumor or somepin'. I don't want to be getting' anyones in trouble when I don't know what's for certain and what's not."

"Why don't you let us be the judge of that? We're not gonna accuse someone without the proper evidence. So tell us what you know."

"I heared that this boy had somepin' to do with it. That's the word goin' round."

"This boy have a name?

"Yeah. Jones. Marvin Jones."

"And where's this Jones live?"

"Jes up the street some. On Fulton."

"What else you know about him?"

Willie jumped in.

"Yeah, I know he lives in an apartment a few blocks up like Smiley says. Lives alone, I guess, 'cept for his occasional woman friend. If you know what I mean. Works over at some print shop on Kirk Avenue."

"Anything else?"

"Well, I knows he's got a taste for junk and stuff."

"And how would you know about all of that?"

"Let's jes say I seen the dude making some buys."

"How about one of you taking us up the street and showing us his apartment?"

Smiley walked the officers up the street and pointed out the place. When they knocked on the door, there was no answer.

The next morning, the police showed up at the printing plant over on Kirk Avenue at eight in the morning, about an hour after the first shift started. They asked the owner if he had an employee named Marvin Jones. The owner said he did and the police asked what he knew about him. He had been working at the shop for about nine months, the owner said. A decent employee. Never any trouble. Always came to work on time. Didn't miss time. Did his job up to expectations. Then they had the owner call Jones off the shop floor and report to the front office. When he walked through the door the police did a double take. Marvin Jones was six foot eight and two hundred twenty pounds plus. Dark skinned. Nothing like the description from Margaret Jackson. Or me.

"Marvin Jones?" the one officer asked and Jones nodded. "We're going to need you to come with us down to the station."

"What's this about, officer? What is it that you think I done?"

"We'll explain that to you at the stationhouse."

"Can I get my jacket?"

Both of the officers accompanied Jones back to his locker and stood on both sides of him as he opened the door. On the top shelf, above the hook that held his coat, was a pistol. Marvin was stunned to see it sitting there, because not only had it not been there when he opened his locker earlier in the day, he didn't even own a gun.

One of the officers grabbed it.

"This belong to you?"

"I ain't never seen it before, officer! I swear."

"Then what's it doing in your locker."

One of the officers pushed Jones against the locker and put him in handcuffs.

"I think you have some explaining to do."

Once they arrived at the station, the police took him to an interrogation room and bombarded him with questions. Where were you at noon on Christmas Eve Day? At work, he told them. Did he know anything about the robbery at the grocery store on Mount Street? Only what he had heard on the street. And the gun, how did he come into possession of it? He repeated what he had said at the printing shop. That he had never seen it before. Then what would it be doing in his locker? Someone must of placed it in their by mistake. It must belong to someone else.

The questioning went on for three hours. They asked if he knew Smiley and did he know Smiley claimed to see him running from the store. Jones held his ground and maintained that he had nothing to do with the robbery, that he had not been anywhere near the store that day.

Yes, he admitted to them that he used drugs now and then. That's how Smiley and Willie knew him because he had bought those drugs from them. And that was the only illegal thing he had ever done. Unless you count his sneaking into a high school in Baltimore County as doing something illegal. But there were adults that told him it was ok to attend that school. Until an article appeared in the Baltimore Gazette talking about it being illegal. But he wasn't the one who had arranged it. It was about basketball anyhow. He paid the penalty for that because he was kicked out of that school. And yes he had wandered around for a few years after he dropped out of high school. Wasted his time. Was high a fair amount of the time. Up to no good but up to no bad either. Just hanging out. But now, he had a job. An apartment. He was trying to do something with his life. Working and going to night school to get his high school diploma. He was a law abiding citizen.

By this time, the police had located Margaret Jackson and brought her to the station. They threw Marvin Jones into a line up. With four other tall, dark skinned men. And, Margaret Jackson picked him out of that line up and identified him as the man she had seen in the grocery store that day. *Yes sir that's him. Second one on the left.*

And when the police said the description she had given them previously did not match Marvin Jones in any way, she told them that she must have been mistaken. Confused. She was never real good at describing people. Never real observant. Because this was surely the man she saw that day in the store. Here he was. Standing right on the other side of the glass.

Later that day, they brought in Smiley and he identified Jones as the man he saw running from the store. Without any hesitation.

Within hours, the police charged Marvin for Charlie's murder and the robbery at the grocery store. Threw him immediately into a cell. Then they went back to the print shop to check on his alibi. They asked the owner if he could confirm that Jones had been at work that day. The owner produced a time card that showed that Jones had clocked in a few minutes before seven and clocked out at three. But, he couldn't say that he had personally seen him.

With the sound of printing presses churning out sheet after sheet of brochures in the background, the police questioned his co-workers and one of them admitted that he had punched Jones' card for him that day. Said that Jones told him he had some debts to take care of and he had to run out for a few hours to get some money from someone he knew. But he never came back and so this employee had punched his card in and out for lunch and then again at the end of the day. He hoped he wasn't going to be in any trouble because he was just trying to help out a friend. He mentioned that Jones once did the same thing for him.

A few days later, the ballistic tests came back and the gun found in Marvin Jones' locker proved to be the gun that fired the fatal shots into Charlie. There were traces of hair and skin on the barrel, which was consistent with my being hit on the head. There were no fingerprints, however, as the gun had been wiped clean. But the police felt good about the case. They had the weapon, an eyewitness identification from Margaret Jackson and Smiley, the motive and means from the co-worker. The only inconsistency in their case was my description.

I was brought to the station house the following day to see if I could identify my assailant in the line-up. I stood in front of the window, watching the five men enter the room. I gasped.

"Are you okay Mr. Sanders?"

"I am. It's just that I recognize one of the men."

"The man who attacked you?"

"No, I recognize one of the men from years ago. I played basketball against him a few times. I wrote a story about him."

"Which one?"

"It's number four. I think his name is Jones."

"Is he also the man who attacked you in the store?"

"No. There's no way it was him. I would have recognized him that day. And the guy I remember was much shorter and light skinned. Are you saying it was him?"

"I can't say. You have to tell me if you recognize your attacker."

"None of these men could be the one. They're all the wrong height. Wrong complexion."

"Take your time Mr. Sanders. Look again."

"No I'm sorry but none of these men could be the one."

After the men were led out of the room, I again asked the officer if they thought one of the men in the line-up was responsible for the crime. The officer confirmed that Margaret Jackson had identified Marvin Jones. They had found the murder weapon in his possession and had blown a hole in his alibi.

"Mr. Sanders, you said you wrote a story about the guy."

"It was years ago. I was in high school. I wrote a story about city kids playing basketball for county schools. He was one of the players. It was printed in the Gazette."

"What happened after the story was printed?"

"Nothing. Jones was kicked out of the school. I heard he dropped out rather than re-enroll in a city school."

"So, maybe he had a grudge against you. Saw you in the store. Remembered what happened and decided to even the score?"

"Why in the world would he hold a grudge against me?"

"Because you derailed his dreams. Maybe he had visions of playing basketball in college and then the pros and making a lot of money. Your article destroyed those plans."

"Maybe he had a grudge against me but I'm telling you that he was not the guy who attacked me and shot Charlie."

"Are you sure? You weren't able to recall much about your attacker other than his height and complexion. You couldn't describe his face, his hair, his clothing. You admitted to having a few drinks. You were anxious to get out for the holiday. Then, you were hit in the head and you admit that you don't remember things. Maybe you are mistaken."

Everything the officer said was true, to an extent. But I knew that Marvin Jones was not the man in the store that day. I thought about everything the officer told me. Certainly all of the evidence they had accumulated pointed to Jones. There was no way to explain away the gun, Margaret's identification, the false alibi. But how could I have not known Marvin Jones that day?

Despite my misgivings, I did not question the police officer any further and, a few minutes later, left the station. Marvin Jones was arraigned the next day and assigned a public defender. Charged with murder and armed robbery. Charges, which if he were to be found guilty, could land him on death row.

# CHAPTER TWENTY-THREE

In the days immediately following the incident, there was a constant flurry of activity in the hospital room. Nurses coming in and out to check my blood pressure, temperature and pulse and to change the dressing on my wound. Doctors testing my progress from the concussion. Police asking questions. And then returning to ask more questions. There was the constant presence of my mother from mid-morning until visiting hours ended at eight. When not being poked, pestered, questioned or observed, I slept most of the time. There was no time to absorb what had happened or to think about what needed to be done at the store.

What little did need to be done at the store, Mr. Watkins had taken care of. He contacted the employees immediately after I was taken away in the ambulance. Paul came down to the store to help lock up and post a sign in the window. But the neighborhood already knew what had happened. Police tape covered the front door announcing, in no uncertain terms, that this was a crime scene and there would be no entry for days to come.

On the first morning of my hospital stay, Mr. Watkins was also the first person to come visit. He poked his head through the door, early Christmas morning, and said, "You feeling up for some company?"

"What are you doing here? It's Christmas. You should be home celebrating with your family."

"Under the circumstances, I don't feel much like celebrating. Besides, I brought my family with me."

He held open the door and Mrs. Watkins walked in. Carrying one of her cakes. And then Darnell who I had not seen since our rough parting a year ago. We spent the next hour talking about everything except what had happened the day before. By the time my mother arrived, I was feeling tired again, so the three Watkins excused themselves.

But before leaving, Mr. Watkins said, "Michael, Celia is coming in next week. I told her what happened and she wants to know if she can visit you. If it is ok with you. I mean if you're feeling up to it. I imagine you'll be home by then."

"Yes. That would be great. Just have her give me a call when she gets in."

The only other visitor that came to the hospital was Mr. Perl who had read about the hold-up in the Gazette. He stopped in the day after Christmas on his way to the office and spent an hour with me. He assured me that the job was there for me but that I should take as much time as I needed. I told him that I'd let him know but obviously there were things to tend to in order to reopen the store. I didn't want it all to fall to my mother and intended to do what was necessary to get things restarted.

Two days later, when I was released from the hospital, I returned to my apartment despite my mother's protestations. Since she had to come by each morning to change the dressing on my head, she preferred that I stay at her house. Given my condition, there was not a lot that I was able to do other than rest. And that's exactly what I did for the next four days. Just laid in bed, watched television and slept.

On New Year's Eve day, the police called and asked me to come down to the station for a line-up. Since I was unable to drive, my mother took me. Shortly after I returned home in the early afternoon, Celia called.

"Is it all right to come visit you today?"

I was tired and upset from the visit to the police station so I told her that I wanted to take a nap.

"But, I'll be ok in a few hours. If it fits your schedule, then I would be happy to see you later in the day."

"Then why don't I bring some dinner. We can hang out for as long as you are up to it. You can be my date for New Year's Eve."

I told my mother that Celia was coming over and that she would take care of dinner that night. My mother left and I climbed into bed and dozed off. And then I had a dream, a nightmare that would startle me from my sleep. It was something that I had expected would come, given the trauma. But the dream was not about the incident. At least not in the sense of reliving what happened. I didn't dream about the hold-up and the gun against my head. About Charlie's murder. About my attacker and my injury.

Instead, I dreamt that I was standing in a bathtub taking a shower. As the water poured over my head, I heard a creaking sound. And then a cold air swept against the shower curtain, rippling it from end to end. Blowing inward until the curtain ballooned against my body. Suddenly, a hand grabbed the curtain and pulled it aside. Exposing my nakedness. And there stood Celia. In front of a large crowd of people, all of whom I recognized. My parents. Coach Schwartzwalder and the boycotting black football players. Mr. Perl. Mr. Watkins and Darnell. Jimmy

Hightower. All my roommates—Blake, Doug and Danny. My former so-called girlfriends Becky and Ellen Wagner. The four guys who beat up Darnell and me. The ladies of Mount Street Cakes and Pies. Lenny. Mrs. Garrett. Mr. Bailey. The entire 1969 New York Mets team. Even the woman I met that day of the Vietnam moratorium. And finally Coach McCaskill with Hicks but not with Jones.

Celia peered into my eyes.

"I've been watching. We all have."

"Why?"

"You know why."

"No I don't. Have I done something wrong?"

But Celia and the others just stared. For what seemed like hours. Then Celia spoke again. More forcefully than before.

"Michael, you know why."

And then I awoke. Lying there, staring at the ceiling. Perplexed. That dream would revisit me. Over and over again for years. Always starting the same way. And ending the same each time. And each time, I would awake unsettled. When Celia visited, later that afternoon, I told her about the dream.

She arrived carrying two shopping bags filled with food. I reached out and grabbed one of the bags, in my one good arm, as she entered my apartment.

"Wow, those bags are heavy," I exclaimed.

"Well, I was planning to cook for you. But then my mother offered. I figured, since I'm no wizard at the stove, we would be better off if I accepted her offer. But you know how she is. She just can't cook for two people. There must be enough, in those bags, for a dozen people."

I placed the bags on the kitchen table and turned to face her. It had been four years since I had last seen Celia or spoke to her. So much had happened in that time. We stood facing each other. Just breathing in the moment. Taking in each other, looking. Her face was a mosaic of emotions. Her lips curled up in the tiniest of smiles. Her eyes watery. But no tears seeped out. For a moment, she tilted her face toward the floor. Took a breath. Her shoulders sagged just a bit as she exhaled.

"Michael, it's been too long," and she stepped toward me and we hugged.

She nestled in against my chest, turning her head so that her left ear pressed against my heart. We embraced for a minute, saying nothing. And then she stepped back, her hands still grasping my forearms, and smiled again.

"So let me check out your bachelor pad."

We strolled through the apartment.

"So, what do you think?"

"It's nice."

"Sounds like you're being kind. What do you really think?"

"It looks comfortable. Plenty of room. But I don't know. It's just that it could be anyone's apartment. I don't get the feeling that it's you. That you made it your own."

She was right on target with her assessment. In the time that I had lived there, I hadn't done much more than furnish the living room with a two-piece beige sofa and a television sitting on a table. A bed and a small dresser for the one bedroom and nothing for the second bedroom. The dining room was totally empty except for stacks of records and a turntable and speakers that sat directly on the floor. I hadn't covered one inch of flooring with a rug or taken the time to hang one picture on a wall. There was a table with two chairs in the kitchen. A cabinet with a few plates and bowls and another with one pot and one frying pan. Since I brought home only what I needed for dinner each night, even the refrigerator showed few signs of a person living there.

"Probably because I never thought I would be here that long. Maybe now that things have changed, I'll do some decorating," I explained but Celia flashed an expression that indicated she took no stock in what I said.

As we sat on opposite sofas, there was a sudden silence. For two people, who had known each other for many years, we groped for what to say next.

"Listen, Michael. I know the last two years have not been what you expected. And what happened to you last week. And Charlie. It's beyond words, it's horrible. No one should have to go through that. I don't want to pry. But I'm here. You can talk to me about whatever you want, whatever you're comfortable with. "

"I don't want to talk about the store or what happened there. I just want to get over it and forget about it. I know it will take time. But, at least, there's a beginning to the end. They arrested Marvin Jones today."

"That's good news. Did you know the guy? Had you seen him before?"

"Yeah. I think you'll remember him too. He was the guy I wrote the story about. Back in high school. The basketball player. You criticized me over that." Celia nodded her head.

I continued, "Here's the thing. They found all type of evidence implicating him. Someone who was shopping in the store, at the time, recognized him. But I don't think he's the one who did it."

"Did you tell the police?"

"I did. But they told me that my memory was shaky. That my recall was affected by my injuries."

"Do you think they're right?"

"I could understand their doubts if it was only that I couldn't identify the attacker. If I couldn't remember him. But I know Marvin Jones and I know he was not the man I saw in the store that day. I may not know who did it. But I know who didn't."

"So, what are you going to do?"

"I don't know. It's only been a couple of days since they arrested him. I haven't had time to think it through. I guess I'll wait for his defense attorney to contact me."

"I just hope you do what you can, if you're sure. I hope you will do the right thing."

"Listen Celia. I want to talk about something else. Can I tell you about a dream I had today? Is that okay?"

I described the dream, repeating what each of us had said.

"So, what do you think it meant? Why would you, and the others, be watching me?"

"I don't know Michael. It wasn't my dream. It's something you have to figure out."

"You must have an opinion, though."

Celia shrugged, "Maybe it doesn't mean anything. Or maybe it's simple. I'm not a psychologist but it seems that these are all people who had different impacts on your life at different times. They're your past. Maybe the dream is about your future. What your next step will be. How you process what has happened and go forward. What you do with the rest of your life."

"You know that dream starts out exactly like that day you surprised me in the shower. Before you left me that day, you said that you hoped that I would find my way out of the darkness. I was never sure what you meant. Can you tell me now?"

"That's what you remember from that day. What I said. I would think, I would hope that you would have remembered something else."

"Oh believe me. I do. For instance, I remember exactly what you were wearing. From top to bottom."

"Ha Ha. As I recall, it wasn't the first time you checked out what I was wearing in the bathroom. But it was the first time I checked you out. From top to bottom. Every inch of you."

"So are you going to tell me what you meant?"

"I think I told you. Later. When we came back from the Gwynn Oak rally. You needed to take a hard look at yourself. Especially your relationship with Darnell. I had hoped you would do that after our brief encounter in the shower that day. But you were young, what thirteen or so. It was probably more than what you were capable of at the time. So, I kind of spelled it out to you that day after the demonstration."

"Do you thing I have changed since then? That I did what you wanted?"

"I don't know Michael. We haven't seen each other much since then. My parents tell me what's going on with you. There are times when I think you've figured it out. Like when you defended Darnell against those four white kids. Or the Mount Street Cakes and Pies. Those are both good things. But then I hear what you are saying about the police arresting the wrong man today and I think that you are back to playing it safe."

"I told you that I'm trying to do what I can about that."

"That's the point. You have to make something happen. You have to do more than you think you can. You can't settle for just trying."

"I get the feeling that you are always holding me to a higher standard. Maybe that's what the dream is about. All of you expecting something from me that is beyond what I can do."

"Like I said. It's something that you have to figure out. I'm not passing judgment on you. I'm just glad to spend some time with you. What do you say we check out what's in those bags my mother sent?"

We went to the kitchen, unpacked the two grocery bags and sat down to eat. It had been a few years since I had enjoyed one of Mrs. Watkins meals. And this one did not disappoint. We barely made a dent in what she sent.

"My mother said you should keep the leftovers so you'll have something to eat for the next few days. You can return the dishes next time you're in the neighborhood."

After cleaning up, we returned to living room. This time, however, Celia sat down on the same sofa as I did. I was feeling a bit tired but I didn't want the evening to end. I didn't know when I would see Celia again.

"Can I ask you something, Michael?"

"Sure, anything."

"How come you never hooked up with me? I know you were attracted to me."

"I don't know. I never thought about it."

"You never thought about being attracted to me. Or you never thought about why you didn't do anything about it?"

"No, no. I knew I was attracted to you. I thought about it all the time. But you were older. And I was intimidated. I didn't think you were interested."

"I think you know better than that. I gave you plenty of signals. I waited for you to make a move. But you never did. What were you afraid of?"

"I don't know. I just wasn't ready. I wasn't sure."

"Of me. Or of yourself."

"I'm sorry Celia. I'm not ready to have this conversation. Can we talk about something else?

"We can. But first I have to tell you something."

She paused and looked down toward the floor. When she raised her eyes back to meet my gaze, she said, "I want you to know that I am engaged. I'm getting married next summer."

# CHAPTER TWENTY-FOUR

I did my best to hide my disappointment and congratulate Celia on her news although I wasn't sure that I was entitled to feel any disappointment. Despite my interest over the years, I had never done anything to build a romantic relationship with Celia, just as she said. Instead, I had been fearful, hesitant. Worried what people would say. Now any chance had disappeared. Not that I was any more prepared to do anything about it today than I was before.

"Then we're ok. You and me."

"We are."

We turned on the television to watch the countdown from Times Square and I fell off to sleep not long after the ball dropped. When I awoke the next morning, Celia was curled up on the other sofa. We spent the day together and, three days later, she sat with me at Charlie's funeral before returning to New York that afternoon.

Charlie's funeral on January fourth was the first time I had left my apartment since the visit to the police station. The church was crammed with people paying their respects. There was a host of eulogies from family and friends, each one describing Charlie as a caring, loving man. Pastor Brown spoke eloquently.

"Who can explain why such things happen," he implored. "Why the good are taken from us before their time. Charlie was such a good and caring person. As a policeman and then as a security guard, protecting us from the very evil that struck him down. Always with a smile and a hello. Holding open the door as we carried our food from the store where he worked. We will miss him. But we know, when our time comes, Charlie will be standing at the gates of Heaven. Holding open the door. Welcoming us again."

Three days later, I was scheduled to meet Paul at the store in order to put the place back in order.

When I pulled my car to the curb a few feet from the store, Paul was already standing at the front door. I turned off the engine and then just sat there. My hands gripped the steering wheel and I just stared at the street. Paul was holding the door open. He bent over so he could get a view of me sitting there.

"Come on," he shouted, "it's cold out here."

But I remained frozen in place. Staring out at Mount Street. At the people scurrying along the sidewalks. Past the liquor store and the hardware store. The barbershop and the nail salon. The fried chicken carryout place. And my grocery store.

Paul sensed something was wrong. He closed the door and walked around to the driver's door.

"Michael, are you okay?"

I didn't answer. I just sat and stared. Paul banged on the door, pleaded with me to open the door, to answer.

After a few more attempts to rouse me, Paul ran over to the barbershop and summoned Mr. Watkins, who rapped on the window by my ear.

"C'mon Michael. Open the door."

I leaned forward, pressed my forehead against the steering wheel and then sat back and unlocked the door.

"Maybe it's not such a good idea you trying to come into work today. Darnell's still home and he can stay with you. How about I have him drive you back to your apartment? I think Paul can take care of the store."

I nodded my agreement and climbed over to the front passenger's seat. Darnell showed up a few minutes later.

"Hey Michael. I'm really sorry that you're going through this. Whatever you're feeling, you're entitled to feel. It's tough to digest what happened."

"You know, it's funny how things turn out, Darnell. Truth is I'm not having any problem with what went down at the store. I mean I am but it doesn't make me afraid. You want to know what's really bothering me? Why I didn't go into the store today? It's that I was never supposed to be there in the first place. I should have been in school and then working as a writer. I did the right thing. I gave up my plans to help my parents. And look how it turned out. "

"I know you're angry. And you need to let it out. But you suffered a trauma. You need to give yourself time to heal."

"I've had an ongoing trauma for the last two years. This is just the final straw. I don't need to heal. I need to move on. To get on with my life. And it starts today. I am done with that store."

"Are you planning to just walk away?"

"As quick as I can. For now, I'm physically staying away. I'll do what I have to, to make sure it survives, to help my mother."

With Darnell as my witness, I had vowed to make a change that day.

What I hoped would be a change for the better would prove to be something else though.

My mother had given up on the store as well. Although the store had provided a comfortable living for her, it had now become associated with only bad things. Throughout her marriage, a husband who had spent most of his waking hours at the store and any leftover hours thinking about it. Then the death of my father in the street in front of the store after flying out in a fit of rage. And now, the assault on her son and the death of an employee.

Like the previous time when I had been assaulted, my mother was quick to act. That first time, she had placed our house on the market in the first week after the beating. Within days the house had sold and we had purchased a new home and moved to Baltimore County. This time, she put the store on the market the third week of January 1974 but the sale would take much longer to complete. It was a balancing act. Appearing too eager to sell would undercut the value of the store. Yet, since neither my mother nor I intended to return to the store, it was critical to find a buyer as quick as possible.

Of course, there was also a cloud hanging over the place. The local newspapers continued to report about the incident and its aftermath. A fact that was pointed out when my mother met with John Stallings, a business broker who was recommended by our lawyer.

"I don't want to temper your hopes but this may be a tough sale right now. Prospective buyers will be cautious because of the violence associated with the store."

"Then you need to be aggressive about it. Don't deny it. Don't be afraid of it. Let them know there is nothing to worry about. This was an isolated incident. The store has been successful for generations. It's an opportunity for the right person."

"And what should I tell them when they ask why you want to sell?"

"Tell them my husband passed away and we can no longer manage it. My son needs to return to school and pursue his career. Otherwise, we would still be there."

As it turned out, it took only six months to sell the store. During those intervening months, Paul and the other employees managed the day to day operations. I continued to supervise but now it was from my apartment. We replaced Charlie with two security guards to make sure the floor was constantly watched. Since the employees had stepped up to compensate for my absence, I provided a monthly bonus to each on top of their salary. And I was transparent about my mother's effort to sell the store. We intended to protect the employees and secure their jobs with the new owners as best we could.

It was Paul who actually initiated the contact that resulted in the sale. He had taken my place at the Grocer's Association, attending the monthly meetings. He befriended an African-American family who had joined at the same time. The Jenkins were a well-respected family who owned a drug store on Dolfield Avenue in northwest Baltimore. Their twenty-nine year old son, a recent graduate from the University of Maryland MBA program, had opened a grocery store next to the drug store a few years prior. Now the family was looking to expand and open up other locations. Mount Street became an attractive option because the store was sustaining its profit margins and, by retaining all the employees, they were able to seamlessly take over and maintain the same public face to the customers.

They paid a fair price with fifty percent up front and the balance in monthly payouts over five years. As she had promised after my father died, my mother also had added me as a forty-nine percent owner. In the summer of 1974, I was suddenly in terrific financial shape and free from any obligations. Free to resume my dreams and goals. Free to do whatever I wanted. Free to try to rid myself of the stagnancy that had engulfed my life.

When Darnell had driven me home that day in January, I was invigorated, excited and intent on mapping out a new game plan. I spent the next few days thinking about what I would do and quickly determined that I would no longer settle for anything less than what would make me happy. That meant dedicating my entire time to becoming a creative writer and eliminating anything that would distract me from my goal.

Which meant that I had to call Mr. Perl and decline the position with the Gazette. Although the job would allow me to resume my journalistic career, on a level that would have taken years for someone starting out in the industry to attain, it also would make it more difficult for me to do any creative writing. I knew from my college days that when I tried to juggle a lot of balls at the same time, it was always my creative writing that suffered. There had to be no distractions.

Throughout the month of January, I spent mornings jotting down ideas and making notes, trying to develop storylines. In the afternoons, my time was still occupied with store matters. After a few weeks, I was unsure if I had made any progress. There were plenty of ideas, yellow sticky notes posted along the walls of the kitchen table and sheet after sheet of paper filled with random thoughts. Most of them ultimately found their way to the garbage can. What seemed like a good idea one day, didn't seem very good a day or two later. It was like milk on the verge of turning sour. One day it was okay to drink and the next day it was being poured down the drain. My typewriter remained zipped inside its case. For all the effort I had put forth, there was still nothing to show for it.

And then the new routine was broken when the bathtub dream, as I came to call it, visited me again. It had been a month since the dream first occurred on New Year's Eve. This second time played out exactly as the time before--the curtain pulled open, as I took a shower, and Celia standing there in front of the same group of people, all wearing the same expressions as the previous time.

Again, the dream unsettled me. It was two o'clock in the morning and I was awake and staring at the ceiling trying to determine what it all meant, if it meant anything at all. Was there some hidden message that I was supposed to figure out? The first time I had described the dream to Celia and then quickly forgot about it. This time, there was no one to talk to about it so I tried, as best I could, to dismiss it from my mind.

But the dream was relentless and gaining steam. There had been a one month respite between the first and second time but the third came right on the heels of the second, only one week later. The fourth time came two days behind the third time. The frequency was increasing and by March, the dream came every other day. I began to dread nighttime but not because I was afraid of the dream. It wasn't a nightmare, at least not the type that people complained about, the kind where they bolted up from their sleep, drenched in sweat, seeking comfort from someone. No, my dream only served as an interruption from sleep. It would leave me quizzical. But there was also a cumulative effect. I was fatigued during the day and unfocused. Trying to determine the meaning of the dream not only occupied my time during the night, when I should have been sleeping, but also during the day when I would ponder what it all meant rather than spending my time constructively.

Finally, after a few weeks, desperately needing to talk about it with someone, I called Celia.

"Michael. This is a surprise. I don't think you have ever called me before."

"I'm sorry to disturb you but I didn't know who else to talk to."

"What's wrong?"

"Nothing really. It's that dream I told you about. I am having the same dream every other day. I can't figure out what it means and I feel like if I don't figure it out, it will keep haunting me."

"Maybe you should seek some professional help. Talk it over with a therapist."

"Maybe I should go to the palm reader down the street. Maybe she can explain it. Or I know this Rastafarian. I could smoke some weed with him and ask for an understanding from Jah. If I only had the time, I could fly to Nepal, climb a mountain and find a guru to explain it all."

"Be serious Michael."

"I'm not crazy, Celia, and I don't need to talk to a therapist. I just want to understand the dream."

"But why call me? I'm not a dream interpreter. What is it you think I can do?"

"I think you can explain it. You have insight."

"I wish I could help you. But I can't. I told you that before."

"Ok. I understand. I'll figure something out," and I hung up.

The dream continued to recur at such an alarming rate that, on the nights when I would not have the dream, I would lay awake wondering why. On the nights it did come, I would awake and shout at the ceiling, *Will someone tell me what the fuck this means. Someone please tell me what I am supposed to do?* But nothing changed. There were no answers, nothing that I could figure out. And the dream just kept repeating, the same damn thing every other night. Week after week.

And then the dream changed.

It was the early fall of 1974 and I had been called into the state attorney's office to discuss and prepare my testimony in the State of Maryland versus Marvin Jones. The trial was scheduled to begin in the middle of October. The prosecutors felt they had a slam dunk case. John Gavitt, the lead prosecutor, brought me to his office and asked me to recall the sequence of events and I described what happened that day in the same manner I had eight months earlier. And then came the big test question.

"Michael can you identify who committed this crime. Is he in the courtroom today?"

"I remember certain things about him. And I don't think you arrested the right man," I confessed.

Gavitt shook his head in disgust.

"Michael, we need you to identify Marvin Jones as the person who did this. We have all the evidence and it all points to him. If you could identify him, it would seal the deal for a quick conviction. Can you do that?"

"I can't. I know my memory is foggy. Being knocked out didn't help. But I remember a light skinned man who was about my height. Marvin Jones is dark skinned and a good six or seven inches taller than me. You don't want me to lie do you?"

"Of course not." Gavitt paused for a moment. "I'll tell you what we're going to do. We'll put you on the stand and simply ask you to recount the events as you did today. You can do that right?"

"Yeah. That won't be a problem. But what if the defense attorney asks me if his client is the one who did what I had just described. What should I say?"

"Tell him the truth. Tell him that you can't be certain, that between the drinks, the panic of being attacked and being knocked out by a blow to the head, your memory is foggy. After the defense attorney is finished his cross-examination, I'll have the chance to ask you additional questions if we need to clarify your answers."

When I left Gavitt's office that day, I placed a phone call to the public defenders' office intending to talk to the person who had been assigned Marvin Jones' case and tell him my doubts about his client's guilt. But that individual was in court at the time, so I left my name and number and asked that the lawyer contact me as soon as possible as I had information that would be critical to the case. A week passed and there was no return call. I tried again and once again left my name and number with an urgent message. There was no call back.

The trial started two weeks later on July 25 and a jury was seated the same day. Gavitt seemed pleased. The public defender, who had been assigned to represent Marvin Jones, raised few challenges. The jury consisted of only two older black women along with ten whites, seven of whom were men, a jury make-up that appeared heavily slanted in favor of the prosecution. The judge adjourned at the end of the day, declaring that the testimony would begin the following morning. Outside the courtroom, I tried to corral the public defender, a young man named Solomon King.

"Excuse me, Mr. King. Do you have a moment?"

"Yes, how can I help you?" I was surprised that he didn't know who I was.

"I'm Michael Sanders."

"Oh the store owner." He seemed puzzled by my presence.

"Mr. King, I left several messages for you. I have information which I believe raises questions about the guilt of your client."

"Oh yes. I remember getting those calls and I'm sorry I didn't get back to you. It's been rather hectic. You know they overload us with cases. But I definitely want to talk with you."

"When do you plan to do that? I mean the trial starts tomorrow."

"I promise I will call you. But I have another engagement now. Please bear with me."

The next day, the testimony began when Gavitt called his first witness, one of the cops who had responded to Mr. Watkins phone call for help that day. He described the scene when he first arrived, finding one victim sprawled on the floor by the rear door with a gunshot to the chest and bleeding profusely. Dead at the scene. His weapon still in the holster. A second victim behind the counter with a gash to the side of his head. Money missing from the open cash register drawer. Groceries sitting on the counter, the ones that I had bagged, that day, before being hit on the head.

When the defense attorney had his chance, he asked whether there was any evidence, at the scene, indicating that his client had been there. Any fingerprints. Any pieces of clothing. Hair. Anything that pointed to his client. The officer answered that there was no evidence at the store indicating who had committed the crime.

The next witness was Margaret Jackson. She explained that she had been shopping in the store when Mr. Michael (that's what everyone called me just as they had referred to my father as Mr. Al) had shouted out that the store was closing in a few minutes. At the time, there was only one other shopper in the store.

When asked if she recognized that other shopper, she pointed to the defense table and said Marvin Jones was the other person in the store that day.

"Are you sure that's the man you saw in the store that day just before closing time?" he asked.

"Yes sir," she replied.

When it was his turn to cross-examine, the defense attorney asked about her initial identification of the assailant.

"Mrs. Jackson, isn't it true that you first gave the police a description of the person in the store that day. And you described him as being about six feet tall and light-skinned?"

"Yes sir."

"If you would permit, your honor, could I have the defendant rise?"

"Mr. Jones, please stand up," the judge ordered.

"Now Mrs. Jackson, please take a look at the defendant. Would you say he is about six feet tall as you originally stated."

"No sir. He's a good seven, eight inches taller than that."

"And would you describe his complexion as light skinned?"

"No sir."

"Then Mrs. Jackson, can you explain to the court how your original identification varied so greatly from the identification you are swearing to, under oath, today?"

"I think I mixed him up with someone I passed on the street on my way home that day. That's what popped into my head when I tried to remember. When I went to the police station for the line-up and saw the defendant there, I realized I had made a mistake and I corrected it. I'm sorry for that but I promise you that the defendant is the man I saw in the store that day."

The defense attorney then asked, "Do you have any reason to lie, Mrs. Jackson? When you compare the defendant to your original description, it's hard to believe you could make a mistake of that magnitude."

"Well sir. It's like I said. I confused him with someone I seen on the street. I mixed up the guy I seen on the street with the guy in the store and put him in the wrong place. But, my mind was set clear once I seen him in that police lineup. I knew it was him 'cause I remembered thinking how tall he was when I passed him in the aisle."

Listening to the testimony, I was irate. Surely the defense attorney knew I had given the police a similar description as Margaret Jackson's original description. And if he had only called me back when I had tried to reach out to him, he could have set in motion some reasonable doubt on the part of the jury. But he didn't pursue the line of questioning any further and stood in front of the table and simply looked at his pad.

"Do you have any further questions for this witness," the judge asked.

"Yes Your Honor. Mrs. Jackson, can you confirm that no one entered the store after you had left?"

"Of course not. I wasn't there. But Mr. Michael said it was closing time so I 'spect no one else came in," she replied.

"But it's possible that someone did enter the store after you left and committed the crime."

"Objection. Calls for speculation," the prosecutor interjected.

"Sustained."

"Mrs. Jackson, were there other people on the street when you left the store?"

"Yes sir."

"And some of these people were in the vicinity of the grocery store?"

"Yes sir."

"Were some of these people men?"

"Yes sir."

"Then to clarify, Mrs. Jackson, you have no first-hand knowledge whether anyone else, anyone who was on the street that day passing right by the entrance, entered the store after you left."

"No sir."

"That's all I have for this witness."

In my mind, the defense failed to do enough to discredit Mrs. Jackson's identification and plant the seed that someone else may have entered the store after Margaret Jackson had left. Maybe he had a plan and was laying the groundwork. But there was little to indicate that this lawyer knew what he was doing.

Gavitt next called Smiley to the stand and first asked him if he was in the neighborhood on Christmas Eve.

"Yes sir, I was standing on the corner, up the street from the grocery store, a bit before noon."

"And what did you see?"

"I seen *Margaret* Jackson leave the store, carrying bags of food, and then a few minutes later I seen this tall boy run from the store."

"And did you notice anything about this man you saw running."

"Yes sir. He was wearing a jacket that said *Lions Basketball* across the back."

Gavitt pulled a plastic bag holding a jacket and approached the witness. "Like this jacket?"

"Yes sir."

"Your honor. We would like to enter this jacket into evidence as exhibit one."

Returning to a spot in front of Smiley, Gavitt asked, "And do you see the man here today, the man you saw run from the store on Christmas Eve around noon? The man you saw wearing the jacket that said *Lions Basketball.*"

"Yes sir that be him sitting at that table over there".

"Let the record show that the witness pointed to Marvin Jones. I have nothing further for this witness."

When the public defender had his chance, he asked Smiley which direction the man ran from the store.

"Down the street and turned the corner."

"How far away were you at the time?"

"I don't know, I ain't the best at judging distances."

"Would you say you were at least fifty yards away?"

"Probably so."

"And he was moving fast?"

"Yes sir."

"And he was running away from you?"

"Yes sir."

"So, at best you only saw him briefly, from a good distance away, and he was running away from you and yet you are positive that this is the man you saw?"

"Yes sir, but I knows that's the man I seen that day. He be the right height and I seen enough of him to remember his face. And I remember the jacket."

As King looked down at his pad, a man sitting immediately behind him stood up quickly and walked out the courtroom door.

"Mr. Smiley. Do you consider yourself a good observer of what goes on around you?"

"I ain't sure I understand the question."

"Well on the day of the incident at the grocery store, you were standing on the street and there had to be a bunch of things going on. People passing by. Cars driving down the street. Yet you were able to spot a man running away from you from the distance of half a football field away. So you must be a good observer?"

"I guess so."

"Sir, can you describe the man who was sitting behind me and left the courtroom less than a minute ago?"

Gavitt leapt to his feet, "Your honor, the defense is trying to pull a stunt here. We object to this question."

"I'm just trying to make a point about the witness' ability to make an accurate identification in the midst of a lot of activity."

"The objection is sustained. The witness does not have to answer."

"Then I have no further questions Your Honor."

And with that the judge adjourned the proceedings for the day.

On the second day of the trial, Gavitt started by calling the lab technician who had performed the ballistics testing and he confirmed that the gun, placed into evidence, was the one that fired the fatal bullets. Mr. King did not cross-examine the witness.

Then Gavitt called to the stand one of the detectives who arrested Jones at the printing shop in December. He described finding the gun in a locker belonging to the defendant, the very gun that proved to be the murder weapon.

"And did you find anything on the gun?"

"Yes we found traces of skin and hair, on the barrel, which would be consistent with the attack, since the store owner was hit on the head opening a wound."

This was the same policemen who questioned Jones at the station later that day. Gavitt then asked if the detectives had checked into the defendant's alibi.

"Where did Mr. Jones claim he was on the day in question?"

"At work."

"Did that turn out to be the case?"

"No sir. He did report to work that day. He punched his time card and worked for about one hour before leaving for the day and directing another employee to cover for him by punching the time card later in the day."

"Thank you detective. One more question. When you went to the print shop that day, was there anything else in the locker? "

"Yes, there was a jacket which Mr. Jones put on before we departed for the station."

Walking over to the evidence table, Gavitt held up the jacket and said, "Is this the jacket that the defendant had in his locker."

"Yes sir. He put it on. Once we reached the station, we took possession of it since the eyewitness accounts described a man wearing that very jacket."

"Thank you detective."

Jones' lawyer, never raised any issue with the alibi and only directed his questions to the alleged murder weapon.

"Were there any fingerprints on the gun?"

"No, the gun was wiped clean except for the barrel."

"And was the gun registered to Mr. Jones?"

"No."

"Did he claim the gun belonged to him?"

"No, he said he had never seen it before."

"Were you able to find out how Mr. Jones came into possession of the gun?

"No sir, other than finding it in his locker." And that was it for the cross examination.

Next up was John Carter, the employee who claimed he had faked the time card that day and would testify to the same blowing a hole in

Jones' alibi. Carter said that Jones had arrived at work a few minutes before seven, as was his habit. They were assigned to pack out a job together in a section of the warehouse and no one else was around when Jones said he had to run out to take care of some business. Since he had done the same for him in the past, Carter had agreed to cover for Jones and punch his time card at lunchtime. When he didn't come back, Carter punched his card at the end of the day.

"And what time did he leave work?"

"A few minutes after ten."

"Did he say where he was going?"

"He said that he had some debts that needed to be taken care of and he was running out to take care of them."

The defense attorney declined to cross-examine Carter. The prosecution rested its case.

The defense only provided two witnesses, neither of whom could speak to the crime but only about Marvin Jones. His mother was first. She talked about how laid-back Marvin had always been. Never raised his voice. Never got in a fight in his entire life. He was just incapable of doing something as despicable as this murder. He had always been such a good boy.

When it was his turn, Gavitt treaded lightly, lest he raise any sympathy for a devastated mother. Did she know he did drugs? No. Did she know he had debts? No. When was the last time he had lived with her? Over six years ago. And when was the last time she saw him. It had been months.

"So", Gavitt asked, "maybe you don't know as much about your son as you think you do."

The only other defense witness was Quentin Berry, who had coached Marvin Jones at the rec center. His testimony was much the same as what Jones' mother had offered. Jones was a gentle giant. Never aggressive. That was his shortcoming on the basketball court and that was his shortcoming in life. He never pushed anyone around. He would be the last person you would think of committing a crime.

When Gavitt cross-examined, he immediately pounced on the article that appeared in the Gazette years before.

"Isn't it true that Jones was caught playing illegally for a high school in Baltimore County?"

"Yes."

"And there was a story written about it and one of the victims, the store owner, Michael Sanders, was the one who wrote about it."

"Yes."

"So, maybe Mr. Jones still carried a grudge and the hold-up was payback?"

Berry shook his head and said he couldn't imagine that would be the case. Marvin was not the type to hold a grudge, certainly not for that many years and that he was getting along fine in this life and, anyway, he probably didn't connect the store owner with the incident.

The defense chose not to call Marvin Jones to the stand and simply rested its case. The judge announced there would be a break for lunch and then final summations would begin in the afternoon. I couldn't understand why Jones' attorney had not followed through and contacted me to hear what I had to say.

In his summation, the lawyer, for Marvin Jones, offered very little to exonerate his client other than to say the evidence was circumstantial. In a voice lacking any real conviction, he argued that the woman who said she had seen Mr. Jones in the store, before the crime, could not say he was there when the crime occurred or that someone else had entered the store, after she left, and committed the crime. A witness who said that he saw Mr. Jones running from the store but in a direction and at a speed that made it virtually impossible to positively say that the defendant was that man. Yes a gun had been found but why would Mr. Jones take the effort to wipe it clean only to put it in a place where it could be found and, in fact, lead the police right to it. His client lacked the cunning to plan and carry out such a crime. The people who knew him best, agreed that he was too meek to have done this.

On the other hand, Gavitt told the jury that the evidence was overwhelming in favor of a conviction. Marvin Jones had the motive to commit the crime because he harbored a long-held grudge against the store owner and had huge debts that needed to be taken care. He had the means because he faked his alibi, enlisting a co-worker to make it seem that he had been at work that day when actually he had left early. He was seen in the store and identified by another shopper. He was seen running from the store by another eyewitness. The gun that was used in the crime was found in his locker at work. Hell, the only thing missing was actually seeing Marvin Jones fire the weapon. He planned the crime and he carried it out and as a result a man lost his life. Now, Marvin Jones must be held accountable for his actions and found guilty.

It took less than an hour for the jury to agree and return its verdict of guilty. Everyone, except Marvin Jones' mother and perhaps his old coach, felt justice had been done. The crime had been universally condemned from the beginning by every part of the Baltimore community. The media applauded the quick and unequivocal decision of the jury for a man who had shown no remorse and no sympathy to the families involved. The police and prosecutor were satisfied that they had done their job thoroughly and that the system had worked. The neighborhood and Charlie's family, while still shaken by the act, were comforted to a degree, knowing that someone had been held accountable and punished. Even the lawyer for Marvin Jones was satisfied. He was heard to tell a colleague, as he left the courtroom that day, that this was one verdict he wasn't going to lose any sleep over. Marvin Jones was sentenced to life in prison for his crime.

I was probably the only one who left the courtroom that day with any doubts about his guilt. But even I had been impressed by the preponderance of evidence that had been presented and the fact that a jury had considered the evidence and reached a unanimous decision in very short time. Even if my doubts about Marvin Jones being the one who had committed the crime had been presented in open court, it seemed one tiny piece of countervailing testimony against a tidal wave of incriminating evidence. I believe I would have reached the same conclusion had I been on the jury. Perhaps, up to that point, I only wanted to believe that Marvin Jones did not commit the crime, to believe that my past had not come back to haunt me and make me feel that I had sent Marvin Jones down this terrible path. Perhaps, I had blocked him from my mind that day and that's why I was confused as to the identity of the attacker.

That night was the night when my dream changed. The beginning was as it had always been. But when I called out, *what I have done wrong,* this time there was an answer. Hicks, who had been standing next to Coach McCaskill, took one small step forward, looked me in the eye and said, "You done wrong by my man."

Was he talking about the trial or about the story I had written years ago? I didn't see what I had done wrong then and certainly I didn't see what I had done wrong now. I wasn't the one who had convicted Marvin Jones. I had tried to do what I could as I had told Celia I would. I expressed my doubts to the prosecutor and I had tried to contact Jones' lawyer, more than once. What was I supposed to do? Why should his fate rest in my hands? Nevertheless, that dream continued to haunt me for the next twelve years. Every day and night for twelve years. Until one night in 1987.

# CHAPTER TWENTY-FIVE

It was September and out of the blue I received a phone call from Darnell. It was a surprise. A shock, in fact, because we had not spoken in over twelve years since that day in January when he had taken me home from work. The day that I had vowed to change my life. A vow that had not met with much initial success. Yes, there was an initial flurry of activity, efforts made at rebooting my writing career. But my recurring dream had zapped me of my energy, sent me down a path where I used drugs, on a daily basis, and sidetracked my efforts.

Once I had walked out of the courtroom after the Marvin Jones trial, I found myself treading water, with nothing to do. The store had been sold and I had not returned to Mount Street since that day in January. The trial no longer occupied any of my time. I was completely unencumbered. And, after a few months, completely bored and listless. I began to contemplate my options and had a change of heart. I decided to contact Mr. Perl.

"Mr. Perl. It's Michael Sanders. I know I have no right to ask this but, if by chance there is still a position available at the paper, I would be interested."

"I don't know Michael." There was a moment of silence, "What's going on? You turned me down a year ago. Why the change of heart?"

"Because I made a mistake. Now, I realize that I need to get back to what I like doing. Sports writing was the first thing I did and I always enjoyed it. I was good at it. You said it yourself. It's sort of like returning to my roots."

As it turned out, the Gazette needed a new beat writer for the Orioles for the upcoming season and the job started immediately. Perl overcame any initial reluctance, reluctance that was more than justified, and offered it to me. But with a requirement, "Get your ass in your car and drive here right now. The job starts in thirty minutes. If you want it, you have thirty minutes to get here and claim it. But, before you do, be honest with yourself and with me. If you're taking it because you have nothing better to do, then forget it. But if you mean to put your heart into it, then welcome aboard."

I did want it so I drove directly to the Gazette's offices and twelve years later, I was still covering the Orioles for the Gazette. Perl had warned me, back when I first talked to him at the Maryland State Fair, that the life of a sportswriter was difficult. And that seemed to be the case for many of the guys who I met on the beat because they were always complaining about the travel, especially as the season wore down. Too many anonymous hotel rooms. Too many hot dogs and nachos consumed during the season. Too many late night dashes for fast food after filing a story. But, most of all, too many days and nights away from their families.

None of those things ever bothered me. I was used to living in places that were never really my own. From the last years at my parents' house. To living in Darnell's room, after high school, surrounded by his trophies, his posters and his memorabilia. To the non-descript cinder block dorm room and then a run-down over-used apartment in Syracuse. Even now, my place in Baltimore still lacked any touches that made it seem like mine, something that Celia had pointed out to me years ago. And, unlike my colleagues, there was no family that I left behind. My mother had moved to Florida a few years after selling the store. The Watkins' were the closest thing I had to family in Baltimore and years had passed since I had seen any of them, up until Darnell's call.

If anything, the new job actually afforded me the chance to see her more often than when she lived in Baltimore. The Orioles trained in Miami and I rented a condominium each year for the six weeks during the spring season, not far from my mother's place and we would meet once a week for dinner. Like me, she had moved to Florida to get a new start.

When she informed me of her intentions to move, it was with the normal speed which she had tackled all the other moves in her life. She sold the house and had packed up or disposed of most of the furnishings before she mentioned it to me.

"Michael, I've sold the house and bought a new one in Boca Raton. I'll be moving in two months. All of your stuff has been sitting in boxes in the attic and you can either come get them or let them go with everything else that will soon be thrown out."

Years before, I had walked out of my parents' home with what, at the time, I thought were my entire earthly possessions, two suitcases of clothes and a few books. Upon moving back in during my father's illness, I realized that there were things I had left behind up in the attic, but they had very little meaning for me. Those items represented things from my past, things that were from a different period of my life and I wasn't looking for any reminders of that time. Now faced with the prospect that whatever had been piled into the boxes would be lost forever, I decided to take a look.

The boxes were piled neatly in a stack, with no markings on the outside of each carton to indicate what was inside. Once I opened the first box, I realized that my belongings had been piled in with no organization other than its relative location in the room. My mother had simply started at one corner of the room and deposited what was in front of her into a box and then moved to the next spot. Everything that was on the bookshelves had been placed in two boxes, the closet in another, the night table in a third and everything that had been hanging on the wall in a fourth carton.

The last box contained the contents of my desk and I initially saw nothing worth keeping. And then I came across two three-ring binders, the binders that held my collection of writings, from my pre-teen and teenage years, starting with that first story about John Hancock. I flipped through the first binder, scanning the pages to check out all the names that I had once written about, names that brought back memories of the hours spent writing and the joy it had brought. I closed the first binder and dropped it back in the box. As I picked up the second binder, a sheet fell out. Actually a photograph and when I picked it up, from the floor, and turned it over, there was the picture of my third grade class. Mrs. Garrett's class.

I looked at the faces. I remembered all the names of my classmates and thought back to the day when we each told Mrs. Garrett about our career plans. I knew Ellen Wagner had become a lawyer and for a brief time my girlfriend. Maybe there was still time for her to become President. As for the others, I had no idea what they had become since I had long lost touch with every other person in that photograph. I wondered how many had achieved their goal, how many had fallen short, how many changed their mind or had their mind changed for them. How many settled for careers because they had to. Like me. At least I had been given a second chance and although it was not exactly what I had in mind, back in third grade, it was close. I rolled up the photo and took it with me. I trashed everything else.

When I returned to my apartment, I found a picture frame, placed the photo in it, and hung it above my desk. I had seen other people tack quotes and sayings above their desks in college and at work. Wise words from the Beatles or Kahlil Gibran. Jonathan Livingston seagull posters. *Carpe diem plaques.* Even Richard Nixon--*A man is not finished when he is defeated. He is finished when he quits.* Words to live by. To inspire. I had never felt motivated to hang someone else's words. But today I felt the urge for the first time. I didn't need inspiration or motivation. Just a reminder.

While my life may not have proceeded on the course I had hoped, for Darnell Watkins, things had happened exactly as he had planned. From the time we first met, he was focused and intent on realizing his dream. He took all the right steps. Top of the class grades. Summer enrichment courses. An internship in a well-respected Baltimore law office. Harvard undergraduate and Harvard Law School. When he graduated, he took a position in the Civil Rights Division of the United States Department of Justice. Whereas his brother, George, had been the challenger, the person who called out the injustices and broke down the doors at the sit-ins and protest marches, and his sister, Celia, had been the one to empower people, when she took a year off and went to Alabama to register the disenfranchised to vote in what was to become a lifetime effort, Darnell took the role of defender. The person who would work inside the system to make sure the system obeyed the law and see to it that people were treated fairly and equally.

That worked fine for a few years. While Jimmy Carter was in office. But when Ronald Reagan assumed the Presidency, civil rights took a back seat and Darnell soon found himself frustrated by the "go-slow" policies of the new administration. Over the years, he had been watching the work of the Southern Poverty Law Center and their efforts on behalf of victims of hate groups. When he had reached his breaking point with the Justice Department, he turned in his resignation and decided to open up a practice in Baltimore, dedicated to fighting racial discrimination and segregation. Within months he had filed suit on behalf of dozens of clients who had suffered from racial bias on the job, in the housing market and in the school system. The need was great and Darnell was soon overwhelmed with cases. He began hiring additional lawyers for his firm so that he could handle the most challenging cases. It was in regard to one of these cases that he called me.

"Hi Michael. It's been a long time. How you doing?

"Pretty good Darnell. How's your family?

"They're all good. My father reads you religiously. But he says he misses the days when you gave him the inside information before it hit the paper. It always made him seem the savviest of sports fans when he talked to his customers at the barbershop. Everyone was always impressed when his predictions came true. Do you have some time when we can get together?"

"Well the Orioles are off on Thursday. So I have the day off as well. You want to meet for lunch?"

"Well I was thinking. Do you still play basketball?"

"On occasion. What do you have in mind?"

"Why don't you meet me at the Downtown Racquet Club around eleven o'clock. We'll shoot around and then grab lunch."

On Thursday, I walked over to Darnell's club which was only a few blocks from my office. He was waiting in the lobby. We changed in the locker room and headed up to the courts which were usually busy at lunchtime into the early afternoon. But we were ahead of the rush and we had one of the half-courts to ourselves. We played a game of horse to warm-up.

"Michael, do you remember the first time we shot hoops together?"

"Sure it was behind your father's barbershop. We were both in sixth grade and it was the first time we met. As I recall, I kicked your butt. Even though you had home-court advantage with that lousy backboard."

"Only because I let you. But, you know, I think a lot about those days. We became good friends. We had a lot of good conversations while we played on Saturdays. I think I really got to know you. That's why I wanted to meet you on the basketball court first. Because there is something I need to talk to you about. And I think you were always most honest when we played."

"Go on."

"I started a law practice a few years ago. For the most part, it is discrimination law. Probably what you would expect from me. I'm working on a case and I could use your help."

"My help. What kind of case could use my help? "

"It's an appeals case. On behalf of Marvin Jones."

"How in the world did you get mixed up with Marvin Jones? That case was resolved years ago. What the hell's going on Darnell?"

"One of his cousins came to me. He had heard some rumblings on the street. I think Marvin Jones was wrongly convicted. And, as I understand it, so do you."

"What I think doesn't matter. A jury convicted him. The evidence was overwhelming. He got a fair trial."

"Did he? You, of all people, know that he didn't get a fair trial. He got railroaded. You know he wasn't the one who killed Charlie and I understand you've had nightmares about it."

"I told that in confidence to Celia. She should have never said anything to you."

"Maybe so, but she did. And she did for the right reason. Do you still have the dream, Michael?"

"I do."

"Did you ever think that you're having the dream because you're the only one who can get Marvin out of prison? To get his conviction overturned. You told Celia you wanted someone to tell you what the dream meant. I'm telling you. You help Marvin, you help yourself."

"What is it that I can do? If I wanted to do it."

"Did you ever stop to think why you were never called to the stand during the trial?"

"Because the prosecutor didn't want to take a chance since I couldn't positively identify Marvin. And they had plenty of evidence without my testimony."

"Yes. And because the prosecution never said anything to the defense attorney that there was potential exculpatory evidence. They never said a word about your contradictory description. If they had, it would have confirmed Margaret Jackson's original description and shed a lot of doubt on their case. At the very least, it would have been cause enough for them to do a more thorough investigation and to look for other suspects."

"But I reached out to the public defender. He never returned my call. I tried several times to let him know that I doubted it was Marvin Jones."

"Marvin's attorney was a neophyte. It was only his third trial. He never questioned the evidence. He never mounted a decent defense. He thought Marvin was guilty so he never bothered to learn what it was that you wanted to tell him. There was too much pressure to get a quick conviction. Everyone was screaming for Marvin's neck. His lawyer capitulated. It was the easiest path. I only wished you had tried harder."

"You think it would have made a difference if I had testified?"

"Probably not. Like you said they had other evidence and they would have explained away the inconsistencies. They needed a conviction and they had Marvin in their sights."

"So what difference will it make now?"

"I have plenty of evidence which I'll tell you about later. But I need a witness. I need someone whose integrity is beyond doubt. If the man who was attacked that day steps forward and questions the verdict, well, it's something that could get Marvin a new trial."

"I'm gonna have to think this over, Darnell. I'm not sure I'm prepared to relive the events of that day. I feel bad for Jones but I'm just not sure."

"Michael I'm glad you feel bad but I'm not looking for your compassion. I am looking for your courage. This can't be about you. You need to get past your feelings, your guilt and do something about it."

By this point, the courts started filling in. We joined a game of five-on-five and played for the next half hour before grabbing lunch at the Women's Industrial Exchange on Charles Street. For most of the meal, we talked sports and politics.

Before we went our separate ways, I asked, "Darnell, if Marvin Jones did not commit the crime, do you know who did?"

"I do."

# CHAPTER TWENTY-SIX

It took me only one night to decide to help Darnell. Whether or not Darnell was correct about me needing to help as a way to rid myself of the dream, it was the right thing to do. People didn't quit on me. I couldn't quit on Marvin Jones. I called Darnell the next day and told him I was on board. It would take two years to get a new trial for Marvin and another year before the trial actually started.

Darnell was right. Back in 1974, everyone was clamoring for a quick trial and conviction. The media had latched onto the story as the horrific Christmas Eve killing and stoked the flames of public opinion. The neighborhood wanted the police to find the attacker and get him off the streets quickly. As the police uncovered evidence and secured identifications against Marvin Jones, they never bothered to investigate any deeper. Arresting Marvin Jones would satisfy the media and public hunger and, with the spate of evidence, no one would question the outcome.

Now, thirteen years later, the Marvin Jones case was long forgotten. Even in the Mount Street neighborhood, no one ever mentioned the killing and most of the current residents were not living there when it happened. There was no shortage of new crimes being committed every day. No one cared about something that happened over a decade ago. They cared about what was happening now.

Darnell realized that he had to drum up public interest along with filing an appeal on behalf of Marvin, who had always maintained his innocence. It was not uncommon for lawyers to claim there was new evidence to exonerate their client, to request a new trial, especially when they thought there was a systemic racial bias at work. But the courts were reluctant to reopen most of these cases. Especially in the case of Marvin Jones. He had his day in court and the jury had returned a guilty verdict in less than an hour. There was no one who felt that justice had not been served. No one except for Darnell and me.

"Do you think, if Marvin had been white, that things would have been different? Of course they would have. The police would have investigated more thoroughly. He would have had a competent lawyer or at least someone who might have thrown up some challenge to the prosecution's case. No one cared if they found the person who committed the crime. They only cared that they found someone that they could convict easily."

Darnell explained his strategy.

"First we need to plant a seed with the media and get them on our side. We need the Gazette to question the case. I've seen other situations where there was plenty of evidence to demand a new trial and still the request was denied. We need to create an atmosphere that will force the judge's hands."

We all knew the power that the media wielded and it was that power that Darnell wanted to harness. A story in the Gazette would go a long way to giving credibility to his effort. It was a post-Watergate world where the media had expanded its role as an investigating presence. If the police were not going to do their job, then it was the media who had to do it. If the prosecutors and courts would not see to it that justice was served, then it was the media who would see to it. The Washington Post reporters, Bob Woodward and Carl Bernstein, had proved the power of the media when they brought down the Nixon presidency by tracking down leads and evidence while the authorities covered up and blocked any real effort to determine what had happened.

Over the years, the Gazette had done its share of investigative reporting, writing articles on improprieties in the Maryland State mental health hospital system and corruption among building contractors and government officials in Baltimore County. Darnell planned to turn their focus toward the criminal justice system and, in particular, the case of Marvin Jones. No one loved a good fight and a good story more than the reporters at the Gazette. Someone could make their name with this kind of story.

I arranged a meeting with two reporters, who covered the local news. Eileen Fitzsimmons, a fellow Syracuse alumnus who had attended the university, years after me, and loved to share stories about the harsh winters. And James Everett, a graduate of Northwestern University and a twenty year veteran with the Gazette. Eileen was young, a recent hire at the Gazette, after having spent time at newspapers in Tennessee, Florida and Atlanta. She was confrontational in her approach, relentless in her pursuit of the involved parties until she wore them down and she got her interview. With a disarming charm and a natural beauty, that she underplayed by dressing plainly, keeping her hair tied back and minimizing any use of make-up, she would provide enthusiasm and intensity to our plan. Everett was more of a back door type of reporter. He cultivated his sources, spent long evenings drinking with them and was quick to do them a favor. When the time came, he would call in his markers. Usually dressed in a gray tweed jacket and bowtie, with one pocket stuffed with a pipe and pouch of tobacco and the other pocket stuffed with a notepad, he would provide the experience and gravitas. He carried weight with the editors and, if we could hook him, we would have a story.

We met at Darnell's law offices, on Calvert Street, and, after the introductions, Everett asked, "So, what have you got for us?"

"We have a story about a gross miscarriage of justice. About a man falsely accused and convicted of a crime he did not commit. He deserves to have a new trial. But, more importantly, the system needs to be exposed. To be held accountable, for this mistake, because it goes far beyond this one example," Darnell replied. "This story is on the same level as the building contractor corruption story that appeared in your paper last year."

Everett was the one who wrote that story and Darnell knew the comparison would pique his interest.

"I'm going to let Michael give you the background."

Both Fitzsimmons, with pen in hand and a notebook on the table in front of her, and Everett, fiddling with the stirrer straw in his Styrofoam cup of coffee that he had purchased at the carry-out on the corner, turned and looked at me.

"Before I worked for the Gazette, I owned and operated a grocery store in West Baltimore. It was my father's store, my grandfather's before him. When my father had a stroke, I left college and took over. Then my father died, in 1973, and I accepted a job with the sports department at the Gazette. It was only a matter of weeks before I would be done at the store. On Christmas Eve, my last Christmas Eve there, we were getting ready to close when someone held-up the store. My security guard, Charlie, was killed. I was hit on the head."

Darnell went on to explain that Marvin Jones had been arrested and convicted of the crime. The evidence against him seemed substantial and conclusive at the time.

"Except that Michael's description of the assailant did not match the person who was arrested. The police and prosecution buried this fact. Told Michael that his memory was clouded by the hit to the head. He was never called to the stand during the trial. Michael tried to contact the defense attorney, who was a public defender on his third trial, but the guy never got back to him. He tried multiple times including at the courthouse."

"The police built their case on two other identifications and evidence that they found at the printing plant where Jones worked. As it turns out, the identifications were fake and the gun they found in Jones' locker was planted. The police and prosecution knew for certain that the one identification was questionable and the other was from a known criminal. But the defense attorney never raised enough doubt during the case. As for the evidence they found, the police accepted things on its face and never bothered to ask any questions, totally disregarding the statements from the accused. The defense attorney did nothing more than ask a few questions when the witnesses took the stand. He never talked to anyone. He was bullied by the prosecutors, who wanted to make sure that they got a swift conviction to satisfy the political pressure. That attorney now manages a restaurant which says something about his legal capabilities. The bottom line is that Marvin Jones has been in prison for twelve years for a crime he did not commit."

"Do you know who committed the crime?" Fitzsimmons asked.

"I do. His name is Raymond Ward. They call him Ray-ray and he's serving time in Jessup for another armed robbery."

"Give us a few minutes to talk it over," Everett suggested.

We stepped out and Fitzsimmons and Everett discussed what Darnell had told them. After a few minutes, they waved us back into the conference room.

"This story is intriguing," Everett said, "and we want to look into it more. I think if what you say holds up, the paper will be anxious to run with it."

Darnell turned over all the names and information to Everett and Fitzsimmons. After the two reporters left, Darnell was pleased.

"Now, I did promise that I would tell you everything I know."

As he had previously told me, one of Marvin Jones' cousins had asked Darnell to take the case. He had heard that Willie Boyd, the drug dealer who operated on one of the Mount Street corners, had schemed to get Jones fingered for the crime. Jones had taken up with one of Boyd's old girlfriends, shacking up with her on occasion. But Boyd wasn't finished with her. He wanted her available when the whim hit him. One night, he showed up at the girl's house and found Marvin there. They weren't doing anything, just sitting on the sofa talking and listening to a Marvin Gaye album. Boyd wasn't happy about what he imagined was going on but he was too small to challenge Marvin physically. Even though Marvin had avoided fights his entire life, you didn't go after a six foot six guy. So, Boyd told him that he didn't want him messing with his girl anymore. When he didn't listen, Boyd decided to take care of Jones. To teach him a lesson. The grocery store murder provided a perfect opportunity. He fed the police information, implicating Jones, and it had worked. When Boyd was killed in a drug deal, a few years later, word began to leak out about what he had arranged.

Margaret Jackson, who had been in the store moments before the hold-up, had originally provided the police with the same description as I had. Margaret, like many of the people in the area, bought drugs from Boyd and he reached out to her. How did he know about her being in the store that day? Because, as soon as she heard what had happened, she came up to the corner to buy drugs, something to calm her down.

"Can you imagine," she had told Smiley, "if I had been in that store two minutes longer, I may not be alive today."

In exchange for fifty dollars of free drugs, she lied to the police and identified Jones. The detectives did ask her why her identification varied from the initial description she had provided and she had no answer, said she was mistaken the first time but got it right now. The police noted the discrepancy and passed it onto the prosecution and that information was passed on to the defense but the attorney never aggressively questioned Margaret Jackson about her flip-flop on the identification. When Fitzsimmons and Everett approached her, she recanted her identification and gave the two reporters the description she originally gave to the police. After the trial, she told the reporters, she saw Ray-ray on the street and knew he was the one but she had to keep quiet.

Smiley was easier to manipulate for Willie Boyd than Margaret Jackson since Smiley was in his employ. Smiley claimed he saw Marvin Jones run from the store but Smiley was not standing on the corner that day and had not seen anyone. What Smiley had seen was the gun sitting in a trash bin down the street from the grocery store. He grabbed it and put it in his pocket. Later, in the day, he told Willie that he had found a gun, not knowing that it was the gun that had been used to murder Charlie. Willie was the one who figured it out and hatched his plan. He approached another one of his customers, a guy named John Carter, who worked with Marvin Jones at the print shop. Another exchange of drugs for a favor and the gun was planted in Jones' locker. But, first, Willie put some skin and hair on the barrel knowing that I had been hit on the head. Carter then put the gun in the locker and told the police that Jones had left the shop that day and had never returned. The police never questioned any of the other employees but, when Everett and Fitzsimmons talked to the employees who were there that day and still worked for the print shop, they all remembered seeing Jones at work. The entire day.

The police never asked Smiley why he hadn't come forward with his information. A crime had occurred and, yet, he had done nothing until the police mildly threatened him on the corner days later.  And why had none of the other employees, at the print shop, stepped up to alibi Jones. Because they didn't want to cross a drug dealer, one who would do whatever he needed to do. That's what they told the reporters. And why hadn't the police wondered why Jones would take the time to wipe his fingerprints from the gun and yet leave hair and skin on the barrel and then put it in his locker. Wouldn't he have stashed it in a safer place?

Everett and Fitzsimmons weren't able to track down John Carter, the employee who had cooperated in setting up Jones for the fall. He had become a victim of the streets years before, dying from an overdose. But, they did locate his sister, who confirmed that Carter had told her what he had done. Told them that he had planted the gun. Darnell was certain that a new test, called DNA technology, that had first been used in England in 1986 to overturn a man's conviction and then, for the first time, in Florida in 1987, would show that the skin and hair on the gun was not mine.

In March of 1988, the Gazette reporters contacted Ray-ray's lawyer and asked if he would be willing to talk to them. Surprisingly, he agreed and Everett and Fitzsimmons drove down to Jessup on a sunny afternoon. Ray-ray confessed to the hold-up and murder. He hadn't meant to hurt anyone but he panicked. And he felt sorry for that boy who took the rap. He had found religion and he wanted to do right. Hoped his confession would help get Jones out of prison. Ray-ray was serving a fifty year sentence, as a repeat offender. The hold-up at the Mount Street grocery store was his first. There would be a dozen more before he was caught and locked up at age forty-two. Most likely, he would die in jail so he had nothing to lose. He wanted to do something good, something that people would remember that he did right. Something that Jesus would remember when the time came. Freeing Marvin Jones could be that ticket.

Armed with this new information, Everett and Fitzsimmons

approached the prosecutors and showed them the inconsistencies in the case. And the response from them was to say that the crime had been thoroughly investigated at the time and the evidence was accurate. The prosecutor's office stated that the evidence had been presented to a jury and that Marvin Jones had the opportunity to present a defense. The jury had spoken.

Everett and Fitzsimmons wrote their story and the article appeared in the Gazette in the spring of 1988 splashed across the front page and two full pages inside with pictures of the store, Marvin Jones, Charlie, Margaret Jackson and Ray-ray. The article generated no more than a ripple of attention and interest. Most people, I spoke to, sympathized with Marvin Jones' plight saying it didn't surprise them that the police took short cuts and the prosecutor's office withheld information, after all, those people with the power didn't worry about fairness when it came to black people. So, if Marvin Jones was to have justice, it was still up to Darnell to convince the courts that he deserved another trial.

Shortly after the article appeared, Darnell filed his appeal. In his brief, he wrote about the new information, information that pointed to someone else. There had been prosecutorial misconduct. Pertinent information had been withheld from the defense. The store owner was unwilling and unable, at the time, to corroborate the identification of the suspect because Jones was not the one who committed the crime. He had tried to warn the defense but was ignored and was now anxious to step forward to see that the man convicted received a new trial. The other identifications also were inconsistent and the prosecutor knew it but withheld the information because it would hurt his case. So he buried it. To top it off, Marvin Jones had not received competent representation. There was more than reasonable doubt that Marvin Jones had committed the crime. There was absolute evidence that he had not and that Raymond Ward had. It was time to correct the verdict.

Darnell prevailed and won a new trial for Marvin Jones, although he would have to remain in jail until the trial started. In September 1989, Marvin Jones got his second day in court. Margaret Jackson recanted and identified Raymond Ward. Smiley was not called to testify. John Carter's sister revealed his secret and confirmed that he had planted the murder weapon. Four employees of the print shop testified that Jones was at work that day. The DNA test confirmed that the skin and hair, on the gun, was not mine. And I testified that Marvin Jones was not the man that killed Charlie. What seemed like a slam dunk, in favor of the prosecution in 1975, now appeared to be a slam dunk for the defense.

On September 23, 1989, Marvin Jones walked out of a Baltimore City courtroom a free man. The police could take some satisfaction in that the right man had been found and confessed to the crime. Mount Street and the black community were relieved that justice had been served.

That evening, I joined Darnell and Mr. Watkins for a celebratory dinner, prepared by Darnell's mother. As was his manner, Darnell took it all in stride. When I congratulated him on his tenacity and brilliance, he told me it wasn't about him. It was about making the system work for everyone.

"And that's not the only good news we got today," Mr. Watkins chimed in. "Celia's moving back to Baltimore. She's taken a position at Hopkins, starting in January."

I guess she did turn out to be an east side girl after all. So, we toasted the good fortune of the Watkins family. It was like old times. When I was ready to leave, Darnell walked me to the door.

"Michael, I want to thank you for what you did. You got the ball rolling. You stood up. I hope you will rest easier now. "

We stepped out on the front porch. "If you don't mind, I like to make an observation, but last time I did, you didn't take it too well."

"No go ahead."

"I've known you for over twenty-five years and it seems to me that you've lived your life in a revolving door. You step out and you do good things, for the right reasons. And then you step back into the door and you're back on the wrong side. Hunkered down. Doing nothing or doing things for the wrong reason. I think you've made it back to the outside. With your job. With what you did for Marvin. I just hope you stay there. I hope we can continue to hang out together."

"I'd like that Darnell."

As I began to walk down the steps, Darnell said, "Michael, there's one more thing I need to tell you. About Celia. She never did get married. I thought you might like to know."

# CHAPTER TWENTY-SEVEN

On the drive home, that night, I was looking forward to sleep, for the first time in a long time. To see if my dream would be gone. Much to my disappointment it wasn't, although it had returned to its more benign version. Hicks had stepped back into the crowd and no longer shouted at me. At least I could live with this version of the dream. And, as it turned out, over time the dream slowly disappeared.

The baseball season ended a few days later and that meant that work would be less hectic for me. There would be stories to write, mostly about what the Orioles were doing in the offseason, but I would be freed from the daily grind of reporting the results of the games. It would give me more time to spend in the office and at home, rather than on the road. Be able to take a breath. Even a long weekend.

One day, I was sitting at my desk, when Mr. Perl called me into his office.

"I have some news. I wanted you to know that I am retiring at the end of the year. Hey, don't look so surprised. Even crusty old guys like me want to do something other than spend their entire lives at the newspaper."

When Perl's final day came, we held a farewell lunch at Tio Pepe's, his favorite restaurant, where we ate mussels in a garlic sauce, Spanish prawns and tournedos in sherry sauce. And drank lots of sangria. We returned to work and, late in the afternoon, he again called me into his office.

He was boxing up the last pieces from his desk, packing away forty years of work. He stopped and took a seat and motioned me to do the same.

"I came across something while I was cleaning out my desk."

He handed me a lined file card and taped to the front was a cut-out copy of the first letter to the editor that I had sent to the Gazette. A letter that challenged Mr. Perl's review of the Orioles 1967 season. A letter that ultimately led to my hiring. And a friendship.

"Don't ask me why I kept it. I guess I thought it might mean something to me, or to you, someday. It's yours now."

I tucked it into my shirt pocket.

"You know I've had a pretty good run. I've seen a lot of good things.

Yeah, there were plenty of bad days but, when I think about it all, I wouldn't trade a day of it. I wonder if you'll be able to say the same thing when it's time for you to retire. I know you enjoy sports writing and covering the Orioles. I'm just not sure you love it. Maybe you settled for it rather than doing what you really wanted to do. But you're still young. There's still time."

He stood and we shook hands. "You stay in touch now. I'll still be reading the paper to make sure you don't use any of those sappy leads like you used to."

It would be great to say that Mr. Perl's little farewell speech inspired me to chase the thing I had always wanted. The thing that I declared back in third grade. To write stories. But it didn't. Because I had already started to write creatively again. It had been my choice to stop writing when it had become too difficult. I had stopped because I wanted to and now I had started up again because I wanted to. Oh, it was still challenging. I would write and, the next day, toss it away because it didn't feel right. But I found the joy in it again. The failures didn't stop me this time.

I had scheduled vacation time between Christmas and New Year's, figuring I would spend the time writing, hoping to finally break through. I had no other plans other than to write, although I had been invited to the Watkins for a New Year's Eve party, which was doubling as a welcome home party for Celia. So, most of the vacation, I did exactly what I had planned to do, relax and write. Lines. Thoughts. Ideas. Lots of yellow sticky notes. Crumpled pieces of paper filling the trash can. Nothing went very far.

On the morning of New Years' Eve, I again sat at my desk and began pecking at my typewriter. And, for once, the words began to flow. It was a start and something to build on.

The sun had set and it was now dark outside and time to go to the Watkins house. I gathered up the sheets I had just written, folded them and placed them in the breast pocket of my shirt. For once, I was pleased with what I had accomplished. Hopping down the steps of my apartment and skipping to my car, I was anxious to get to the Watkins. Life felt better, on track, and I realized that I had been unable to say that for a lot of years. I was looking forward to this night and seeing Celia and tomorrow, when I would sit down and write again. I was ready to move forward. Fifteen minutes later, I arrived at the Watkins' home. I jumped out of the car and bounded up the front steps. Like an eight year old boy. Filled with equal doses of enthusiasm and wide-eyed optimism.

The End

.

.

.

## AUTHOR'S NOTE

In trying to add realism to the story, I have used the names of several actual individuals, locations and historic events. In most cases, these are meant simply as a point of reference and to provide a feel for the time period covered in the novel.

In a few instances, I have written about events where the descriptions of what happened were gathered from research from various sources. The sit-ins at Reads Drug Stores, the desegregation rally at Gwynn Oak Park and Reverend Baucom's sermon, the incident at Mandell-Ballows restaurant, the 1969 World Series, the black players boycott at Syracuse University, the Kent State protest and other anti-war rallies are all drawn from newspaper articles in the archives of the Baltimore Sun, Syracuse Post Standard, Syracuse University on-line archives and Wikipedia. Using some literary license, I have added descriptions and words as further texture for the reader.

Regarding the interview with Ben Schwartzwalder, coach of the Syracuse University football team, the words attributed to him are from an actual interview that he gave at the time and culled from the same sources noted above. The fictional main character, Michael Sanders, is used as the interviewer, although that was obviously not the case. However the interaction, between Michael and Mr. Schwartzwalder, is based on personal experience when I, as a reporter for The Daily Orange, interviewed Mr. Schwartzwalder, and his reaction to my appearance was, in fact, the way he greeted me.

Beyond the ones cited above, all other characters are fictional and are not drawn from any actual people, living or dead. Any similarity to actual events or individuals are also purely coincidental

# ABOUT THE AUTHOR

Steven Wasserman is the author of Barriers, his first novel to be published. He studied Journalism at Syracuse University and lives in Pikesville, MD. He is married with five children and four grandchildren. He is currently working on his second novel, Lucky Matty.

Made in the USA
Coppell, TX
24 July 2021

59406880R00125